FREEDOM OF EXPRESSION AND PARTISAN POLITICS

STUDIES IN RHETORIC/COMMUNICATION
Carroll C. Arnold, *Series Editor*

Richard B. Gregg
Symbolic Inducement and Knowing:
A Study in the Foundations of Rhetoric

Richard A. Cherwitz and James W. Hikins
Communication and Knowledge:
An Investigation in Rhetorical Epistemology

Herbert W. Simons and Aram A. Aghazarian, Editors
Form, Genre, and the Study of Political Discourse

Walter R. Fisher
Human Communication as Narration:
Toward a Philosophy of Reason, Value, and Action

David Bartine
Early English Reading Theory:
Origins of Current Debates

David Payne
Coping with Failure:
The Therapeutic Uses of Rhetoric

Freedom of Expression and Partisan Politics

by Craig R. Smith

University of South Carolina Press

Copyright © University of South Carolina 1989

Published in Columbia, South Carolina, by the
University of South Carolina Press

Manufactured in the United States of America

Library of Congress Cataloging-in-Publication Data

Smith, Craig R.
    Freedom of expression and partisan politics / by Craig R. Smith.
        p.   cm.—(Studies in rhetoric/communication)
    Bibliography: p.
    Includes index.
    ISBN 0-87249-611-2.—ISBN 0-87249-638-4 (pbk.)
    1. Freedom of speech—United States—History. 2. Political
oratory—United States—History. I. Title. II. Series.
JC599.U5S556   1989
323.44'3'0973—dc19   89-30556
                                                              CIP

To my father, who first introduced me to the fine art of political argument and to my mother, who taught me that there was more to a good argument than logic.

CONTENTS

Foreword

Freedom of expression is central to the constitutional rights upon which our representative democracy is based. We are careful to avoid and quick to condemn any violation of this right. In this work, Dr. Smith provides insights into the uses and misuses of persuasion in America, a neglected component of the American experiment.

In free societies, persuasion is the thread from which we weave the political tapestry. That is not to suggest that all public discourse is free of cheap talk. Far from it. When a political leader promises peace knowing he or she will deliver war, his or her words may seem to be of no more value than those of a common demagogue. But if the politician's talk is cheap in that instance, it provides a record by which he or she may be judged. And, perhaps more important, it affords others the chance to react with their own version of reality. The result is open discussion and debate.

Those active in political affairs are perhaps the most adept at persuasive speech. Political leaders use persuasion to promote significant, even radical changes by mobilizing public support for their views. As Dr. Smith shows, open discussion and debate mediates change in America.

The guns that fired upon British troops won freedom for the American colonists from King George III. But it was the persuasion on both sides of the Atlantic that formed the battle lines.

Prior to the American Civil War, public discourse sharpened the debate and defined the issues. It was a cruel and bloody war, but the rhetoric of the leaders on both sides gave full meaning to the words "secession" and "union."

Franklin Roosevelt convinced Americans that we had nothing to fear but fear itself; he mobilized a nation first to survive a devastating economic crisis and then to join a world war against tyranny. It was Roosevelt's voice across the airwaves that united the nation in peace and steeled it for war.

John F. Kennedy once said that Winston Churchill had mobilized the English language and led it into war. When England stood as the last outpost of freedom in Europe and defeat seemed inevitable, Churchill rallied England to a defense few had thought possible.

Martin Luther King, Jr., eloquently advocated the rights of black Americans. His speeches tapped a powerful wellspring of support that overcame years of hatred and violence. His inspirational dream of racial equality spurred the marches and sit-ins without which essential civil rights legislation would not have been enacted.

Each of these leaders possessed a remarkable ability to describe a problem in vivid terms and propose a way to solve it. Each was able to seize the public's imagination and direct it toward needed action.

Thomas Jefferson rightly claimed that the American experiment would not work unless the electorate understood the issues of the day. Jefferson's electorate was an elite group of propertied white males over the age of twenty-one. Today's electorate is far more pluralistic: a black man finished third in the race for the Democratic presidential nomination in 1984; in the same year, a woman was nominated for vice president by her party. Furthermore, the issues Jefferson's electorate faced were less complex than the issues we face two hundred years later. And the means to persuade the public have become vastly more sophisticated as new communication technologies have evolved.

As a theorist, historian, practitioner and participant-observer of contemporary political persuasion, Professor Smith has developed a rich and incisive understanding of the relationship between the First Amendment and American political persuasion. His contributions to scholarship are well known. But he has also participated in the political marketplace as a speechwriter for President Gerald Ford, George Bush, and Lee Iacocca, to name but three. He has served as Director of Senate Services for the Republican Caucus of the U.S. Senate and as Deputy Director of the National Republican Senatorial Campaign Committee when I was its chair. Since 1968 he has worked with CBS News as a consultant for political conventions, elections, and presidential inaugurals. This experience allows him to view the uses and abuses of political persuasion through a unique set of lenses.

After reading the following text, I am convinced that few works could do more to open the eyes of voters to the new technologies of political persuasion and the regulations that control them. I hope those who read this work will pass their understanding on to others thereby bringing us a step closer to Jefferson's dream of a responsive and responsible electorate.

Senator Bob Packwood
March, 1988

FREEDOM OF EXPRESSION AND PARTISAN POLITICS

1

INTRODUCTION

American history is characterized by periods of relative stability and periods of fluid change, the one presaging the other, sometimes almost imperceptibly. The American experience can be conceptualized as continuous adjustments of a dynamic tension between the status quo and the pull of new ways of thinking and doing. Characteristically, pragmatic *reality* has been preceded in our society by someone's discernment of idealistic *potentialities*. It is largely through the art of persuasion that this conversion of ideals to pragmatics has been accomplished, precisely because both freedom of expression and social stability have been uniquely prized in the United States.

To study the role of persuasion in American history is to study transformations of ideals into realities through debate and discussion. In the United States, as in most other democratic societies, *change* is *deliberated*. Deliberation entails raising certain conventional questions again and again. Where there is critical analysis of an old policy—of the status quo—one asks: What problem or problems is the status quo not satisfactorily resolving? How widespread and serious are those problems? Are the problems physical or psychological in nature? Conversely, those who argue for change must also deal with such standard issues as: What are the specifics of the new proposal? Does the proposal solve the problems that the status quo cannot? Is the new policy more advantageous than the old, or does it result in significant new disadvantages?

These issues, normally addressed in political persuasion, are as ancient as political rhetoric itself. They were "stock issues" even to the early Greeks. They imply a critique of reality: the proposal of ideals and conversion of the ideals into practices. They identify "burdens of proof" that specify the persuasive work of those who *defend* the status quo and those who *propose changes*. Freedom for everyone to express his or her views, as is promised by our Constitution, has the further effect of producing endless social tensions between forces for change and forces

1

resisting change. If I am free to propose, you are free to oppose, and vice versa. This tension always exists in the social and political discourse of a free society. In this book I propose to assess that tension as it has been specifically experienced in the history of the United States. I do not propose to add much new historical data to the already well-covered record of American politics. What I intend is to look at that record in a special way—seeking to discover how the ideal of freedom of expression has been treated in political persuasion and what practical influences the ideal has had and still has on the nature and the course of public political persuasion.

I will focus on the interplay among the democratic ideal of freedom, commitments to other values, and the patterns of public controversy that emerge in a society such as ours. At the same time, I shall show the complexity of the processes of persuasion by which the contest between forces of order and those of freedom has been carried on. That exploration will reveal that public persuasion develops, evolves, and even mutates into subtle forms that we frequently do not even recognize as persuasive. It will also note that freedom can drive change, just as order can drive stability.

The ideal of freedom of expression was strongly held from the very beginnings of the British colonies in North America. Historians have clearly established that the Founders of the Republic believed freedom of expression was the *sine qua non* of democratic society. Even before the nation was founded, it was for freedom of speech that new colonies were started in Rhode Island and Connecticut. Freedom of expression was the leading "cause" supported by some of the most persuasive tracts written in the revolutionary period. It is not remarkable, then, that a major criticism of the Constitution of the United States, as originally drawn, was that it did not guarantee freedom of expression as a *national* value. Hence, when the early amendments were worked out, the guarantee of freedom of speech and press was the *first* amendment added in 1791. Among arguments used in support of this national guarantee was the reasonable one that unless the marketplace of ideas is open, it cannot provide citizens the information they need to make electoral decisions. Those who were fearful that elites would seize control of governmental machinery argued even more strongly that the democratic process must be self-correcting: abuses in and of the system must be revealed in an open environment so they can be removed by the citizenry or its representatives. It was clearly intended that the new system should be constantly examined, criticized, and purified through open debate and deliberation on policies.

The authors of the Federal Constitution and its first amendments

2

wanted an open marketplace of ideas because they firmly believed that understanding is better than censorship. Censorship "protects" citizens from knowledge that their "rulers" judge to be harmful or inexpedient. Free and open discussion of all ideas allows citizens to make decisions for themselves about the merits of an idea, a product, or a candidate. Assuring that this would always be possible *on a national scale* was a primary concern of those who argued for and finally secured passage of the first ten amendments. They believed their colonial experience and the history of political societies in the world amply demonstrated that where the populace was patronized and treated as incapable of understanding the principles and details of government, tyranny followed.

Under the new system, it was generally understood that in those rare cases where national security required that information be withheld from the general public, notably in times of war, some restraints might be put on freedom of expression and the citizens' right to know. This understanding can be traced to the state constitutions written just after the Declaration of Independence and to the Articles of Confederation. Treason and subversive activities were concerns in the early days of the Republic. Recognizing this practical necessity was admitting that another form of tension often arises between the ideal of an open marketplace of ideas and the practical needs of sometimes conducting statecraft away from the public eye. The tension between practical survival and faithfulness to the Founders' ideals is a strong one. In our time, the courts have leaned toward openness unless a "compelling government interest" can be demonstrated that necessitates closing down access to national security information. In the past, however, the courts have been more supportive of the government claims for the need for security. In the chapters that follow, I shall illustrate this tension and discuss how its problems have been resolved without permanent loss of freedom to express. It is enough to point out here that this tension is inevitable. It escalates when executive privilege or some other form of control is invoked to limit information that might prove useful to the public's understanding of an issue. The censorship and eventual release of the Pentagon Papers is a case in point. The Nixon administration sought to suppress the information. It did not put national security at risk but was clearly critical in educating the public about our war effort and in helping them decide what course should be followed in the Vietnam War. The government was unable to prosecute those who released the Papers because of the long tradition and legal status of the guarantee of freedom of expression and information, but in other circumstances, in the short run, suppression of such information sometimes serves the public's interest. For example, during World War II, it was vital to keep secret the

3

fact that the Allies had broken the German cryptography. *When* such suppression is warranted is a familiar subject of debate in free societies.

I shall examine some attempts to undermine the guarantee of freedom of expression. The clashes I shall look at were contests in persuasion *about* freedom of expression and information. These clashes, others like them, and the pervasive tension between desire for change and desire for order have created an environment in which persuasion is pervasive and often highly sophisticated. I shall begin my survey with some philosophical clashes that helped to establish the tradition of freedom in portions of the country where it did not originally exist and I will conclude by exploring the nature of modern political campaigning and its involvement with modern technology.

Our nation was founded by people who sought freedom of expression for themselves and their kind, as did the Puritans; by people who sought this kind of freedom for all people, as did the Quakers of Penn's woods; and by people who carried into the New World British constitutional and Enlightenment theories of individual rights. In colonial and early national times, these kinds of people did not see "freedom of expression" as a value in precisely the same ways. Joining their views had to be worked out over time, as we shall see. Yet ours is a history of retaining individual freedoms in the face of socio-political threats against these freedoms. Despite inevitable controversies over how best to implement freedom in this or that socio-political moment, freedom of expression has been generally valued in America. I hope to shed some light on *how* this has happened *here.* To do so seems both historically and contemporaneously important because survival of freedom of expression is by no means the norm in Western civilization, even though it has long been the West's avowed ideal.

A part of the obligations of a responsible citizen in a free society is to be aware of the persuasive strategies that operate in the pursuit of freedom. These are rhetorical-persuasive processes that interpret and create political and social realities. They are processes that, for a nation as a whole, are largely controlled by the leaders of society. What I aim at in this volume is a *description of the major strategies employed to accomplish change in a free and open system.* I do not suggest that persuasion is or has been the sole means of socio-political development.

THE BOUNDARIES OF PERSUASION

Since its origins in the Revolutionary War, the United States has undergone dramatic political and cultural changes without experiencing

4

the upheaval associated with revolutions in France, Russia, and more recently China. It is true that this nation grew out of a violent revolution, but that violence erupted to preserve rights that the colonists claimed had evolved over the previous century and a half. Furthermore, the country has withstood pressures for change without disintegrating. For the most part, radical thought has been tempered by accommodating the prevailing mood through public debate and because of a long-standing tradition that accepts the vote of the majority and the rule of the Constitution as interpreted by the Supreme Court. But this is an idealized view of the American experiment; our history is certainly not devoid of strife and violence. The Civil War grew out of inability to settle, through public debate, conflicts over values and constitutional issues. Labor strife has certainly not been unknown to us, and during the Vietnam War Americans took to the streets, rioted, and threw stones at their president. To be realistic, we must grant that even in the United States the possibilities of public persuasion are limited. We should look closely, then, at what the resources of public persuasion have allowed in our society and what they have not provided.

Abraham Lincoln's first inaugural exemplifies public persuasion struggling with impending violence. Lincoln appealed for adherence to traditional institutions of public and political order. He told the seven states that had already seceded from the Union that their action had no legal basis, and he relied on the Constitution to justify his armed action to preserve the Union. These appeals and appeals to love for and the expediency of union failed to persuade all parties, and the war came. When it was over, however, the Civil War had made the "United States" a singular noun, and the union became more stable. Post-Civil War America was less likely to tolerate political actions that went beyond the boundaries of persuasion. The nation was on the way to a "nationalism" based on a continuity of thought about the importance of government-by-law-and-persuasion.

Historic, institutionalized decisions yield traditions to which persuaders also can and continually do appeal, but persuaders also reshape our traditions. History is perhaps not as much "what happened" as it is "what people have been led to *think* happened." When Lincoln reinterpreted the Constitution as precluding secession, he was building illusions as much as was Jefferson Davis when he tried to prove that the Constitution allowed for secession. What the Founders really meant by "separation of church and state" is under heated debate today, and probably the decision will evolve from arguments before the Supreme Court and in the Congress. Just how our stabilizing traditions should be perceived is itself a serious matter of public persuasion—persuasion in which the institutions of society, such as church, state, educational establishments, geographic blocks, and historical and legal research tend to pull the various disrupting sides toward a conceptual middle. Our stabilizing institutions are subject to gradual change, but they do stabilize by their continued existence: they comprise what Edmund Burke called the "fabric of society."

Since the framing of the Constitution, "mainstream" political leaders have had a large part in institutionalizing the nation's central values: Freedom of speech and press; accepted legal procedures; routine transfer of office from one officer to another; separation of legislative, executive, and judicial power; and a host of others. On the whole, the conserving values have given birth to a set of phenomena that function to maintain social stability. When issued from established institutions—the law courts, the executive, and even segments of the press—persuasive appeals to these values take on the force of law both because of their standing as *values* and because of the institutional *source* by which they are affirmed. They even have a coercive cast that limits the subsequent role persuasion can play in the society. For example, judicial interpretations of the doctrine of equal rights have by now made it difficult to persuade by arguing that merit, *without* regard for race, creed, or sex, should be valued above policies of reparational "affirmative action."

One sees the conserving and constraining thrusts of institutionalized values in the First and Tenth Amendments to the Constitution. The First Amendment, which is the bedrock of all other liberties, protects freedom of press, speech, and religion. It prohibits the Congress from making any law abridging these freedoms. The Tenth Amendment vests in the states all powers not specifically delegated to the federal government. These and the other Bill of Rights amendments were intended to maximize individual freedom and to constrain the active powers of the national government. The Bill of Rights exists because of vigorous criticism of the Constitution during the debates over its ratification in 1787—88. Interpretation of these amendments has been the subject of continuous debates across two centuries. The same perennial problem or tension motivated that discourse: How much individual and group freedom is consistent with the collective good and stability? Assuming that our democratic-republican system continues, it would be folly to expect debate on that question ever to cease. On the other hand, because *both* freedom to change *and* the worth of stability are paramount values built into our laws and traditions, those who would promote change primarily through actions, rather than primarily through persuasion, have been

6

institutionally placed at a disadvantage. I want to portray the ways in which public discourse in the United States has usually channeled radicalism toward reform rather than toward revolution and ideology toward compromise rather than toward political and social fragmentation. We appear to be destined to function within the tensive framework of freedom and order. Accordingly, it is worthwhile to understand the uses and limits of persuasion in a freeing-constraining society. Perhaps the strongest reason for doing so is that if persuasion cannot ameliorate conflicts between freedom and order, applications of force become the alternative.

PHILOSOPHICAL CONFRONTATIONS

I begin this study with an examination of persuasive processes that grow out of philosophical confrontations. The two cases I shall discuss illustrate how philosophical ideals are converted into pragmatic realities through persuasive interchanges of considerable duration. In the first instance we shall see how, in one part of the nation, freedom and individualism were born out of a philosophical/theological struggle. In the second case we shall observe how utopian political ideas were gradually compromised by persuasive processes, permitting their incorporation within the mainstream of political thought.

By *philosophical confrontations,* I mean conflicts about *values.* Such confrontations can occur with a person or in a society. For example, during the Vietnam War many young men had to decide between service to a country they loved and rejection of what they perceived as an immoral war. Questions of patriotism, survival, courage, and self-worth had to be worked out in inner dialogue before action could be taken.[1] Conflicts between philosophies also occur in public arenas. What *kind* of *person* a black human being is was a philosophical question much argued in politics during the nineteenth century. The relative values of free enterprise and collectivism have been the subject of innumerable twentieth-century arguments. In the discussion to follow I propose to reflect on both intrapersonal and interpersonal conflicts over values.

What happens when conflicts concerning values and value systems occur depends on how an individual or a group is able to cope rhetorically with several predictable problems in "making a case." Those problems include:

1. Showing that a particular philosophy explains and rationalizes past and present experiences
2. Showing that one's philosophy "fits" and explains *new* experiences as they arise

3. Adjusting one's philosophy to new circumstances without seriously compromising the fundamental principles of that philosophy
4. Exposing the weaknesses of competing philosophies and thereby impairing the persuasive appeal of alternative philosophical assumptions and positions
5. Showing and sustaining the claim that a given set of philosophical principles and concepts can be *applied in practice* with plausible and desirable results—as in a political program
6. Showing that to act on the principles of a given philosophy will or will not bring about confrontations among different religious, social, and economic classes

These are what might be called the "strategic" issues on which outcomes of confrontations between philosophies depend. Outcomes are, of course, also affected by events, especially when confrontations continue over a considerable period of time. Philosophies derive in part from experiences of those who espouse them. But the course of events and the new experiences they generate can outrun a philosophy by providing grounds for opposing or altering it. For example, to most of us, no amount of persuasion can integrate contemporary experience with the philosophy of the Flat Earth Society. In general, a philosophy that is unable to explain or adapt to changing social, economic, scientific, and political conditions will fall by the wayside, and no amount of persuasion can save it. We shall see both rhetorically generated and event-generated developments at work in the cases treated in this chapter. In either case, however, rhetorical success in sustaining philosophical positions will depend on the six rhetorical considerations I have just enumerated.

I propose to ask and answer how philosophical confrontations tend to be handled in American rhetoric and how rhetorical resolutions of such conflicts have shaped our history. I shall examine two decidedly different historical cases: the confrontations associated with Puritanism and those associated with Populism. The Puritans arrived in America in 1630, and they almost immediately began a long debate about their values. Populism had its roots in the Grange movement of 1872 and was carried to the pinnacle of its persuasive power in the presidential campaign of 1896. Examining the rhetorical management of the cases argued in these two disparate philosophical controversies will reveal important features of how our history has been made, and it will suggest ways that we ought to think about public philosophical confrontations in general.

10

PURITAN VERSUS REVIVALIST

The spirit of nationalism grew out of the breakdown of feudalism, the growth of a middle class, the emergence of guilds, mercantilism, corporations, and awareness of the importance of land ownership. The Renaissance generated interest in cultivating secular life, exploration, the arts, and trade. The Reformation forced a questioning of church-state relations, religious individualism, and tolerance. In rough outline, these were changes in the European milieu that occurred before immigration to America began.

In 1630, ten years after the landing by the Pilgrims, the Puritans came to Massachusetts. In various ways the culture they brought with them was a product of the European changes I have just mentioned. They were driven from England by the rise of Bishop Laud and by the Anglican resurgence of 1629.[2] Like later American protest groups, the Puritans would use the persecution they had suffered as an argument to vindicate their movement and justify their own excesses. The stories of the persecuted—John Foxe (1516–1587), William Perkins (1558–1602), and Thomas Shepard—would serve to punctuate the cry for freedom and to rationalize the need for conformity in the New Zion.

In an early sermon, John Winthrop, the first governor of the Massachusetts Bay Colony, set the tone of the Puritan venture. He used for his text Second Samuel, 7:10, "Moreover I will appoint a place for my people Israel, and will plant them, that they may dwell in a place of their own, and move no more: Neither shall the children of wickedness afflict them any more, as before time." Here would be a New Zion, a Bible Commonwealth, highly ordered, theocratic, and pragmatic. It would be a "Shining City upon a Hill" in the New World. (This Biblical allusion has been used by Ronald Reagan and Mario Cuomo in recent years.) Winthrop's sermon was not very different from those he had given in England. It became a model for other preachers in the New World. It set out theological lines of argument that would run through the revolutionary period and the growth of America as a nation. We hear them even today from the rostrums of our political conventions and religious ceremonies: We are a chosen people; we must keep our society cleansed; we have a manifest destiny; we grow in purity while the Old World decays in sin.

For Puritans, the New Zion was the ideal to which they aspired; the Old World was the reality they sought to escape. They would advance man to his more perfect state in order to rectify his relations to an omnipotent God. All of these goals were set into a Covenant Theology, and that theology became the basis of the philosophical/theological confrontation that developed over the next generations. Winthrop was trying to create more than a moral Republic, he was in fact asserting that the Puritans were carrying out God's work in a religious Zion.[3] Winthrop and his band of Puritans heard a "calling." They had survived the crucible of persecution in England, a rough crossing of the Atlantic, and much suffering in the New World. Having paid such dues, when forced to defend their values, they would do so zealously. Thus, "justification by hardship" became a theme often used in philosophical arguments. It is even a safe generalization that the founders of a philosophical movement who endure hardships will be more committed to their philosophy than those to whom they pass it. It can also be generalized that those who later evangelize for the philosophy will commonly use the episodes of hardships the founders endured to justify their own actions and interpretations and to motivate new followers.

The hopes of the new Puritan community, and its assurances, were embodied in Covenant Theology. By His grace, God established three covenants with the faithful: the Covenant of Church, the Covenant of Society, and the Covenant of Grace. The first two were promises and directions for socio-religious action, and the third dealt directly with the terms for personal salvation. The marvelous power of the "covenant rhetoric" that developed from the three covenants was that it not only reinforced uniformity in the religious and secular communities but it held out hope of a saving *personal* experience for each member of the community. The sin of one person in the society became the sin of all, but the Covenant of Grace promised the possibility of personal salvation from the consequences of sin.

The Covenant Theology and its associated rhetoric softened the austere notions of John Calvin's *Institutes,* which were the keystones of Puritan theology in England and America. Unmodified, Calvin's strictures excluded from eligibility to the true church all but a select handful of the "saved." Many of the Puritan clergy appear to have sensed that Calvin's formulations, if taken literally, were too rigid for a thriving and continuing Church and society. Over time, their explanations and defenses of Covenant Theology produced a good deal of controversy and a remarkable compromise.

The Covenant of Church essentially involved God's exchanging His pledge to be their God for the Puritans' total acceptance of Him. Those who had saving experiences provided evidence that the spirit of God was

12

among his chosen people, so "saving experiences" became the heart of Covenant Theology.

It developed that children of the settlers were not having saving experiences. One theory was that because the colony had become more secure, and even somewhat prosperous, the second generation of Puritans had not been purified by the hardships of their parents. They were therefore less open to emotional conversion based on appeals to God's wrath. In other words, they felt less need of God in their newly secured world because they had less direct experience of His power.

The church fathers adapted by creating a "half-way covenant." It allowed members, especially children, to attend church but not to partake of communion. The hope was that these half-way members would eventually "see the light." The half-way covenant allowed them into the church in the hope that they would earn their way to the altar.

But the breadth of the covenant was only one of the problems the Puritans faced in trying to sustain their ideology. A more devastating problem arose when "visible saints," those who were recognized by the Church as being saved, could not agree among themselves on who in the community had been saved. Confusion was compounded in 1641 when the King forced the colony to accept religious tolerance in secular affairs.[4] The new Massachusetts Charter of 1641 said: "Every man whether inhabitant or foreigner, free or not free shall have libertie to come to any publique court, counsel, or Towne meeting, and wither by speech or writing to move any lawfull, seasonable, and materiall question, or to present any necessary motion, complaint, petition, bill or information, where that meeting hath proper cognizance. . . ." The opening of society's affairs to the voices of non-covenanters was not contemplated by Covenant Theology as originally promulgated.

In 1662 a Synod was held to attempt to clarify the confusion. Partial church membership was granted to those who professed faith, and lived righteously. The half-way covenant was reasserted, now specifically with respect to the Church.

The conception of an inner church of "visible saints" and an outer church of half-way members led to a change in the style of preaching. Early ministers, conceiving themselves to be addressing homilies to small congregations of informed and concerned adherents to the faith, had generally made sober appeals to the intellect and careful analyses of scripture and Covenant Theology. Now, with the awful fate of half-way members avowed, ministers began to make hortatory efforts to move the half-way members toward saving experiences. This became more and

13

more reasonable as time passed because half-way members and non-members came to outnumber visible saints by larger and larger ratios. Ministers literally had to call out to the half-way members in the rear of the church, over the heads of the saints in the front pews. The physical situation of sermonic address was symbolic of the intellectual problem Covenant Theology faced.

The change in Puritan sermonic rhetoric was dramatic. It was a logical and practical adaptation to a new reality in church audiences.[5] But the original version of the Covenant of Church authorized no such change. In consequence, the philosophical root of Covenant Theology was put in question. Changes in theological interpretations came more slowly than changes in homiletic style, but roughly a century after the Puritans arrived, Solomon Stoddard, in 1725, was directly ripping away at the impossibilities of the Church Covenant as originally interpreted.[6]

Logical and practical impossibilities in the original interpretations of the Social Covenant also soon presented serious problems. The Social Covenant had been conceived from Biblical sources and nurtured aboard the good ship *Arabella*. As initially conceived, the covenant required God's chosen people to fulfill the "mission" of Christ on earth by founding a New Zion. The government of the New Zion was divinely ordained. Second Kings 11:17 expressed member-government relationships in terms of a King's loyalty to his people and their loyalty to the King.

The Social Covenant was conceived as binding all citizens together, as *one body,* to God. They were to be "knit as one" in their conformity, said Winthrop. The sin of one member of the body would therefore fall on the entire body. The whole community was thus responsible for the actions of each member. Twenty thousand incoming settlers were expected to conform in this Zion. The people, the civil government, and the ecclesiastical domain were conceived as one in thought and deed. If you were not a church member, you could not become a freeman; if you were not a freeman, you could not vote and hold office.[7] Church membership required that one had had a saving experience verified by other church members. The society was monolithic and theocratic, and it was natural and even necessary that ministers exercise direction over the Colony's development, though they did not serve in secular office.

Not surprisingly, the clergy was a coercive group of guardians.[8] They worked diligently to keep the community unified and sinless. Those expressing nonconforming theological positions were banished and formed new settlements, as in Rhode Island and Connecticut. To the Puritan preachers, including Winthrop and Cotton Mather, variety was

14

sin. But variety was inevitable given the influx of settlers, the change of generations, and the end to frontier insecurity. This is why the Social Covenant collapsed. The sea of immigrants simply overwhelmed the small band of purists who had established the covenants in 1630. As early as 1634, civic leaders had to share legislative powers with "deputies" elected by freemen because of provisions written into the Massachusetts Royal Charter. Local affairs were debated in town meetings, a tradition that continues to this day in New England. When open forums were imposed in 1641, and Roger Williams lobbied for separation of church and state in 1644, the Social Covenant was severely threatened. In 1675, measures were "adopted to suppress, among other things, the pride displayed in immodest and costly fashion."[9]

By 1679, the forms of sermonic persuasion were changing again. Young preachers were beginning to experiment with new forms of organization and more emotional appeals.[10] In that year, yet another Synod was called to protect the Social Covenant from reform. Sins were cataloged; duties detailed. Again, *structure* was seen as the best means to save the philosophical movement. But it was to no avail. In 1684 the original New England Charter was revoked; the 1691 Charter again demanded religious toleration, a provision of the 1641 Charter that had been ignored after the rise of Cromwell in England.

In this period of philosophical/theological tension, preachers made further adaptations. The accepted argument that God would not punish good was, for example, extended by some ministers to assert that God would *reward* good. Eventually freedom of thought and religious interpretation could not be contained in the Christian community. Prosperity, security, and practicalities of maintaining congregations eroded the need and justifications for the Social Covenant. Something different was needed to make the faith acceptable and motivating. That need was answered by evolution of revivalism, and revivalism undercut Covenant Theology by legitimating emotionalism and individualism.

We should note here the intellectual character of the shift in Puritan theology. The issues being controverted were theological, and they concerned the highest values—man's relation to God. The actual argumentation, however, tended to focus on practical decisions. Initially, Puritans argued about who was saved and what the half-way covenant meant about the nature and structure of the Church. Still more practically, the half-way covenant notion raised the rhetorical issue: *Who* is preaching *for?* Such considerations became the foci of strife: Was the Church's main business to save the unsaved or to sustain the faith and understanding of the visible saints? By what homiletic *means* could either or both ends be best served? Inability to answer such questions on the basis of received theory undermined Covenant Theology and at the same time gave detractors evidence for arguments against the received doctrine and its defenders. Revivalist preachers often combined debate about theology and its ultimate values with ridicule of the practices with which the old theology was presumably being maintained. The Puritans' experience was prototypical in this respect. Where theory or philosophy cannot deal with practical realities, the theory is opened to ridicule. As we shall see, in a later day Populists who were theoretically and ideally concerned with helping the poor were eventually caught up in debate over the practical merits of free coinage of silver.

The flavor of early debate over Puritan theological issues can be perceived in the printed exchanges between Roger Williams of Rhode Island and Puritan leaders. In 1644, Williams wrote his famous *Bloudy Tenent of Persecution for Cause of Conscience*. In it he refuted a tract prepared by the Massachusetts ministers. He wrote: "Magistrates . . . have no power of setting up the Forme of Church Government. . . . And on the other side, the Churches as Churches, have no power . . . of erecting or altering formes of Civill Government. . . ." John Cotton answered Williams in 1647 with a tract of his own to which Williams responded in 1652:

> I fear Master Cotton would create some evil opinion in the heart of the civil Magistrate. . . . Master Cotton and others have thought (me) too zealous. . . . The daughter New England, separated from her mother in Old England, yet maintains and practices communion with the Parishes of Old. Who sees not then, but by the links of this mystical chaine, New England Churches are still fastened to the Pope himself?

The arguments of Williams were answered by many. But no one was more prolific or influential than Increase Mather's son, Cotton. Here is an excerpt from his "election sermon" of 1690:

> The God of Heaven has good thoughts for those men, whose good works render them Servicable to His People. . . . Our God has a People in the World . . . a people who have chosen the Lord Jesus for the Redeemer of their souls; a people who have Believed and Practised according to the Scriptures of Truth. . . . Tis the prerogative of New England above all the Countries of the World, That it is a Plantation for the Christian and Protestant Religion. You may now see a land filled with Churches, which by solemn and awful Covenants are Dedicated unto the Son of God.

16

In the years that led up to the "Great Awakening," theoretical and practical argument continued energetically and sometimes vitriolically. There was a veritable propaganda war between the "New Lights" and the "Old Lights" of the Church. Theologically there was an antithesis between the received doctrine of predestination and the much looser doctrine of the Covenant of Grace. There were also practical difficulties in maintaining congregations of "the elect" only. As a result of the theological inconsistency, the half-way covenant, the influx of immigrants, and persuasive New Light arguments, the notion of a Social Covenant was gradually eroded and soon even the Old Light preachers began to alter their basic messages and their sermonic style. Theocracy was visibly dying out as more and more people began to share Roger Williams' views on the separation of religion and statecraft. The theological antithesis gave the "opening" for theological change in the direction of religious individualism while the practicalities of holding audiences and sustaining the churches provided impetus for the change.

God's mercy, argued the orthodox Puritans, granted the Covenant of Grace. This covenant existed between God and Abraham's offspring. Violating the covenant, Winthrop often warned his followers, would bring travail upon the New Zion. But if the covenant were adhered to, it was possible, if faith were properly placed, to experience saving grace despite man's corruption. Christ provided the redemptive power that gave Puritan preachers their most optimistic message. The theological problem was to find rational procedures to attain grace without violating the notion that only a few were destined to be "saved." The rhetorical genius of the orthodox system was that the Covenant of Grace was to energize people to seek to be "saved." Listening to the Word was one way to salvation since it aided the *understanding,* which could move the *will* to salvation. The parishioner thus had nothing to lose by "attending the Word," and surely was unsavable if he or she ignored the Word.

According to traditional theology, the Covenant of Grace, known by some as the Covenant of Good Works, had been violated by Adam. Thereby all God's creatures were damned. From this condition, God could elect to save whom He pleased. Their salvation was a grant of mercy since God did not have to save anyone. Since man was corrupt, the Puritans believed his faculties were corrupt also. Corruption of understanding paralyzed the will, so that only a merciful rebirth in Christ could free these faculties. Such rebirth was predestined by God but prospects of its happening were expanded in the covenant of redemption through Christ.

How then were Puritan preachers to recommend actions by which to attain grace without violating the older doctrine of predestination? The method hit upon was to synthesize "faculty psychology" with the "morphology of conversion." Faculty psychology held that the various aspects of the psyche were located in different parts of the body. The understanding was in the head; the will in the heart; the appetites and affections pervaded the body. Man could be remade. The understanding could guide the will to accept faith. Once faith was embraced and professed, the emotional rebirth was possible.

How was this movement to salvation accomplished? Sense data (incoming perceptions) were identified by the understanding, embraced or rejected by the will, which then directed the emotions (the affections) to respond. As conceived by the Puritan ministers, understanding was the key to opening the individual to God's world; the emotions were reached *through* the understanding by rational speech.

This belief that the intellect moved the human will explains why early Puritan sermons were dry, pedantic, and expository. Careful, analytical listening was expected: the emotions were believed to interfere with clear understanding. Accordingly, preachers directed their persuasion at the understanding and minimized appeals to emotions. This was a reasonable response to prevailing psychological notions, but it made for dull sermonizing. However, a new psychological theory was beginning to take hold.

At first a few, then many preachers began to think of the human psyche as a single entity, instead of conceiving of the understanding, will, and emotions as separate entities having a chainlike relationship. The idea spread that to influence one "part" of the psyche was to influence the whole person. Appeals to emotions were thus psychologically legitimized and they increasingly appeared in sermons. The ultimate result was the gradual emergence of a new style and form of preaching. This style often took the form of a "jeremiad" because in the manner of the Old Testament prophet, Jeremiah, the sermons were direct and often threatening calls for immediate change in the life of each listener.

The first "jeremiads" began to appear early in the 1640s and their appearance led to considerable theological debate about the relative merits of intellectualism and emotionalism in preaching. As strict Calvinist doctrines began to disintegrate, the emotions were increasingly seen and used as avenues to the will, and emotional preaching came into ascendancy.

The evolution from one persuasive mode to the other was slow, but the change was evident and conscious. For example, Michael Wigglesworth's lectures on oratory at Harvard reflected a more unitary view of man's psychological makeup than was commonly understood by traditional

18

preachers.[11] Eventually, laymen were expected to *seek* the light as they listened; they were no longer conceived of as passive though rational listeners. Moreover, an obligation to *motivate* now fell upon the sermonizer.

Even Cotton Mather was converted to "Glorious piety," and this caused him to ignore the covenants in his later sermonizing. Solomon Stoddard, who began as a pillar of the old church, moved sermonic practice toward emotionalism by condemning erudite preaching. He claimed that "God leads me through the whole work of preparation partly by fear, and partly by hope." Jonathan Edwards' slow, frightening delivery of highly colored discourse brought many to conversion, and others—including his uncle by marriage—to suicide.[12]

With the "Great Awakening," the change was complete; the covenants were gone; doctrinal upheaval had set in. But, as I have already said, the shift had been gradual, and a new set of theological-philosophical premises had to be worked out. Wigglesworth's lectures on eloquence (1653) presaged change, but no single minister better represents the change from intellection to emotionalism in *both theory and practice* than Solomon Stoddard (1643–1729).

Stoddard's *A Guide to Christ,* published in 1714, offered theological-psychological principles by which a preacher was to "guide souls through the work of conversion." Stoddard reversed the traditional order of steps to salvation. Instead of addressing the *understanding* and thereby the *will* to guide listeners toward salvation, Stoddard emphasized influencing them through *hope* and *fear*. In short, *emotions* must be addressed directly. His most radical theological notion was that "[t]here is an absolute connection between faith and salvation: if you believe in Christ that will be a sure sign of election. . . . You will not be rejected if you come." Perhaps in his zeal to increase church membership and inspire preaching, Stoddard went farther than his colleagues were willing to go in overturning the doctrine of predestination, but his doctrine that salvation is open to all and his teachings about how to preach were to become the bases of religious theories and practices entirely antithetical to traditional Puritanism.[13] Revivalism flowed from his initiating spirit.

The "Awakening" is generally chronicled as running from 1735 to 1745 in New England, from 1725 to 1758 in the Middle Colonies, and from 1739 to 1780 in the South. The extent to which evangelism freed the American spirit is of great moment to current historians. Some argue that the "Awakening" was the opening of the political revolution to come. Surely, religious activation of the lowliest of men, and the corresponding radical emphasis on individualism had great impact. In

19

this sense, at least, there can be little doubt that the rhetoric of revolution began in the sermons of ministers caught up with new theories of obedience.[14] Suddenly, the world witnessed a massive revolution of thought and action countenanced by the religious doctrine of the colonies of one nation.[15]

Jonathan Edwards' preaching was the culmination of Stoddard's doctrine and style of sermonizing. When Stoddard died in 1729, Edwards assumed the old man's pulpit. His fame was achieved, however, through his revivals at Enfield, Connecticut in 1734 and 1735. Later, in 1741 on July 8, Edwards returned to Enfield to deliver his most famous sermon: "Sinners in the Hands of an Angry God."

"Sinners" specifically reveals Edwards' reliance on the linkage between persuasion and psychology. He believed in shifting the attention of the minister from God's truth (*logos*) to God's beauty (*pathos*). Edwards' sermonizing was *sensational* both in terms of the senses it aroused and the reaction it got. Edwards believed the entry to the will was through the senses (and feelings) of an audience:

> O sinner! Consider the fearful danger you are in. "Tis a great furnace of wrath, a wide and bottomless pit, full of the fire of wrath, that you are held over in the hand of that God whose wrath is provoked and incensed as much against you as against many of the damned in hell. You hang by a slender thread, with the flames of divine wrath flashing about it, and ready every moment to singe it and burn it assunder; and you have no interest in any mediator, and nothing to lay hold of to save yourself, nothing to keep off the flames of wrath, nothing of your own, nothing that you have ever done, nothing that we can do, to induce God to spare you one moment.

He painted vivid pictures of imminent fiery damnation to create in listeners a state of mind conducive to the saving experience. He sought to reach the will not with reason but with frightening appeals to the eye, ear, nose and touch.

What Edwards did to kindle the new spirit in New England, George Whitefield did in England and in most of the American colonies. In America, Whitefield helped to transform a growing schism in religion into a gigantic gulf. He preached in fields and streets and held out the possibility of salvation to any person. In his published works, he held fast to the doctrine of predestination, but his sermons implied a more democratic God.

If Stoddard filled more pews, and Edwards expanded preaching's use

20

of emotion, Whitefield opened the floodgates of democratized religion. His anti-intellectualism and his outdoor preaching made him a celebrity in America and England. Of 110 anti-Methodist pamphlets written in England before 1740, 82 were directed at Whitefield. In Foote's plays, he was Mr. Squintum; novelists Tobias Smollett and Henry Fielding satirized him; he was Hogarth's "Cross eyed clerk" and Richard Groves' "Wild Goose." But Whitefield's drawing power helped him fend off critics almost as easily as he made converts. His message was radical: Christ can save us all. In his most famous sermon, "Abraham's Offering up of His Son Isaac," he exhorted:

> We do not love God or Christ as we ought to do: if you admire Abraham offering up his Isaac, how much more you ought to extol . . . the love of God. . . . O! Let us love him with all our hearts and minds and strength. . . . Unless you get a faith of the heart, a faith working by love, you shall never sit with Abraham. . . . From hence we may learn the nature of true justifying faith . . . that salvation is God's free gift.

Instead of predestination for a few, Whitefield's preaching offered a democratic opportunity to all. Instead of dry intellection, he brought emotional rejuvenation. Most important, instead of focusing on a single conformist congregation, Whitefield presupposed a radical individualism unknown to early New England Protestantism. Up to thirty thousand people at a time, mostly belonging to the lower and middle classes, heard Whitefield's sermons, and a scattering of the wealthy could be seen in carriages at the edges of the crowds. Much weeping, wailing and convulsiveness characterized such gatherings; much money was collected, even from the poor. Whitefield's sermons were so powerful that when one was read in his absence in Maryland, a revival began.

Revivalism created a spirit in America that was congenial to the Revolution.[16] Revivalism was first and foremost a break with authority; it established a psychology that could accommodate other religious change.[17] Elisha Williams (1694–1755), rector of Yale from 1725 to 1739, made a formal plea for the broadest freedom of expression in religion in 1741:

> That the sacred scriptures are alone the Rule of the Faith and Practice to a Christian, all Protestants are agreed in; and must therefore inviolably maintain, that every Christian has a Right of judging for himself what he is to believe and practice in Religion according to that Rule.

21

It was no step at all from this religious belief to the position that each citizen was free to make and interpret secular laws.

Revivalism also taught radical democracy. If anyone could be saved, then all men were equal before God. In fact, the rationalizations religious leaders used for the sake of revivalism were later transformed into political rationalizations, as in the Declaration of Independence and other discourses intimately involved in the campaign to overthrow British rule. An early example of this linkage was Jonathan Mayhew's preaching.[18]

Mayhew's most famous sermon, "Unlimited Submission and Non-resistance to the Higher Powers," was delivered in 1750. In this one sermon delivered twenty-five years before the Revolution, we find *couched in religious doctrine many of the crucial appeals later used by Henry, Jefferson, Adams, and Madison to justify revolt.* And they are used in our time by politicians discoursing on the sacred heritage we must protect—mainly by electing them. It is no wonder modern historians have called Mayhew's sermon the "morning gun of the revolution." We do well to remember, too, that such a sermon could not have been delivered had not the conformist pressures of theocracy been undermined and freedom of expression about religion and politics come to be protected in New England society.

Mayhew's sermon presented a facet of the kind of persuasion that tends to resolve philosophical confrontations. The sermon, ahead of its time, merged the best thoughts and outlooks of both philosophical "sides" into a single philosophy. Mayhew's avowal of independence and individualism was a synthesis of the best thinking of enlightenment philosophers and the soundest justifications offered by revivalist theologians. Like the early Puritans, Mayhew was rational in his approach to listeners, yet he also gave attention to their feelings. Mayhew brought together thoughts and attitudes about religion and politics that had been evolving for 120 years, but his tone remained intellectual and expository in the manner of the best Puritan divines. Some excerpts from the sermon illustrate these qualities:

> It follows, by a parity of reason, that when he turns tyrant, and makes his subjects prey to devour and to destroy . . . we are bound to throw off our allegiance to him and to resist. . . . We ourselves . . . are indispensably obliged to secure and promote as far as in us lies the opportunity. . . . For a nation thus abused to arise unanimously and resist their prince, even to the dethroning of him, is not criminal, but a reasonable way of vindicating their liberties

22

and just rights; it is making use of means, and the only means which God has put into their power for mutual and self defense. . . . If those who bear the title of civil rulers do not perform the duty of civil rulers, but act directly counter to the sole end and design of their office; if they injure and oppress their subjects, instead of defending their rights and doing them good, they have not the least pretence to be honored, obeyed, and rewarded.

In 1673, in reaction to attempts from England to control the Anglican church in America, Mayhew wrote a pamphlet called *Observations on the Propagation of the Gospel*. In it he clearly expressed separatist and individualistic thoughts: "[I]s it not enough that they persecuted us out of their world? Will they pursue us into the new to convert us here?" These themes of personal and national independence, of the *right* of a people to displace their "rulers," of a divinely ordained *American* destiny presaged the major themes of our most honored political documents: the Declaration of Independence, the Constitution, and the Bill of Rights. Indeed, as I shall later show, these same themes appear in virtually every political campaign, whether it be to elect a president or to protest ecological abuses.

These themes are contributions of the pulpit to political discourse in America. They constitute parts of an American heritage that defines fair play in governance and the paramount importance of individual rights. Any past or present politician perceived to be tampering with or disregarding this heritage has been popularly judged to have violated the American civil religion that emerged in parallel with evangelism.

In the United States issues raised by philosophical confrontations are characteristically rendered political. In that process modifications occur as the issues and propositions are shaped by the self-governing people. The result is that what is finally accepted by the populace is less absolute, final, or arbitrary than the philosophical premises that gave those propositions birth. Significantly, this cannot be said of certain other philosophical confrontations elsewhere—such as those between the rights of "the people" and the established government in the French Revolution or that between "democracy" as represented by the Weimar German Republic and the doctrines of National Socialism. At most points in our history a consensus existed that things must be settled by free and open debate in *public forums*. The result has usually been that pragmatic compromises are derived from, but not fully expressive of, philosophical positions.

The struggle between theocratic dogmatism and individual freedom

23

was a formative part of colonial New England's experience, and it was an early instance of this movement from doctrine to pragmatics. The controversy illustrates and tends to explain how and why we have acquired a "civil religion." Indeed, most philosophical confrontations in the United States become "settled" in terms of that civil religion. As the New England theological controversies and the early documents of our nation illustrate, *fairness* was very early defined as action consistent with the values generally propounded by Judeo-Christian tradition. This same standard was manifested in settlements of such controversies as those over slavery and establishing the Thirteenth, Fourteenth, and Fifteenth Amendments to the Constitution. In these and many other cases the settlement reasserted the *moral right* to freedom, independence, and equal treatment of persons. Today, arguments about abortion reflect the same tendencies. The central, technical issue is: At what point in its development does a fetus acquire the full, historic, human rights to equal protection under the nation's basic laws? This is but one of the contemporary philosophical confrontations in which the *morally* generated rights of individual persons are being weighed in public argument. I suggest that in all such cases, political changes, if they are to be made, will have to be shown advantageous *without endangering the moral rights and privileges hammered out and articulated in New England's confrontation between theocratic dogmatism and democratic individualism.*

POPULISTS VERSUS SOCIAL DARWINISTS

The Origin of the Species was published by Darwin in 1859. While the Civil War raged across the American landscape, the debate over Darwin's thesis raged in British and eventually American pulpits, classrooms, laboratories, and the press.[19] With the end of the Civil War came America's great industrial surge. Capital formed rapidly and fortunes were made quickly, but working conditions were often an abomination. A few in society saw in Darwin's thesis a persuasive tool for rationalizing contemporary social and economic conditions. Ironically, many Social Darwinists were initially horrified by Darwin's thesis that natural selection of species explained how man evolved from lower forms of life. Nonetheless, the persuasive force of natural selection and its corollary that only the fittest survive was translated into a strong rationale for a competitive economic system: If the free enterprise system were to continue to advance, its weaker members would have to give way to the stronger. This was the "law" of social as well as biological life.

24

Other people, loosely called "Populists," believed that a better world could be built by restructuring the realities of the environment. Not deterministic "selection" but rational and idealistic management of social and economic institutions could and should direct the evolution of society, these opponents of Social Darwinism contended.

Populism as an organized movement was born out of the frustration of the Farm Alliance movement. Even that movement was preceded by the Patrons of Husbandry, a group that emerged after the Civil War to try to overcome the abject poverty of the rural South. The Patrons were imitated by many other grass roots organizations, which eventually merged to form the Farm Alliance. In 1889, the Western Farm Alliance gave way to the more diverse Populist or People's Party. In 1892, the Southern Farm Alliance, numbering nearly three million members, joined with the Populists to give them new impetus. Their candidate for president won twenty-two electoral votes, and they won the governorships of two states. In the 1894 election, the Populist vote increased by 42 percent over 1892. Populists were able to count six United States Senators and seven members of House in their ranks.

The positions of Populism as a political party derived from a miscellany of generally agrarian sources. With the depression of 1872, farm agitation became highly articulate. In 1873, for example, the Illinois State Farm Association listed its grievances. Besides attacking business monopolies, they claimed that the railroads were arbitrary in setting freight rates and were as opposed to free institutions and commerce as any feudal barons of the Middle Ages. These claims and their associated arguments would eventually become staples of Populist discourse, but the claims had an erratic history prior to formation of the People's Party.

In 1874, when wheat prices fell to $.67 a bushel, farmers gave support to a new movement, the Greenback movement. The Greenback Party was a pro-inflation party that wanted the government to print more paper money. The Greenback Party faded as a political force in 1877 when wheat prices shot up to $1.05 a bushel, but management of the economy was now added to the collection of ideas on which the Populists would draw. When wheat prices plunged below $.70 in 1887, a new agrarian entity, the Grange Movement, emerged and promulgated the general philosophical outlook of the still existing Farm Associations and the Greenback Party. Ultimately, such nostrums as abolition of national banks, free coinage of silver, Greenbacks, government ownership of railroads, and regulation of grain markets became parts of the heritage of the formally structured Populist Party.

In 1890, a United States Supreme Court decision in what was called the *Minnesota Rate* case effectively ended government regulation of the railroads by reversing the *Munn* decision. The "railroad barons" were free again to gouge their clients and this spurred renewed farm protest. It was at this point, in 1891, that the People's Party was formed by representatives from various existing farm and labor organizations. The new party held its first convention in 1892 and drew up a platform that incorporated all of the demands just named, together with proposals for a graduated income tax, introduction of the Australian ballot, direct election of Senators, and a number of other "radical" demands. In general, the Populists took their stand for redistribution of wealth, political reform, and aid to the destitute. It was a full fledged political party and had such election successes as I have already mentioned. It was not without political difficulties, however.

As the Populist movement grew, it became clear that it had both positive and negative appeals. Xenophobia, paranoia, and racism were present in the rhetoric of Western Populists, who looked to the minting of new quantities of silver coins as the cure for their economic plight. They asked that the Treasury coin new specie backed by silver instead of gold so that more money would be put into circulation. The resulting inflation would relieve farm debt and stimulate the economy. Their hatred for the "Eastern Banks" is the basis for Richard Hofstadter's conclusion that they were tainted with anti-Semitism, but an examination of primary source material fails to support the claim.[20]

Southern Populists were more positive.[21] They attempted to include the Negro Alliance in the Populist movement and proposed detailed programs of land reform, railroad regulation, and antitrust legislation, which they believed were more important than coinage of silver. Generally, the southerners perceived silver conversion as only one of many answers to the problems of the 1890s. They seemed to understand more clearly than their midwestern brethren that equity in a land of plenty could not be accomplished with a single kind of legislation alone.

The Populist Party Platform of 1892 was an attempt to unify the disparate rhetorics of the West and South by stressing that only cooperation would bring the nation back from the verge of moral, political, and material ruin into which it had fallen. Ignatius Donnelly wrote in the Preamble to the platform:

> The conditions which surround us best justify our cooperation: we meet in the midst of a nation brought to the verge of moral, political, and material ruin. Corruption dominates the ballot box . . . and touches even the ermine of the bench. . . . The national

26

power to create money is appropriated to enrich bond holders. . . . A vast conspiracy against mankind has been organized on
two continents, and is rapidly taking possession of the world. . . .
We declare that this Republic can only endure as a free government
while built upon the love of the people for each other.

He went on to articulate the Populist litany I have already reviewed.
James B. Weaver was nominated as the Populist presidential candidate.
He received 10 percent of the electoral vote and two million popular
votes in the ensuing election.

Two years later, the Populists had taken control of state legislatures,
won governorships, and held Senate and House seats. Their appeals were
clearly attuned to the times. The Populist successes convinced many
leaders of the Democratic Party that the Populists would have to be
appeased if the Democrats were to win the presidency and the Congress
in 1896. They tried to lure the Populists by adding to their own party
platform a resolution calling for the conversion to a silver standard.

When William Jennings Bryan was called forward in the Democratic
Convention to sum up for the silver side, few realized how effective his
rhetoric would be. "The Cross of Gold," which had been delivered by
Bryan dozens of times, popularized the Populist mentality and on this
occasion swept up the delegates before it like leaves in a whirlwind. Said
Bryan:

> The humblest citizen in all the land, when clad in the armor of a
> righteous cause, is stronger than all the hosts of error. . . . You
> come to us and tell us that great cities rest upon our broad and
> fertile prairies. Burn down your cities and leave our farms and your
> cities will spring up again as if by magic; but destroy our farms and
> the grass will grow in the streets of every city in the country. . . . If
> they dare to come out in the open field and defend the gold
> standard as a good thing, we will fight them to the uttermost having
> behind us the producing masses of this nation and the world,
> supported . . . by the laboring interests, and the toilers everywhere,
> we will answer their demand for a gold standard by saying to them
> you shall not press down upon the brow of labor a crown of thorns;
> you shall not crucify mankind upon a cross of gold!

That Bryan was less than logical hardly mattered. Like early revivalists,
he was appealing to the common man, and he knew that emotion was a
more powerful persuader in that moment than was logic. What was
important was that he elevated Populism to a philosophical level, in

confrontation with the forces massed on the side of the status quo. Bryan rendered Populism a philosophy rather than a mere call for specific changes by constructing a string of paired oppositions that divided the country ideologically. He pitted rural interests against urban, the interests of laboring masses against those of the business elite, and the forces of religion against those of the new science. In his discourse, Democrats and Populists were divided from Republican and business-oriented urbanites by *moral* outlook.

When the debate over the gold standard came to the floor of the Democratic Convention, Bryan argued so persuasively for adoption of a silver standard that Populist and Democratic delegates to the convention joined to nominate him for president. That Bryan's ideological approach to political action struck a popular chord was to be evidenced by his repeated, later nominations and by his appointment as Secretary of State. The moralism of his kind of Populism would be further shown in his final rhetorical struggle with the atheist Clarence Darrow in the Scopes trial in 1925.

Bryan lost the election of 1896 to William McKinley, and when prices of farm goods shot up again, farmers largely abandoned their organized quest for political reform. The moral unity Bryan had preached could not hold together the special interests represented in the Populist Party. Still, many Populists craved identity as a separate political party, and this led to divisions over whether to join with the Democrats in supporting fusion candidates. The appeals used by Populist leaders did not reflect unity. Some in the South, like Tom Watson, who had wanted to include blacks, now played to racism. Some in the Midwest resurrected isolationist paranoia and focused on anti-Eastern appeals. As a political party, the Populists lost support and fragmented as economic conditions improved; on the other hand, Bryan's synthesis of Populist doctrines remained popular within the Democratic Party.

The catch-all character of the original Populist demands and the general negativism of their argumentation were seeds of confusion and ultimate decline. Populist appeals worked in "bad times" but not in good; hence, at the end of the nineteenth century the majority of voters supported McKinley's "full dinner pail." And there were foreign distractions. Ideas of expansionism and Manifest Destiny drew attention away from domestic issues, and the Populist movement died away as an organized force when Admiral Dewey blew apart the Spanish fleet in Manila Bay and American Marines landed in Cuba.

The idealisms that gave birth to Populism were compromised by a political process of acquiring consensus. As had been the case in New

England, utopian ideas had to be given practical applications because expression was free and practical politicians turned ideals into promises. The Populist doctrines were adapted to political realities in the discourse of such as Bryan, but then the Populists lost their distinctiveness. Because the movement was *political* from the start, and because Populists sought a *national* voice, they did not have the freedom of religious leaders, who could separate their followers into sects where radicalism and/or purity can be preserved. By contrast, in order to gain majorities, Populists needed to enter the "mainstream"; that is, accommodate the crowd. A good many did not. Some spoke from case books filled with statistics and dry economic expositions. Others oversimplified, as when they argued that free coinage of silver was the answer to every woe. Still others accented the negative, as did Sarah Emery, who talked about "Seven Financial Conspiracies which have Enslaved the American People." Indeed, imputing conspiracies became a standard topic for committed Populists. The *Alliance Herald* declared, for example, that "The Rothschilds are the head and front of the greatest financial conspiracy ever attempted in the history of the world." Such extreme and often single-issue claims could not gather in a majority of Americans. In the South, for example, conservatives used the threat of radical agrarianism to buttress their own programs. As Paul Gaston points out, "[T]he frenzy of [the Populists'] attack, far from discrediting the mythology, worked rather to strengthen it. Respectable and conservative Americans reacted with unbridled disdain to what they regarded as the wild schemes and subversive tactics of the agrarian radicals so that the new South view of the world seemed, by contrast, to represent sanity, moderation, and security."[22] When the Spanish-American War came, Populists either opposed it as a capitalistic plot or argued that all war was immoral or, at best, an unpleasant duty.

To the extent that Populists claimed to be a *political party* of *national* importance, they had to take positions on issues and events. Most of the positions they took were at odds with their calls for *moral* reform of domestic politics. When they denounced the war, they were attacked for lack of patriotism. When their party-line spokesmen called for divergent domestic changes, they were attacked for inconsistency, internal dissension, and equivocation. Some of their best and most popular themes were being co-opted by the Democrats, and those who sought to be faithful to the original People's Party platform of 1892 tended to view such practical adaptations to political possibilities as moral hypocrisy. All of these factors weakened Populism as a political philosophy.

Why the Populists lost the intellectual battle to the Social Darwinists and expansionists is a complex question. They suffered from philosophical and organizational fragmentation, as I have said, but they suffered also from turns of events that diminished the political appeals. They had other problems, too.

First, they had rhetorically shrewd and appealing opponents. The rationalizers of the status quo were powerful persuaders, but even more important, the Populists as a specifically identifiable group had never been positively perceived by "mainstream" voters. Populist speakers often reinforced the suspicion that they were threatening American institutions. The *Farmer's Alliance* of May 7, 1891, printed in Lincoln, Nebraska, railed that economic "competition is only another name for war." Moreover, Populist speakers and writers were often arrogant and angry in public address. This obscured the fact that, collectively, they were motivated to try to improve the conditions of the weak and poor. Populists' charges of conspiracy and malice hid their shared moral goals. One of their rhetorical practices illustrates this point. On a number of occasions when a spokesperson for the established system refused to debate them, the Populists responded by purporting to present their opposition's case and then attacking it viciously. The fairness of their interpretations of their opposition was, of course, always questionable. And when, as sometimes happened, Populist speakers pretended an opponent was sitting in an empty chair placed on stage, their contrived style could appeal only to those already friendly to them.

The angry and assaultive character of so much Populist rhetoric gave credibility to the perception that avowed Populists were dangerous radicals outside the system. Even when Populism as theory and doctrine was assimilated by the Democratic Party's programs, Populism was still seen as a social "movement" instead of a viable political alternative to Republicanism. The Southern Populist call for a "brotherhood of man" and "social justice" in direct response to Social Darwinism's "survival of the fittest" put them outside the mainstream of American values.

Rejection of the Populist cause in the 1896 election was overwhelming. The defeat was partially due to the fact that labor was coerced into voting for McKinley. Moreover, gold-standard advocates among the Democrats actively opposed Bryan, and banks had refused to extend credit to those supporting him.

Social Darwinism was a convenient way to rationalize accumulated industrial wealth, imperialism, and domestic neglect. It brought together in one social philosophy many disparate tenets that were common in American tradition and experience. It was a philosophy of rugged individualism, survival of the fittest, and minimal governmental participation in the affairs of citizens. Had not the early settlers and pioneers survived because they were fitter than their adversaries? Had not American Calvinism encouraged the piling up of good works in God's name? What could be more natural than demonstrating salvation by being industrious and accumulating wealth? By the late nineteenth century, the U.S. Senate had become a "millionaires' club." The economy was clicking along at an accelerating rate. Captains of industry and those who ran the Republican Party believed that the American dream was being fulfilled. America was becoming a great nation, leaving the bitter ashes of its civil war far behind. Anyone who dared challenge the system was seen as a threat to the nation's newfound greatness. And as the United States embarked on its second century, anything that got in the way of this system was run over, removed, or rationalized.

Unfortunately, as the Populists had made clear, there was a good deal that needed to be rationalized. Wealth, generated by a burgeoning industrial system, was concentrated in the hands of a relatively few persons, and it was made from the sweat of a lower class laboring in often horrendous conditions. Inexpensive agricultural products were being shipped to markets at relatively high costs, a practice that severely depressed the farm economy. Custer's army had been cut down in 1876, triggering a more repressive policy toward native Americans. England, France, and Germany had carried "the white man's burden" to the corners of the globe; now the United States began to look beyond its Pacific and Gulf coasts for islands to add to its empire.

The defenders of the status quo found Social Darwinism, as fostered by Herbert Spencer in England, and John Fiske and Yale's William Graham Sumner in America, a powerful tool because it gave "scientific" and "philosophical" respectability to claims that reforms such as those advocated by the Populists were obstructions to the "natural progress" of the economic and social order.

First and foremost, Social Darwinism espoused laissez-faire government. If the government did not interfere with the economy, then "nature" would take its course, weeding out the sick and weak enterprises while sustaining the strong and vital. A hands-off approach would guarantee a kind of natural selection within the economic community.

Second, property was held to be the *sine qua non* of the social order. It was the "distinguishing mark" of a person who had proved his or her worth. Social Darwinism claimed that property made survival possible and that those with property were the "fittest," the most able, the most blessed. Thus, Social Darwinism reinforced the traditional American belief in life, liberty, the pursuit of happiness and the work ethic that had

31

developed out of Puritan thought. It also went a long way in the South toward justifying the reestablishment of a dominant, white, ruling class.

So did another axiom of Social Darwinism: The notion that Anglo-Saxons had evolved into the supreme race. It was their moral duty, being blessed as they were with superiority, to "bring the word" to the rest of the world. But the Social Darwinist bible was not only composed of traditional Judeo-Christian rules; it also contained economic, social, and political principles aimed at converting the world into a support system for capitalism.

Reformers could take heart from the fact that the active defenders of the status quo were not a cohesive group. Had it been better unified, the Populist Party might have struck responsive chords among minorities—farmers, laborers, the poor—and become a national force. But the Populists were not cohesive, as I have shown. Moreover, to the extent Populists were seen as threats, the defenders of the status quo could begin to reply with one voice. Events, too, had influence. As long as the economic engine produced prosperity for the majority, the defenders of the status quo bore a minimal burden of proof and the advocates of reform bore a heavy one.

The defenders pressed home their advantages of prosperity and of access to important centers of opinion. Sumner and Fiske lectured and proselytized the academic community and through it American opinion leaders. Edward Youmans reinforced this effort in public circles when he began publication of *Popular Science Monthly*. But the Horatio Alger stories of success through earnest hard work probably did more than any other propaganda to lock Social Darwinist thinking into the collective American consciousness.

Not content to show by making money that the system worked, industrialists began to advocate Social Darwinism with fervor. James J. Hill, George Hearst, and John D. Rockefeller became active in the cause, particularly when entertaining political leaders. The immigrant, industrialist, and philanthropist Andrew Carnegie considered himself a patron of the movement in general and of Spencer in particular. By 1889 he was putting out his tracts on the subject. They were not subtle. He asserted that those who sought to overturn contemporary conditions were attacking the foundation upon which civilization itself rested:

> Objections to the foundations upon which society is based are not in order, because the condition of the race is better with these than with any others which have been tried. . . . The Socialist or Anarchist who seeks to overturn present conditions is to be

regarded as attacking the foundation upon which civilization itself rests, for civilization took its start from the day when the capable, industrious workman said to his incompetent and lazy fellow, 'If thou doest not sow, thou shall not reap,' and thus ended primitive communism by separating the drones from the bees. . . .

Carnegie incorporated the naturalism of Charles Darwin, the economics of Adam Smith, and the religion of John Calvin in one short paragraph. Thus, Carnegie and company adapted conventional conservative thinking to the "spirit of the time," and they stole even moral ground from their opponents. According to this creed, if opportunity arose, it belonged to those with talent and industriousness. So the *Gospel of Wealth* proclaimed, "Not evil, but good, has come to the race from accumulation of wealth by those who have had the ability and energy to produce. . . ."

A host of defenders of the status quo could and did confront the Populist "philosophy" with this new philosophical "authority," whether they adhered to Darwinism specifically or not. Evolutionary science gave *intellectual* respectability to decisions and religious pronouncements. The Fifth and Fourteenth Amendments, particularly their clauses concerning no deprivation of property or livelihood without due process of law, were reinterpreted by some to support the economic position of Social Darwinism. In *Pollock v. Farmers Loan and Trust,* the Supreme Court declared the income tax unconstitutional and warned against a "Communist march" in legislation. The same year, the Court undercut the Sherman Anti-Trust Act, which concerned monopolization of interstate commerce, in the *United States v. E. C. Knight* decision. The legislation, later used by Presidents Teddy Roosevelt and William Taft to bust trusts, was an attempt to insure fair competition. In 1896, however, the Supreme Court permitted monopolies in manufacturing, ruling that mere manufacturing was not "commerce" and therefore not covered by the Act.

In rhetoric concerning American foreign relations, the drum beat was even louder. Josiah Strong, a Congregational minister and Congressman, published *Our Country* in 1885. In it he linked "progress" to the ability of the Anglo-Saxon in America to make money and push his way into new countries and he forecast a major role for him in the world's future:

There is abundant reason to believe that the Anglo-Saxon race is to be . . . more effective here than in the mother country. . . . Among the most striking features of the Anglo-Saxon is his money making power—a power of increasing importance in the widening commerce of the world's future. . . . He excels all others in pushing his way into new countries. . . . It seems to me that God . . . is training the Anglo-Saxon race for an hour to come in the world's future.

That hour came in 1898 when Admiral Dewey, acting on instructions from Assistant Secretary of the Navy Theodore Roosevelt, steamed into Manila Bay and destroyed the Spanish Fleet. Thereupon America took on the "white man's burden," and extended tenets of Social Darwinism to its foreign commitments. With the acquisition of Cuba, Puerto Rico, and the Philippines, America became an empire not unlike other world powers.

Perhaps no speaker better presented the philosophy of supporting economic and territorial expansion in order to facilitate "progress" than Senator Albert J. Beveridge. His addresses, "Star of Empire" and "The March of the Flag" rewrote historical fact into a political mythology that justified imperialism. Beveridge accomplished an astute mingling of themes associated with the Puritan "New Zion," the revolutionary claims of Americans' moral superiority, and the theory of evolutionary progress applied politically and socially—all to forge a doctrine of "manifest destiny." No clearer reflection of the Darwinist thesis as Americans applied it exists than in the confrontation between Populist and Darwinist philosophies.[23]

"The March of the Flag" was delivered September 16, 1898. It injected the issue of imperialism into the congressional election of that year. Beveridge's reputation as an orator matched Bryan's and "The March of the Flag" was widely reported and mainly praised by the press. In the speech, Beveridge wove a delicate pattern of argumentation that cited symbols, documents, and precedents from American tradition to reinforce the theme:

> It is a noble land that God has given us . . . a greater England with a nobler destiny . . . a people imperial by virtue of their power, by right of their institutions, by authority of their Heaven-directed purposes . . . a history of statesmen who flung the boundaries out into unexplored lands and savage wilderness. . . .

Beveridge called upon his audience to accept their destiny, reciting the list of America's foreign possessions and posing the ultimate question: How should they be disposed of?

34

He argued that because these possessions were incapable of self-government, and because foreign governments were incompetent and unscrupulous, the United States had no choice but to assume the burden of governance.

Once his theme was established, Beveridge incorporated economic arguments. He claimed that these far flung holdings would expand American markets and thereby increase productivity; more trade meant more jobs. He concluded: "That flag has never paused in its onward march. Who dares halt it now?" The speech was immensely popular, and it became a Republican campaign document. It justified American chauvinism and extended to foreign affairs the philosophical confrontation with Populism. Bryan took up the gauntlet on this issue, as he had on almost every other issue when the conservatives attacked. But Bryan could not defeat the defenders of the status quo and expansion. For reasons I have indicated, their persuasion when combined with economic, political and social conditions, was too effective for even the redoubtable Bryan to overcome.

The fact is that Social Darwinism was never really overcome. Its force as political doctrine was blunted but in part also sustained by the "Progressive movement" which also owed something to Populist thought. The Progressives developed a philosophical position about reform that rested on the traditional American belief that equal opportunities were essential if the talented were to have a proper chance for success. But instead of emphasizing wealth and progress as *results* of American freedoms, as the Social Darwinists had done, the Progressives tended to look at the *causes* of economic and social progress or lack of it. They aimed to reform whatever elements of the system might deter individuals from realizing their full potentials. They rendered attenuated Social Darwinist and Populist doctrines politically operative for specific, pragmatic problems. Progressivism was a reform, not a revolutionary movement.

In the late 1880s, "progressivism" emerged in response to cries for political reform. By the turn of the century, the movement acquired its capital "P" under guidance of reform-minded urban officials such as Samuel Jones of Toledo and John Altgeld of Chicago. Such men initially sought allies in their fights to clean up city halls, but the movement gradually extended its concerns to national problems.

Progressives tended to accept competition as a "good" force that enlarged opportunities for individual and group successes. They argued that there must therefore be an open marketplace for products and jobs, assuring easy entry for new entrepreneurs. Progressives held that if the freely operating system did not allow for an open market, government should intervene to guarantee it. They also held that the interests of business itself dictated high standards of social ethics, for immoral business practices invited government regulation. Government was thus conceived of as an agency of *corrective* social and economic action, not as the designing agency of the society. This was a difficult position for Social Darwinists to cope with since much of their free-enterprise doctrine was assimilated within the action-oriented Progressive movement.

Progressives also incorporated some of the Populists' moral emphasis in their social theory. Government must function morally, as business must be conducted ethically. Not only did the American civil religion dictate morality in government, but if the United States were to have credibility on the world stage, its leaders must act from the best of motives in order to sustain America in its historic role as a shining example of moral democracy.

How was society to assure morality in high places? A vigilant and active electorate was the safeguard the Progressives sought. This implied establishing the fullest possible means by which voters could intervene in governmental processes. Out of such thinking came proposals and ultimately legislation providing for direct election of Senators,[24] ending abuses of voting rights, and using the tools of popular initiatives, recalls, and referenda. Once more, the Progressives were borrowing from both Social Darwinists and Populists, but they constructed a view of governmental activity very different from views fostered by the two doctrinaire philosophies.

These broad tenets of Progressivism were difficult to attack, but their specific applications left ample room for debate. Furthermore, not all Progressives agreed on every point. Like Populism, Progressivism had disparate roots; its urban and rural versions were not identical. But it was a way of thinking that emphasized *practical possibilities*. Not surprisingly, neither orthodox conservatives nor doctrinaire Populists were entirely happy with the synthesis that was called Progressivism. What the synthesis did was open a vista to social and economic reform while professing a truer adherence to the inherited philosophy of American government. It was a response to a variety of discontents—a response that offered specific "cures" for specific faults in the American system.

As early as 1881, Henry Demarest Lloyd had begun a relentless attack on Standard Oil. Wherever he wrote, he raised issues of conscience:

> Nature is rich; but everywhere . . . man is poor. . . . Liberty produces wealth, and wealth destroys liberty. . . . Our bigness—

cities, factories, monopolies, fortunes, which are empires,—are obesities of an age gluttonous beyond its power of digestion. . . . We cannot clean our cities nor our politics. . . . Business motivated by self interest . . . runs into monopoly at every point it touches.

These passages concerned abuse of power. Washington Gladden, the father of the Social Gospel, enhanced Lloyd's themes with his own softer rhetoric. Both sought to pin down those things that had gone wrong with the system, but they did *not condemn the system as a whole*. Such were the beginnings of Progressivism.

We should not neglect the influence of organized labor in creating the Progressive synthesis that would emerge after 1900. No man was more instrumental in developing the labor movement and making its voice heard than Samuel Gompers. He founded and presided over the American Federation of Labor from 1886 to 1924, with the exception of one year. Gompers used the facts that he had worked in a sweat shop and had experience as an immigrant youth to identify with his audiences of commoners. His voice commanded attention, as did the arguments he launched. But Gompers' chief asset was his ability to steer labor into what would come to be called the Progressive mold, away from Populism and socialism. Gompers saw unionism as an integral *part* of broad-based national politics, and every A.F. of L. leader since Gompers has followed the same strategy. Gompers kept the American Federation of Labor from being tainted by any "ism" that might discredit the union's force in the American political system. He knew that "movements" and "radicalism" threatened the middle class, and that that audience was essential in forming any effective majority. Like other Progressives, Gompers courted the center.

The difference in strategy between Populists and Progressives goes a long way to explain the success of the latter group. So, too, does the Progressive habit of relying on responsible, factual, mainly non-threatening persuasion. Progressives did not usually fall victim to stridency, as had the Populists. Furthermore, Progressivism was national where Populism had tended to be regional and where Social Darwinism tended to be urban and elitist. For such reasons, Progressivism was attractive to both major political parties until the Republicans split over it in 1912. Populism stood outside the two-party system until the movement was captured by the Democrats; Social Darwinism as theory, held fascination for only a part of the Republican Party. Progressivism, moreover, was expounded by men of diverse backgrounds often speaking against their vested interest, whereas Populism and Social

Darwinism were almost the exclusive possession of those they benefitted most.

In contrast to either Populism or Social Darwinism, Progressivism gave impetus to a plethora of new magazines, and even a new form of newspaper journalism. Despite the fact that the press, led by the vast Hearst empire, was on the side of the Social Darwinists, reporters and commentators did continue to cover the poor, the abused, the corrupt, and the outspoken. Because freedom of speech was guaranteed, Populists, socialists, anarchists, and even monarchists found their ways into print and became part of the ongoing debate on national priorities. Investigative reporting uncovered corruption; human interest stories put poverty on the front page; interviews came into vogue and brought many a politician out of the smoke-filled caucus room and into public view. Reporters combined moral individualism with concern for the downtrodden. When publishers found that this combination increased the sale of newspapers, the "new" journalism became a fad. *One could argue that the most effective rhetoric of the new synthesis that took hold in the country was the persuasion of Progressive journalists.* Because of free press traditions, they were soon able to build their own organs and solidify the Progressive movement into a counterweight against the conservative press.

If the Progressive press was the engine of the movement, then Theodore Roosevelt certainly supplied the spark that kicked it into high gear. As a member of the elite, a member of the system, and as President of the United States, Roosevelt was able to speak with vigor, authority, and credibility from what he called the "Bully Pulpit" of the presidency. Once he came into the presidency, Roosevelt began to present the country with his action-with-moderation approach to problems. By the end of 1906, Roosevelt fused personal morality, domestic reform, and international leadership with his own persona. Good citizenship, just government, national unity, the elemental virtues, and strength became the five themes of his administration's legislation and rhetoric.

Roosevelt was no stranger to Progressive concerns. As an assemblyman in 1882, he had ruffled many a feather in Albany with his call for election reform. In almost every post he held, including Civil Service Commissioner (1889), Police Commissioner of New York City (1895), and Governor (1897–98), he was ahead of his time in seeking more ways to assure honesty in government. He had also shown concern for abuses of power resulting from rigid class structure. While he was strongly critical of Populism, he often sided with labor against capital, a rare position for a pre-1900 governor, and rarer still for a Republican governor. As a former Assistant Secretary of the Navy, and as the head of the famed Rough Riders in the Spanish-American War, Roosevelt was credible when it came to foreign affairs. More important, he had established his position favoring a strong but fair foreign policy. After he won the presidency on his own in 1904, Roosevelt settled the Anthracite Coal Strike, broke up the Northern Securities Company, and negotiated peace between Russia and Japan. For the last task he was awarded the Nobel Peace Prize.

It was in 1906, at the height of his powers, that Roosevelt chose to deliver his famous speech, "The Man with the Muck-Rake."[25] In no other speech did he so well articulate the balance needed between monied interests and reformers. The major part of the speech attacked those who rake up the muck, the journalists who had gone too far and been too cynical. Roosevelt ridiculed the abusive reformer as "the man who could look no way but downward," who "fixes his eyes . . . only on that which is vile and debasing." Roosevelt knew reform was necessary, but he argued a positive attitude toward the task of improvement. Like most Progressives, he abhorred the "cynical, hysterical, gross and reckless." He strove for balance: "To denounce mudslinging does not mean the endorsement of whitewashing."

But once he had won over the conservatives in his party and politicians who tended to be the target of sensational journalistic attacks, he reversed field and endorsed "relentless exposure of and attack upon every evil man, whether politician or business man, every evil practice, whether in politics, in business, or in social life." Then he turned his attention to the excesses of the wealthy. He called for an inheritance tax on fortunes "swollen beyond all healthy limits." He further surprised his audience by proposing controls over monopolies that abused interstate commerce:

> Again, the National Government must in some form exercise supervision over corporations engaged in interstate business—and all large corporations are engaged in interstate business—whether by license or otherwise, so as to permit us to deal with the far-reaching evils of over-capitalization. This year we are making a balance in the direction of serious effort to settle some of these economic problems by the railway-rate legislation. . . . The eighth commandment reads: "Thou shall not steal."

He warned the rich that:

> [T]hey had sown the wind and would surely reap the whirlwind, for they would ultimately provoke the violent excesses which accom-

pany a reform coming by convulsion instead of by steady natural growth. . . . Materially we must strive to secure a broader economic opportunity for all men, so that each shall have a better chance to show the stuff of which he is made.

This last evolutionary appeal seemed particularly well adapted to the rhetoric of Social Darwinism.

Conservatives praised Roosevelt's attacks on radical reformers, but they attacked his proposed reform. Reformers cheered the call for new restraints on the privileged class, but they ignored the plea for restraints on muck-raking. Perhaps no other president would have dared such a gambit, but Roosevelt's prestige carried the moment and gave a new cohesiveness to Progressivism in American culture.

Republicans, especially those at the Party's convention in 1912, turned away from the Progressive middle—partly on the issue of a third term for Roosevelt—and so again splintered the moderates. Wilson stole some with talk of peace and further reform, while economic conservatives returned to the Republican fold. The Great War would retard reform and help return conservatives to power. Roosevelt was left with the people who believed in him and in his Progressive synthesis and were not offended by a third term.

The Progressive or Bull Moose party convention of August, 1912, revealed the synthetic nature of the party. Senator Beveridge gave the Keynote Address. Later, the delegates cheered Jane Addams, the founder of Hull House, and then lifted her to the podium. She was a delegate from Illinois. Roosevelt greeted her with a handshake that led to a twenty-five minute demonstration. Later in the convention, Addams seconded the nomination of Roosevelt and pleaded for social justice, suffrage, and industrial reform. "A great party has pledged itself to the protection of children, to the care of the aged, to the relief of overworked girls, to the safeguarding of burdened men."[26]

In his acceptance speech, Roosevelt attacked the Republican party machine and recited the litany of Progressive programs. Then freed of the fetters of Republicanism, Roosevelt launched a Populist-like attack on the Supreme Court:

I deny that the American people have surrendered to any set of men, no matter what their position or their character, the final right to determine those fundamental questions upon which free self-government ultimately depends. The people themselves must be the ultimate makers of their own Constitution. . . .[27]

He then called for an easier way to amend the Constitution.

Theodore Roosevelt remains the model of American Progressivism. No other leader better combined the elements: concern for the disadvantaged, guaranteed individual opportunity, public and private virtue, nationalism, and international moral leadership. From the presidency he could issue calls for social reform, national morality, and international strength. He was the "Preacher President" who pointed Americans toward both moral life and the competitive work place. In short, Roosevelt embodied all of the strands of philosophical debate I have examined in this chapter.

While the war and the "return to normalcy" prevented Progressives from achieving all of their goals, they did succeed in reinvigorating public opinion and reforming the economy and the political system under which it operated. Woodrow Wilson, who won the 1912 three-way presidential race, said in his acceptance of the nomination, "There is a vast confederacy of giant industries, a money trust, which is dangerous, controlling both credit and enterprise." Once elected, he began to reform the system by trying to achieve the goals of the Democratic Platform. The "progressive income tax" was instituted nationally, along with a strong anti-trust policy carried out by the Attorney General and the new Federal Trade and Interstate Commerce Commissions. Another amendment was passed, the seventeeth, which provided for direct election of Senators. States such as Wisconsin, California, Oregon, and Louisiana adopted referenda, recalls, and initiatives as ways of doing political business. And well into the 1930s, such leaders as Robert LaFollette in the Senate, and Louis Brandeis on the Supreme Court, defended the Progressive banner.

PHILOSOPHICAL CONFRONTATION IN PERSPECTIVE

In a free society the synthesizers tend to dominate in contests for political and social control. Ideologues of the left and right mark out the range of choices from which the society can choose. But where the majority rules, numerous, diverse interests have to be courted by political persuasion. Ideologues can seldom sustain this; it has been done best in the United States by synthesizers who assemble the most attractive features of ideological and existing ideas and offer them as expedient— not ideological or merely traditional.

Anyone may attempt to create political pressure groups in a free society, but here and in England the survivors have been just two major synthesizing political entities, one leaning toward tradition and the other leaning toward reformation. Only such agencies, it appears, can offer alternative but essentially centrist political solutions. A "mainstream" of pragmatic thinking that still contains alternative choices is thus created and maintained by the persuasions that survive in free marketplaces of political ideas. Ideologues tend to be uncompromising and, in the United States, at least, have been unable to convince a majority of the society, except perhaps in times of extreme national danger. Accordingly, where *philosophies* clash, ultimate decisions await the counsel of those who eschew dogma and espouse pragmatically attractive syntheses of philosophical vestiges.

Pragmatism is inevitable in free societies because the great "middle" pursues expediency. The primary issue becomes: Will this work and with what day-to-day consequences for us? Those who attend to this question hold the reins most of the time, simply because they can deal with issues in ways that are intelligible to persons primarily interested in their own existential well being. Ideologues cannot, without compromising their ideologies.

The two cases examined in this chapter illustrate the operation of these principles of political persuasion in America. The key factors seem to be (1) with everyone free to propose and oppose, confrontations of "systems" are inevitable; (2) but with freedom comes the voice of the pragmatic majority, interested in how things are or will work; (3) so the synthesizers/compromisers ultimately win out *provided there is no resort to force, as in the Civil War.* The fundamental and inevitable tension that informs persuasion in any free society is between ideology (of right or left) and pragmatics. The American record illustrates this, with pragmatism usually the victor.

The reason philosophical confrontations form a special class of democratic controversy and persuasion is that someone argues that a theory or doctrine or tradition takes precedence over pragmatics. In a free society those people are bound to lose debates, but they are not prevented from influencing practical applications of beliefs and values. Other controversies pit advocates of specific political measures against each other. Then things work differently. The peculiarity of cases of philosophical confrontation is that they are instances in which the test is between one theory and another, or pragmatics and theory, whereas most ordinary political controversies in the United States are among advocates of two or more pragmatic alternatives. There, expediency is granted as the prime issue by all or virtually all controversialists.

Issues always have their roots in philosophical problems, as Cicero pointed out. Whether one should be bound by "authoritative" interpretations of Scripture can be pushed back to the question of how and through whom God speaks to humans. Whether to regulate railway rates can be pushed back to the question of what is the ideal role of a

42

government. In the examples of philosophical confrontations I have examined in this chapter, argument *began* at the level of philosophical difference and *ended* with pragmatic compromises for specific cases. This direction of settlement does not *have* to occur. Argument leading up to and during the French Revolution continually addressed *philosophical* differences and seldom focused on matters of immediate expediency.

We need to see that at the level of philosophical confrontation, what is at issue are values rather than policies. Hence, the judgments made are usually comparative: It is better to appeal to the chosen people *than* to convert all of mankind; it is better to provide for all *than* to encourage opportunity for the elite; it is better to abandon one's country *than* to serve its immoral purposes; it is better to assert individualism *than* to obey the law. Whether we examine the oratory of black, gay, or women's liberation, or analyze the persuasion of educational reform movements, we will find value questions brought to the fore.

A majority rule about whether pursuit of beauty is nobler than pursuit of personal independence will simply not be reached—until circumstances in which the choice is to be made are clearly in view. But then the issue has ceased to be a philosophical one and has become a *practical, political* one—a question of expediency as well as nobility. The Anglo-American tradition has left valuing in general to our moral considerations and has focused *politically* on what will be *mutually* valued in specific cases. This being the common practice, philosophical confrontations do not survive as such in American political persuasion. The fates of theocracy in New England and Populism are cases in point.

NOTES

1. Milton Rokeach, Abraham Maslow, and many others argue that values are at least part of an inner psychic core. As values are brought into contact with sensed data, the mind evaluates what it perceives using values as guides. The resulting evaluations are attitudes.

2. See Thomas Shepard, *A Defense of the Answer made unto the Nine Questions or Positions sent from New England against the reply thereto of Mr. John Ball* (London, 1648). In 1640 the Long Parliament asserted itself; the church restructuring was begun. But as Puritans gained power, civil war resulted, lasting to 1645. Persecutions of Puritans in the previous century are recounted in John Foxe, *Acts and Monuments of these later and perillous Days* (London, 1563).

3. John Winthrop, *Winthrop's Journal*, ed. James Savage (Boston, 1825–26); Edward Johnson, *The Wonderworking Providence of Zion's Savior in New England* (London, 1654). Ironically, the *Mayflower*, which landed in 1620 at Plymouth, had been used to run sherry across the Atlantic.

4. In the same year, Charles I fled to Scotland to form an army in an attempt

to regain power from the Long Parliament. The result was civil war from which Oliver Cromwell would emerge first as military leader and then as Lord Protector.

5. See Eugene White, *Puritan Preaching in America* (Carbondale: Southern Illinois University Press, 1971). His book contains an excellent bibliography. The present author wishes to express his indebtedness to Professor White's seminars on Puritan rhetoric. See also Boyd M. Berry, *Process of Speech: Puritan Religious Writing and Paradise Lost* (Baltimore: The Johns Hopkins University Press, 1976). The best primary source is Peter Buckley, *The Gospel-Covenant* (2nd ed., London, 1651). See also Benjamin Colman, *God Deals with us as Rational Creatures* (Boston, 1732); John Cotton, *A Briefe Exposition with Practical Observations Upon The Whole Book of Ecclesiastes* (London, 1654), *The New Covenant* (London, 1654) and *The Way of Life* (London, 1640); James Fitch, *The First Principles of the Doctrine of Christ* (Boston, 1769); Thomas Hooker, *The Soules Preparation for Christ* (London, 1632), *The Soules Exaltation* (London, 1638), *The Soules Humiliation* (2nd ed., London, 1638), *The Soules Implantation* (London, 1637). These last four tracts set out the early view of the morphology of conversion. See also Samuel Willard, *A Compleat Body of Divinity in Two Hundred and Fifty Expository Lectures* (Boston, 1726). For a thorough bibliography on Puritanism see Perry Miller and Thomas H. Johnson, eds., *The Puritans* (New York: Harper, 1965) pp. xxxix-xlvii in vol. 1 and pp. 777–818 in vol. 2.

6. See Samuel Gorton, *Simplicities Defense against Seven-Headed Policy* (London, 1646); Thomas Lechford's attack in *Plain Dealing* (London, 1642) is practical, but George Bishop's attack in *New England Judge* (London, two parts 1661, 1667) is pervaded by his Quakerism.

7. Edmund S. Morgan, *Puritan Political Ideas* (New York: Bobbs-Merrill, 1965) p. xxxi. George Morton compiled Bradford and Winthrop's detailed history of the Plymouth venture into *A Relation or Journal of the beginning and proceedings of the English Plantation settled at Plymouth* (London, 1632). See also Charles M. Andrews, *The Fathers of New England* (New Haven, 1919).

8. Thomas Cobbet, *The Civil Magistrates Power in Matters of Religion Modestly Debated* (London, 1653). See also John Cotton, *An Abstract of Laws and Government* (London, 1640); Worthington D. Ford, "Cotton's 'Moses his Judicials,'" *Proceedings of the Massachusetts Historical Society,* second series, XVI (1903), 274–84; Isabel Calder, "John Cotton's 'Moses his Judicials,'" *Publications of the Colonial Society of Massachusetts,* XXVII (1935), 86–94; John Cotton, *The Controversie Concerning Liberty; of Conscience in Matters of Religion, Truly stated, and distinctly and plainly handled* (London, 1646); William Bradford, *History of Plymouth Plantations, 1606–1646 in Collections of the Massachusetts Historical Society,* fourth series, III (1856); Francis Higginson, *New England Plantation; or, A Short and True Description of the Commodities and Discommodities of that Country* (London, 1630).

9. Edmund Morgan, p. xlii.

10. Perry Miller, *The New England Mind: From Colony to Province* (Boston: Beacon, 1961), 28, 29, 31.

11. He had been influenced by the revival of Aristotelian theory in the late Renaissance.

12. Mr. Hawley committed suicide by cutting his throat after Edwards' revival

in Northampton, Massachusetts during the "little awakening" that preceded the "great" one by five years.

13. Stoddard's revivals of 1679, 1683, 1692, 1712, and 1718 were more successful than Edwards' of 1734–35 and were the first to produce "convulsive conversions." See Solomon Stoddard, *The Way for a People to Live Long in the Land that God Hath given them* (Boston, 1703). Of most use on this point is Stoddard's reply to Increase Mather that Stoddard called, *The Doctrine of Instituted Churches Explained and Proved from the Word of God* (London, 1700). See also, *The Inexcusableness of Neglecting The Worship of God, under the Pretence of being in an Unconverted Condition* (Boston, 1708). This last tract was Stoddard's clearest, and it caused his debate with Increase Mather to fall into bitterness.

14. The seeds of dissent are found in a sampling of early Election Sermons. See Thomas Buckingham, *Moses and Aaron* (New London, 1729); Robert Breck, *The Only Method to Promote the Happiness of a People and their Prosperity* (Boston, 1728); John Bulkley, *The Necessity of Religion in Societies* (New London, 1713); John Richardson, *The Necessity of a Well Experienced Souldiery* (Cambridge, 1679).

15. Edmund S. Morgan, *The Puritan Dilemma* (Boston, 1958), 71–72. See also Emory Elliot, *Power and the Pulpit in Puritan New England* (London: Princeton University Press, 1975).

16. I am quick to point out that freedom varied significantly from colony to colony. Virginians at this time did not enjoy freedom of religious expression. Radical ministers were forced to leave Virginia in the 1740s and "separate Baptists" faced persecution.

17. The conservative thesis is well represented in John Cotton, *The Way of Congregational Churches Cleared* (London, 1648). The antithesis appears in many works. (See, for example, Solomon Stoddard, *An Appeal to the Learned* (Boston, 1709); A. B. Grosart, ed., *Selections from the Unpublished Writings of Jonathan Edwards* (Edinburgh, 1865). See also Ann Kibbey, *The Interpretation of Material Shapes in Puritanism: A Study of Rhetoric, Prejudiced, and Violence* (Cambridge: Cambridge University Press, 1986).

18. The change in the structure of sermons was a reflection of contemporary pedagogy. See Nathanial Appleton, *The Great Apostle Paul exhulted and recommended as a Pattern of true Gospel Preaching* (Boston, 1751) and *Superior Skill and Wisdom necessary for Winning Souls* (Boston, 1737); Thomas Foxcroft, *A practical Discourse* (Boston, 1718) and *Some Seasonable Thoughts on Evangelic Preaching* (Boston, 1740); Hooker, op. cit. Stoddard, *An Appeal to the Learned,* op. cit.

19. The political duel was preceded by intense theological debate. The best of these debates was between Louis Agassiz, who attacked evolutionary thinking, and Asa Gray, who argued that Darwin's theory did not contradict the *Bible*.

20. For an excellent edition of materials published by Populists, see *The Populist Mind*, ed. Norman Pollack (Indianapolis: Bobbs-Merrill, 1967). In the early 1960s, Pollack attacked Hofstadter's thesis, articulated in *The Age of Reform,* that Populism tended to be mean-spirited and anti-Semitic. See also Howard S. Erlich, "Populist Rhetoric Reassessed: A Paradox," *Quarterly Journal of Speech,* 63 (April, 1977), 141.

21. See Robert G. Gunderson, "The Calamity Howlers," *Quarterly Journal of*

Speech, 26 (1940), 401–11; Peter Wiles, "A Syndrome, Not A Doctrine: Some Elementary Theses on Populism," in *Populism: Its Meaning and National Characteristics,* ed. Ghita Ionescu and Ernest Geller (London: Weidenfeld and Nicholson, 1969), 166; Edward A. Shils, *The Torment of Secrecy* (London: William Heinemann, 1956), 98.

22. Paul Gaston, *The New South Creed: A Study in Southern Mythmaking* (New York: Alfred Knopf, 1970), 220.

23. Beveridge's chief antagonist on the issue was Bryan. Bryan's speech represents a full blown example of the antithesis in this confrontation. In his acceptance of the Democratic nomination in 1900, Bryan said, "Behold a republic gradually but surely becoming a supreme moral factor in the world's progress and the accepted arbiter of the world's disputes. . . ."

24. The country had come a long way from Madison's proposal at the Philadelphia Convention of 1787 that the House be elected by the people and the Senate be elected by the House.

25. See Stephen E. Lucas, "Theodore Roosevelt's 'The Man with the Muck-Rake': A Reinterpretation," *Quarterly Journal of Speech,* 59 (Dec., 1973), 452–62.

26. Thomas H. Russell, ed., *The Political Battle of 1912* (New York: American Association of Political and Social Sciences, 1912), 57.

27. Ibid., 101.

3

FREE SPEECH, NATIONAL SECURITY, AND RADICAL SEGMENTS OF POLITICAL PARTIES

Domestic turmoil often has tested America's ability to maintain its institutions and to retain its time tested traditions. Basically, America is a conservative—with a small "c"—country. Our revolution was a battle to conserve rights developed as colonists, rights that early settlers literally fought against nature to preserve, rights that the English Parliament tried to limit by taxation and other legislation. As in the Glorious Revolution of 1688, the American Revolution was undertaken as a last resort and in order to retain rights, not develop new ones. American history is the saga of slow movement toward more and more freedom while incorporating what was useful and beneficial from the past. The checks and balances that the Founders established assured a slow, evolutionary approach to reforming the system of government. The system has provided continuity and stability, but it has also predetermined that needed change will not take place quickly. For example, though widely reprobated, slavery would only end as the result of civil war, the only major disruption of the Founders's system.

Americans are also conservative in the sense that the majority of them are and usually have been predisposed to support the status quo until it is shown to be inadequate to deal with their concerns.

We have, of course, had radicals of right and left. In this book I term "radical" any group wishing to alter the American system in major ways, including the right to freedom of expression. The guarantee of freedom of speech and press insures radicals' freedoms as firmly as conservators' freedoms. But despite the freedoms radicals have had, our institutions have been modified only gradually through the years, and freedom of expression has survived much as the Founders conceived it. Why has that been so? To suggest some answers, I will examine three struggles between zealots and protectors of American institutions. The instances will allow us to perceive the rhetorical strategies used by American radicals and how radical positions have been overcome or blunted.

In exploring radical versus "mainstream" rhetorical behaviors, we should be mindful that all of our institutions and our courses of political action come into being and undergo change *through contests*. Our First Amendment guarantees *the right to challenge* as well as the right to respond to challenges. Furthermore, the cases I am about to discuss are cases in which what was challenged was freedom of expression itself. The cases are historic and rather dramatic, but in principle they illustrate a commonplace feature of American political persuasion about which we seldom think. Challenges to freedom of expression occur continually, for the reason that if I have freedom of expression, I can use it to promote restrictions on your freedom to express, and vice versa. Freedom to persuade has been and is being so used in controversies about appropriate textbooks, defining pornography, protecting national security, and so forth. Yet freedom of expression has been largely preserved over the years. How and why has that happened? I want to illustrate, using three very important instances of this American habit of preserving freedom of expression against radical proposals for limiting it.

First, how did we acquire this guarantee? The First Amendment emerged as first among guaranteed political rights for a number of reasons. Free expression, particularly a free press, had played a large role in shaping the revolutionary movement. Far from the control of the Crown, presses and oratory flourished in the Colonies. When the Stamp Act Crisis of 1765 was brought to life by Patrick Henry's moving speech, publishers made it available throughout the Colonies. It gave new life to the Sons of Liberty and new hope to Thomas Paine, America's leading revolutionary propagandist, whose *Common Sense* would have similar circulation and impact. From Henry's speech of 1765 to the *Federalist Papers* twenty-two years later, presses disseminated the ideas that created the United States and its Constitution. Thus, when the Constitution was submitted to the states for ratification in 1787, it is not surprising that almost all states demanded that a Bill of Rights be added, including especially an explicit guarantee of freedom of expression.

On June 8, 1789, James Madison instituted proceedings in the House to consider constitutional amendments. For his draft of an amendment on freedom of expression, he relied heavily on language that could be traced back to the Pennsylvania Constitution of 1776, the only one that specifically called for protection of both freedom of speech and freedom of press. At each legislative juncture, Madison's amendment was strengthened until it was submitted to the states with the language, "Congress shall make no law . . . abridging freedom of speech or of the press." It became part of the Constitution of December 15, 1791. The version enacted reflected the facts that the colonial press had nurtured the debate that eventually erupted into a war of independence, that new state constitutions and ratifying conventions consistently endorsed a broader interpretation of freedom of expression than what prevailed in England or the Colonies, and that vigorous, partisan, and ofter vitriolic speech was seen as an essential check on abuses by government.

The following three cases are instances of contesting freedom of expression on the national scene. They also illustrate what happens to radicalism in a nation that puts the right to express at the top of its values. Challengers to freedom are always in the position of trying to put some other *value* above freedom of expression. Sometimes it is political power, sometimes it is national security, sometimes it is racial equality, but whatever the value may be, it suffers the burden of trying to secure rank above the specially enshrined value of the First Amendment.

Attacks on freedom are also consistently attenuated by counter appeals to freedom as the ultimate social right. Without the freedoms that flow from the First Amendment, Jefferson would have had great difficulty in overturning the suppression of liberty that occurred with passage of the Alien and Sedition Acts of 1798. Responsible members of the political system would have had great trouble checking the irresponsible actions of the Radical Republicans in 1868. And Edward R. Murrow and those responsible for the unmasking of Senator Joseph McCarthy in 1954 might easily have failed without freedom of press and speech. At least nationally, contests end in favor of freedom not only because ours is a constitutional republic in which freedom of expression is formally and sacredly asserted, *but also because those who employ those freedoms understand how to use their freedom strategically.*

The three sets of historic events I am about to discuss furnish both intense and fair illustrations of anti-system threats and resistance to them, all under the protection of freedom of expression. They are the events surrounding: (1) the passage of the Alien and Sedition Acts in 1798; (2) the passage of the Reconstruction Acts following the Civil War; and (3) the passage of the Subversive Activities Control Act of 1950, together with the actions of Senator Joseph McCarthy which followed its passage.[1]

THE THREAT PERCEIVED

The danger giving rise to each of the developments I will examine was unique, but each perceived threat related to a war, to an external enemy, and to internal subversion. *Security* in the face of such threats was proposed as of higher value to the society than undiminished freedom of expression. While history never repeats itself exactly, these examples suggest that at national levels challenges to freedom of expression recur *in form*. The possibility of such challenges is always present as long as freedom of expression is guaranteed.

The Federalist Party held the majority in the U.S. Senate and House from 1791 to the end of John Adams' administration in 1801. Comprised largely of men from the well-established merchant class and property owners of the North, the Federalist Party favored national, governmental protection for trade, strong defenses, and industrial expansion. In 1798, America was seriously affected by a war between England and post-revolutionary France. France resorted to seizing American ships trading with England because an Anglo-American alliance against France was suspected. Many French leaders believed war with America was imminent. Moreover, America had been experiencing a steady influx of immigrants uprooted by the French Revolution. The conservative Federalists were alarmed by the arrival of these aliens. They suspected that hiding in the influx was a host of Jacobin[2] sympathizers ready to foment revolution and to act as French agents in the anticipated conflict.

The Jacobins were revolutionaries in France. Allegedly they were prepared to spread the reign of terror from nation to nation. The French Revolution, which began with the fall of the Bastille prison on July 14, 1789, had by 1794 become a bloodbath that even its instigators could not escape. King Louis XVI and his wife, Marie Antoinette, had been beheaded, and so had the radical Robespierre. The fear among conservatives in England and Federalists in America was that the terror would engulf the whole civilized world. This fear was not blind. Edmund Burke's *Reflections on the Revolution in France* became a primer for those rallying to stem the radical tide. The Federalist Hamilton, in this country, was quick to realize that the new immigrants almost unanimously supported his political opponents, the Democratic-Republican Party of Thomas Jefferson, James Madison, and James Monroe. At the same time, Jefferson and many of his party expressed sympathy for the French Revolution—especially in its less extreme modes—because they saw it as a natural outgrowth of the Enlightenment.

The Federalists perceived a threat to the sovereignty of the United

States in the all-but-certain war with France. They had reasons. In December, 1797, new French decrees against neutral vessels went into effect. In March, 1798, the peace mission to Paris failed. In April, 1798, the French demanded tribute. Federalist leaders held secret meetings to plot the fate of their party; they carefully monitored the press to be sure their friends were publishing supportive articles. Unfriendly papers were closely examined. It was a moment in history when complete freedom of political expression in America could be called into question—on theoretical and practical grounds. The value of freedom had, in fact, not been historically tested for it had been only seven years since the First Amendment had been added to the Constitution.

THE RADICAL REPUBLICANS

Following the Civil War, the political, social, and economic structure of the South was shattered. President Abraham Lincoln had proposed a reconstruction plan in his proclamation in December, 1863.[3] Under that plan, any Southern state would receive executive recognition as soon as one-tenth of the voters in the state took an oath to support the United States Constitution. Congress broke with the President's plan by passing the Wade-Davis Bill of 1864, a primitive measure requiring far greater obeisance from the Southern states before their governments would receive recognition. The bill was designed to show that reconstruction was the prerogative of Congress rather than of the President. At the Republican Convention of 1864, Thaddeus Stevens of Pennsylvania, Roscoe Conkling of New York, and George Boutwell of Massachusetts wrote radical planks into the party platform calling for what would eventually become the Fourteenth and Fifteenth Amendments.

President Andrew Johnson succeeded Lincoln in April of 1865. He opposed the Radical Republican supporters of the Wade-Davis Act. Johnson, who hailed from Tennessee but had opposed secession, lacked Lincoln's political acumen and credibility, yet he refused to permit Congress to modify Lincoln's lenient policy of dealing with the South.

No precedent existed for the conduct of conquerors who had won a civil war that was fought to preserve national unity. Policy had to be invented despite post-war bitterness. Johnson's unwillingness to compromise and unresolved issues of legislative-executive powers gave additional opportunities to the radicals in the then dominant Republican Party. In the face of the Radical Republicans' vindictive intentions to subjugate the "proud traitors," Southerners assumed a posture of defiance. This not only persuaded many in the North that the Union was

51

about to be cheated of its dearly won victory, but encouraged belief that the South and President Johnson were in league.

Underlying the Radical Republicans' political intolerance was the ideal of racial equality. Racial equality had not been an official goal when the Civil War began. President Lincoln had needed to keep the border states of Missouri, Kentucky, and Maryland in the Union, so he had overruled abolitionists in his cabinet. But after bitter battles and the North's quasi-victory at Antietam (Sharpsburg, Maryland) in 1862, President Lincoln signed the Emancipation Proclamation. Suddenly equality became an uncompromising part of the Radical agenda, and the Radicals resolved to reconstitute the Southern state governments in such ways that Southern representatives in Congress would be unable to shape legislation. Any suggestion of lenience to the South seemed a threat to their program. Opposition constituted a threat. The Radicals took their issues to the public in the elections of 1866 and won overwhelming victories. By March 1, 1867, congressional Radicals passed a law that required Southern states to ratify the failing Fourteenth Amendment if they wanted to be readmitted to the Union. The law was passed over President Johnson's veto and guaranteed the ratification of the Fourteenth Amendment just as two Northern states were rescinding their votes to ratify.

THE MCCARTHY ERA

After 1946, deteriorating United States-Soviet relations evolved into a "Cold War," with fear of nuclear weapons preventing a "hot war." Efforts to stem the spread of communism became a dominant part of United States foreign policy. The Truman Doctrine, the Marshall Plan, the Berlin Airlift of 1948, the North Atlantic Treaty of 1949, and the Mutual Security Act of 1951 were all parts of this policy of "containment."

Containment suffered two severe blows during the second term of the Truman Administration. In 1949, China fell to the Communists led by Mao Tse-tung. The United States had supported the Nationalists led by Chiang Kai-shek, even though there is evidence that American advisors had hindered his ability to retrieve Japanese weapons at the end of World War II. Secondly, in 1950, the United States led a United Nations' "Peace Keeping Force" to protect South Korea from Communist North Korea. During the first phase of that undeclared war, General MacArthur, a World War II hero, pushed the North Koreans out of the South and eventually over the Yalu River, the northern border with Red China. There was bitter division in the Truman Administration about what action to take. General MacArthur advocated bombing the bridges that crossed the Yalu, and he suggested that if Red China entered th nuclear weapons should be used to stop them. As discussion o Arthur's disagreement with the Administration over the conduct of the war escalated, Communist Chinese forces poured across the Yalu into North Korea, driving the Americans back below the 38th Parallel and inflicting severe losses on MacArthur's forces. When MacArthur expressed further dissent from Truman's policy, he was removed, and the war fell into a bloody stalemate. Truman's popularity, already low, plummeted.

Many in America was the conflict in Korea as an indication of a very real threat to all governments bordered by Communist powers. This view was intensified by a domestic crisis for Truman's Administration. In 1948, hearings held by the House Un-American Activities Committee, and led by Congressman Richard Nixon, compromised Alger Hiss, a top State Department official. During the hearings, Hiss was accused by Whittaker Chambers, a former editor for *Time* magazine, of having been a member of a Communist cell. Hiss was eventually convicted of perjury.

Out of these crises, there arose an obsession with preventing persons having unorthodox political views or who might once have entertained such ideas from assuming positions of prominence, authority, and political leadership. Senator Joseph McCarthy, elected to the United States Senate from Wisconsin in 1946, saw the threat of Communist infiltration into the federal government, and he saw the political capital to be gained from an anti-Communist crusade.

Thus, the political instability that prevailed on a global scale and the domestic crisis of confidence in the Truman Administration created political turmoil and fueled fears of subversion. Senator McCarthy saw that American citizens were especially sensitive to and fearful of a Communist threat to their government, the very government that was supposed to be leading the battle to contain communism.

PARALLELS IN EXPOSING THE PERCEIVED THREAT

In each of the situations I have just described, a threat to the existing political system was rendered the more plausible because of national political instability. In each case, armed conflict contributed to instability.

With an undeclared war going on with France, Federalists, not unnaturally, feared disaffected aliens would try to destabilize the national government, and those aliens seemed certain to swell the ranks of the Democratic-Republican opposition to Federalist political power.

The Radical Republicans surveyed the war-devastated South and decided political stability and their own power would be endangered if the South were not reduced to political vassalage. They perceived resistance to their plans as a threat to the ideals of racial equality and a reunited Union for which, in their view, the North had fought.

Senator McCarthy began to make an issue of Communist infiltration into the federal government at a time when the United States' military allies in Europe were recovering from World War II, the United States was deeply embroiled in a United Nations "police action" against Communists in Korea, and the reality of at least some infiltration of the federal government was coming to light.

In each case, rhetoric justified action by calling for purification as the avenue to safety: The Hamiltonians wanted to *preserve* a Federalist America; the Reconstructionists wanted to *redeem* Civil War goals; the McCarthyists wished to *save* the American government from Communist infiltration.

This rhetoric of purification was elucidated by McCarthy at the 1952 Republican Convention in Chicago. McCarthy stirred the crowd with the following charge to purge the United States of all Communists: "I say, one Communist in a defense plant is one Communist too many. One Communist on the faculty of one university is one Communist too many. One Communist among American advisors at Yalta was one Communist too many. And even if there were only one Communist in the State Department, that would be one Communist too many."[4]

The parallel between the situation facing the Federalists and that facing McCarthy is striking. In both cases, a regime born out of violent revolution faced the United States in actual conflict.[5] In both cases, not inconsiderable numbers of people had been displaced by political instability accompanying the revolutionary regime's activity, and many of these had recently arrived in the United States. Their presence, and uncertainty about their political convictions, led to the perception that they and unknown others were bearers of a pestilence by which the foreign regime hoped to infest, weaken, and eventually conquer the United States. Even McCarthy's allegation that Communists had subverted the State Department had its parallel in the late eighteenth century. In the presidential campaign of 1796, which pitted Jefferson against John Adams, Secretary of State Thomas Jefferson was said to have presided over a State Department full of Jacobins and Jacobin sympathizers.

Political self-interest functioned as a motivating force in all three cases. Whether the alleged national threat was real or not, Federalists had much to gain by casting aspersions on an alien group that happened to support

54

their political opponents. It has been argued that Reconstruction was designed by Radical Republicans to exploit the South economically for the benefit of the industrial North. And placement of Republican politicians in power in the South was certain to strengthen the Republican hold on the House and Senate.[6] Senator McCarthy and at least some other Republicans were certainly aware that their political clout derived specifically from their ability to expose Communists in positions of public responsibility. In all three sets of circumstances political self-interest informed action and rhetoric.

ASSUMING THE DUTY OF PROTECTION: IDENTIFYING, CONFRONTING, AND COUNTERING THE THREAT

Once a national party or group has perceived a threat, whether to the United States as a whole or to their political vision, that group naturally undertakes to expose and identify the threat. Only when exposed can the threat be confronted and removed. The problem is that radicals exaggerate the threat and thereby destabilize the governing system and provide opportunities for truly dangerous action. What effective and therefore dangerous strategies did the radicals use in the three historic moments?

Unproven assertion was useful in the identification process. Public pronouncements couched in extreme terms proved effective in drawing attention to threats and in gathering support to confront it. For example, Jonathan Dayton, Federalist Speaker of the House of Representatives, caused consternation in 1798 by asserting (erroneously) that armies were massing in France, preparing to conquer the United States:

> As to the means of invasion, it was known that there were already collected upon the coasts of France, bordering upon the English Channel, a numerous army which, in gasconading style, was called the Army of England. It was known that there were also collected and collecting at various ports in that quarter, ships of war and transports of all descriptions.[7]

Congressman Robert Harper of South Carolina, speaking to the same issue, was more concerned with internal subversion than external threat. As the author of the Sedition Bill and former Chairman of the House Ways and Means Committee, he brought considerable credibility to the debate. He developed a scenario of collapse that revealed the essence of Federalist fears: philosophers of the French Revolution, who were in every country, were paving the way for Jacobins bent on seizing power by violent means—means that had been used during the "reign of terror" in France. Harper put it this way:

> Philosophers of [the French] revolution exist in all countries. . . . They advance always in front and prepare the way by preaching infidelity, and weakening the respect of the people for ancient institutions. . . . The Jacobins follow close in the train of philosophers, and profit by their labors. This class is composed of that daring, ambitious, and unprincipled set of men, who possessing much courage, considerable talent, but no character, are unable to obtain power, the object of all their designs, by regular means, and therefore, perpetually attempt to seize it by violence.

These themes were picked up by the press and the pamphleteers so that in a few months the entire country was exposed to expressions of fear of French Jacobins.

As early as 1866, the Radical Republicans spread rumors concerning President Johnson's alleged allegiances during the Civil War. He had been military governor of Tennessee when Lincoln selected him as a running mate in 1864. For the Radicals, the new President was a serious threat to all they had worked for and won. Senator Charles Sumner proclaimed: "This is one of the last great battles with slavery. Driven from these legislative chambers, driven from the field of war, this monstrous power has found a refuge in the Executive Mansion. . . ."[8]

An even more flagrant, unproven set of assertions was Senator McCarthy's "laundry list" presented in February of 1950 at an obscure GOP women's meeting in Wheeling, West Virginia. There McCarthy claimed that he had the names of 205 Communists in the State Department.[9] McCarthy's general use of exaggeration is clearly documented by a review of his speeches. At times he claimed he could name over 200 Communists in the State Department, then in Reno and Salt Lake City he said they numbered 57, then 81. Later the numbers changed again, first to 121, then to 106. In an attempt to refute McCarthy's accusations, Democratic Senate Majority Leader Scott Lucas of Illinois secured passage of a motion to have the Foreign Relations Committee conduct a full investigation into McCarthy's charges of Communist infiltration. The investigating committee, headed by Senator Millard Tydings of Maryland, called the charges a "fraud and a hoax perpetrated on the Senate of the United States and the American people."[10]

Nonetheless, McCarthy emerged from the early hearings as a hero. In the 1950 congressional elections, McCarthy gained revenge by helping Republican candidate John Marshall Butler defeat Tydings in a vile, unscrupulous campaign. As the 1952 election approached, McCarthy traveled the country drawing large crowds. He was joined by Senators Jenner, Mundt, and Wherry as he pressed his attack. A strong coalition was soon formed.[11] It included some in the Pentagon who vehemently disagreed with Truman's Korean policy and who supported General MacArthur's desire to take the war into Red China. It included Joseph P. Kennedy and other isolationists who had opposed entry into World War II.[12] It included the China lobby, a group dedicated to Chiang Kai-shek's dream of overthrowing Mao Tse-tung.

Radical segments frequently rely on *faulty logic* to make their cases. One of the Hamiltonian contentions was that the French Directory was sending its army to the United States because the army would overthrow the Directory if left unemployed back in France. Given the events of the time, the Federalists had plenty of ammunition to support such an assertion. Armies of revolutionary France did, in fact, invade neighboring European states to spread the Revolution. There was even remote reason to fear invasion of the United States through French territory in the New World. In December of 1797, new French decrees against neutral vessels went into effect. In March of 1798, the United States' mission to Paris was rebuffed and President Adams asked Congress to increase defense spending. In April of 1798, the "XYZ" dispatches, which demanded that the United States pay tribute to France, were made public. Out of these facts, the Hamiltonian Federalists had little difficulty constructing their tortured view of French foreign policy.

There was better evidence of President Johnson's loyalty to the Union than there was of any subversiveness such as the Radical Republicans charged, and McCarthy's inferences as to what acts identified a "Communist" were certainly open to challenge in numerous cases.

Guilt by association is another common tactic used by the radical elements. Radical Republicans reasoned that since President Andrew Johnson was a Southerner, his sympathies lay with the Confederacy. McCarthy and his supporters argued that one former Communist employed by the State Department meant that a large section of the Department had been infiltrated and subverted to communism. McCarthy also used the tactic to great effect when questioning witnesses. Here is a typical exchange between McCarthy and one of his victims. In this case, Reed Harris, a civil servant from the information services division of the State Department had been called to testify:

McCarthy: You attended Columbia University in the early thirties, is that right?

Harris: I did, Mr. Chairman. . . .

McCarthy: You resigned from the University. Did the Civil Liberties Union provide you with an attorney at that time?

Harris: I had many offers of attorneys and one of those was from the American Civil Liberties Union, yes. . . .

McCarthy: You know the Civil Liberties Union has been listed as a front for, and doing the work of, the Communist Party?

Harris: Mr. Chairman, this was 1932.

McCarthy: I know it was 1932. Do you know they since have been listed as a front for, and doing the work of the Communist Party?

Harris: I do not know that they have been listed so, sir.

McCarthy: You don't know they have been listed?

Harris: I have heard that mentioned or read that mentioned.

McCarthy: You wrote a book in 1932. I'm going to ask you again at the time you wrote this book did you feel that professors should be given the right to teach sophomores that marriage "should be cast off of our civilization as antiquated and stupid religious phenomena"? Was that your feeling at that time?

Harris: My feeling was that professors should have the right to express their considered opinions on any subject whatever they were, sir. . . .

McCarthy: I'm going to make you answer this.

Harris: I'll answer, yes, but you put an implication on it and you feature this particular point out of the book which of course is quite out of context. . . . The American public doesn't get an honest impression of even that book, bad as it is, from what you are quoting from it.

McCarthy: Then let's continue to read your own writings.

Harris: From twenty-one years ago?

Here Harris was associated with a "Communist front organization" because he used a lawyer from the ACLU in 1932. He was also badgered and his work was quoted out of context, another rhetorical practice commonplace in fear-arousing public discourse. This passage, and there are many more like it, indicates an assumption of guilt where the evidence is made to fit the crime. The passage also reveals that several tactics are at work at the same time, making it difficult for the defendant to recover, let alone respond in an extemporaneous setting. When written down, such fallacies are not difficult to discern, but when uttered in a highly pressurized dialogic situation, they often prove effective.

Exaggeration of a minimal threat so that it assumes the proportions of a significant crisis is another effective technique widely used by the radicals studied here and by many other such spokespersons. For the Hamiltonians, the example of the Democratic-Republican newspaper *Aurora* "proved" that sedition was rampant throughout the country. The *Aurora* was a Philadelphia paper that supported the Jeffersonians and was highly critical of the Adams administration. In this paper the leadership of the president was often portrayed as imperious and the motives of Hamilton were often called into question not only on the editorial page but in regular reporting. In debate Representative Long John Allen remarked that "liberty of the press and of opinion is calculated to destroy all confidence between man and man; it leads to a dissolution of every bond of union."[13] Other Federalists similarly identified the *Aurora* with sedition, and then claimed that the press in general frequently instigated sedition.

In a comparable vein Radical Republicans published and distributed the words of a few Southerners in an attempt to prove that the whole South might rebel under the new "Southern" president, claiming:

> It is the old troop of slavery, with a few recruits, ready as of old for violence—cunning in device. . . . With the President at their head, they are now entrenched. . . . The safety of the Republic requires action at once.[14]

McCarthy expanded the case of an Army mishap into a congressional hearing. A Private G. David Schine, who was a friend of McCarthy's counsel, claimed he had evidence of Communist infiltration into the Army. By mistake, Schine was prevented from testifying.

> Then McCarthy exploded during the hearing into a personal attack on General Zwicker, roughing him up verbally and humiliating him. In this one act, McCarthy had taken on the full power of the elite officer corps of the Army. . . . The Schine incident was blown into a major crisis when McCarthy claimed that Schine, a private and a friend of Roy Cohn, was being held "hostage."[15]

Clearly, extrapolation from limited instances is one of the most potent methods of making an alleged danger salient for the public.

Finally, radical spokespersons reinforce and compound the sense of danger through *circular support* (sometimes called "milling" by sociologists because cattle and sheep act the same way). Once a threat is perceived as real and its existence gains widespread acknowledgment, those who enlarge upon it are able to associate it with other issues and develop more exaggerations to heighten the intensity of feelings. That is, a threat starts the masses milling, then a second threat renews the activity of the herd and spreads throughout the group in waves that return to excite the leaders further. They, in turn, heighten the intensity of their rhetoric which sets off more waves of excitement.

The Hamiltonians redoubled their efforts to preserve their party from the growing numbers of Republican-Democrats and mitigate their prospect of losing the White House in the election of 1800. The actions they took further excited the crisis situation, setting off more fears among common citizens. The Reconstructionists were re-fired in their activities by a desire to control the South politically as well as militarily. Once their program went into effect, Northerners were excited about the possibility of further reprisals against the South. The McCarthyists were motivated to seek removal of Democrats in order to strengthen their own power and that of Republicans generally. As they charged Democrats with being "soft on communism," they generated added publicity and the public was further excited about problems of subversion. Here, as in the other two cases, ulterior political motives led to renewed and intensified claims about the nature of the alleged threat.

Once milling begins, an *increased sense of danger can be given substance* by the radicals to keep the excitement keen; new evidence of conspiracy can be cited and efforts can be made to dramatize the situation. For the Federalists, the sense of danger from infiltration was increased by pointing to the "outspoken sedition" of certain Democratic-Republicans, who were growing in number. Federalist Congressman H. G. Otis, later to head the ill-fated Hartford Convention of 1812 which called on New England to secede, said in reply to a Democratic-Republican colleague:

> The gentleman . . . vociferates for the evidence of plots and conspiracies against the government. . . . If the gentleman insisted upon evidence of seditious dispositions in our country, *I would refer him to his own speech.*

To Radical Republicans, the danger that President Johnson would veto their legislation was compounded by the danger that if the South regained political power, it could establish a voting bloc in the Senate, and give the Democrats a majority in the House. Worse yet for the Radicals, in January of 1867, the Supreme Court sided with congressional moderates. In the *Milligan* and *Test Oath* cases, the Court overturned the "internal security policies" Lincoln had imposed on Copper-head counties in Indiana. With the war over, the Court decided to come down hard in favor of restoring civil liberties. The Radicals immediately began to plan to amend the Constitution and to use these decisions to stir up public fervor for the elections of 1868.

To the McCarthyists, the danger of communism was expanded by the now partially documented threat of infiltration in the State Department and the Armed Forces. In this exchange between Senators Symington and McCarthy during the Army-McCarthy hearings of 1954, McCarthy feeds the conspiracy claims he first outlined in 1950:

> *Symington:* . . . our people have been urged to entertain serious doubts as to the dedication and loyalty of our armed forces from top to bottom.
> *McCarthy:* . . . one of the subjects of this inquiry is to find out who was responsible for succeeding in calling off the hearing of Communist infiltration in the government. At this point I find out there's no way of ever getting at the truth. The iron curtain is pulled down so we can't tell what happened.

In all three cases, the identification of alleged new dangers served to fuel the radicals' resolve and to increase public excitement.

PROPOSED LEGISLATION GIVES RISE TO GREATER OPPOSITION

As a national threat acquires greater substance and dimensions in the minds of radicals, concrete steps to meet it are naturally proposed. In the United States, radical legislation often borders on or falls into unconstitutionality. In fact, one of the best ways to measure the intensity of radicals' zeal is to examine the legislation they propose.

The Federalists passed the Alien and Sedition Acts in July of 1798. Debate on the Acts in the House of Representatives was marred by both physical violence and slander. Federalists finally passed the Acts by only three votes. The Acts were clearly violations of the First Amendment, though they were never reviewed by the Supreme Court.[16] The "Naturalization Act" extended from 5 to 14 the number of years of residence required before full U.S. citizenship could be granted. The "Act Concerning Alien Enemies" authorized President Adams to order the expulsion of "dangerous" aliens during peace time. The "Act Respecting Alien Enemies" authorized the president to apprehend, restrain, secure, and remove enemy aliens during time of war *or undeclared hostilities.*[17] The "Sedition Act" prohibited conspiracy against the U.S. Government and also prohibited writing, printing, uttering, or publishing false, scandalous, and malicious writings against the U.S. Government.[18] Indicted offenders fell into three categories: (1) figures associated with Democratic-Republican newspapers, (2) leading figures of the Democratic-Republican party, and (3) individuals who were a nuisance to the Federalists. Perhaps the most serious action was the arrest of Congressman Lyon in October, 1798, under the provisions of the Sedition Act. In the ensuing election, he was reelected from his jail cell.[19]

The Federalists were also motivated by the actions of a Philadelphia Quaker, George Logan, who, with no official governmental authorization, journeyed to France to work for peace in the midst of the quasi-war. In response, the Federalists passed a law, the Logan Act, which prohibited citizens from initiating private and unofficial diplomacy with foreign governments. It is still in force today.

Further measures included abrogation of all treaties with France, expansion of the army, arming sea vessels, authorization to attack French vessels on sight, and nominating former President George Washington as Commander of the Army, with Hamilton second in command. Hamilton's modesty fooled few people; most Americans understood him to be the real commander with the aging Washington serving only as a figurehead.

As I have indicated, some of the Federalists' radical actions and proposals were transparently unconstitutional, but it is even more important to notice that their total agenda comprised an extreme threat to personal freedoms.

The Radical Republicans set up the Freedmen's Bureau, a federal agency established to counteract the impact of the black codes that were adopted by Southern legislatures during the sessions of 1865–66.[20] Those codes authorized Southern law-enforcement officials to apprehend unemployed blacks, fine them for vagrancy, and hire them out to satisfy the fine. Radical leaders saw the black codes as a return to slavery. By differentiating Negro labor from other labor, the codes offended Northerners and turned public opinion in favor of Radical Reconstruction. For example, the black code of Louisiana stated:

Sec. 1. Be it enacted by the Senate and House of Representatives of the State of Louisiana in General Assembly convened, That all persons employed as laborers in agricultural pursuits shall be required, during the first ten days of the month of January of each

62

year, to make contracts for labor for the then ensuing year, or for the next year ensuing the termination of their present contracts. All contracts for labor for agricultural purposes shall be in writing, signed by the employer, and shall be made in the presence of a Justice of the Peace and two disinterested witnesses, in whose presence the contract shall be read to the laborer, and when assented to and signed by the latter, shall be considered as binding for the time prescribed. . . .

Sec. 2. Every laborer shall have full and perfect liberty to choose his employer, but, when once chosen, he shall not be allowed to leave his place of employement until the fulfillment of his contract . . . and if they do so leave, without cause or permission, they shall forfeit all wages earned to the time of abandonment. . . .

The Radical Republicans overrode the President's veto of the Reconstruction Acts and amended the Constitution not once but three times. The Radical Republicans shifted their program into high gear on March 2nd, 1867. On that day the Congress passed the Command of the Army Act, which heavily restricted the president's military power; they overrode the veto of their Reconstruction Act; and they passed the Tenure of Office Act. The last was clearly designed to prevent President Johnson from removing officers from his cabinet. The specific motivation for this piece of legislation was to protect Secretary of War Stanton, a supporter of Radical Reconstruction and a critic of Lincoln's and Johnson's softness.[21]

On March 23rd, the Second Reconstruction Act was passed. It gave specific orders to the Army on how to implement reconstruction. Yet another Reconstruction Act giving even more power to the military was passed on July 19th, despite Sumner's feeling that military force should not be used to achieve reconstruction aims. Radicals then made ratification of their new constitutional amendments a condition of any state's reinstatment to the Union. The requirements of the reinstatement process were meticulously spelled out in the Reconstruction Acts: (1) Registration of voters, including all adult black males, (2) each voter had to swear a loyalty oath, (3) voters must elect a convention to prepare a new state constitution providing for black suffrage, (4) the new state constitution must be ratified, (5) the state must hold elections for public office holders, (6) the state must ratify the Fourteenth Amendment, and (7) once the Fourteenth Amendment was adopted by the mandated number of states, a state having fulfilled the other requirements would be readmitted to the Union. By 1868, six states that had seceded were readmitted: Arkansas, North Carolina, South Carolina, Louisiana, Alabama and Florida. The four "unreconstructed" states were Mississippi, Virginia, Georgia, and Texas. Those states faced the additional requirement that they ratify the Fifteenth Amendment. It was not until 1870 that they were all back in the Union.[22]

Like the Federalists in their radical stage, the Radical Republicans offered extreme remedies for the threats they perceived. As in the first case, some Radical actions gained the full status of law whereas others went beyond legal bounds and had to be reversed later.

The McCarthyists were able to pass the Subversive Activities Control Act in 1950 and the McCarran-Walter Act in 1952. The former called for use of various loyalty tests for government employees, and it promulgated several spurious investigations. The Act established a Subversive Activities Control Board to ensure registration with the U.S. Attorney General of communist action and/or front groups. The Act also denied passports to members of the Communist party and its "fronts," and required members of the Communist party to register individually. The Control Board was given power to determine which organizations and individuals were Communist-action or Communist-front groups.

In 1952, the McCarran-Walter Act was passed over President Truman's veto by a vote of 278 to 133 in the House and 57 to 26 in the Senate.[23] It gives the State Department authority to prevent foreigners with alien political beliefs or affiliations from entering the country. This throwback to the Alien Act of 1798 remains in force today. Under the law, current and former Communists as well as homosexuals, anarchists, and those whom the State Department deems "prejudicial to the public interest" may be excluded. The McCarran-Walter Act, a comprehensive codification of the immigration and naturalization system, was amended by Congress in 1987 to say that aliens may no longer be denied entry into the United States on the basis of "past, current, or expected beliefs, statements, or associations."[24]

Attempts to pass legislation, of course, get the attention of the opposition. Until that time, radicals are often not even taken seriously. But when bills are introduced into the Congress or other official action is taken, opposition to the radical segment comes alive.

With the introduction of the Alien and Sedition Bills, the Democratic-Republican party began to rally support in opposition to the measures. When the Radical Republicans presented their plan for Reconstruction to the House and Senate, moderate Republicans and Democrats joined ranks to try to stop the steamroller, and they succeeded in moderating some of the legislation. While Senator McCarthy's speech in Wheeling was ridiculed, responsible elements in the Congress did not move into high gear until the passage of legislation that restricted civil rights.

In each case, concrete action, proposed or accomplished, set the stage for a confrontation that would spill out of the Congress and into the public's consciousness. The media, particularly an organ of national prestige, played an important role in making sure that the arguments of those opposed to the radicals received significant attention.

RADICALS UNDERTAKE TO RESTRICT
FREEDOM OF EXPRESSION

The zeal of national radical segments during periods of their ascendancy usually extends to castigating their opponent's motives and trustworthiness.[25] Federalists, who sought radical change in security laws, frequently resorted to this tactic in replying to challenges during debate on the Alien and Sedition Acts. One such attack was watched closely by members of the House and by a packed gallery. Federalist Jonathan Dayton replied to a speech by Albert Gallatin, a Democratic-Republican leader who had originally come to the United States from Switzerland. Dayton himself was known to be a moderate Federalist, so his insinuations concerning Gallatin's foreign origin and his presumed friendliness to European radicalism were the more striking. Said Dayton:

> And why should that gentleman [Gallatin] be under no apprehension? Was it that secure in the perfect coincidence of the principles he avowed with those which actuated the furious hordes of democrats, which threatened the country with subjugation, he felt a confidence of his own safety, even if they should overrun . . . the states? He might indeed contemplate an invasion without alarm . . . he might see with calmness . . . our dwellings burning. . . .[26]

When Congressman Livingston objected that the new laws required "no indictment; no jury; no trial . . . no statement of accusation," he was answered with the claim that the insidiousness of French intrigue made these objections irrelevant. Said Federalist Congressman Otis, the laws were necessary because the French had "pushed their intrigues into some of the first offices of government." Once again, the perceived threat was magnified by aspersions on the trustworthiness of objectors.

In a like manner, Radical Republicans persistently "waved the bloody shirt" following the Civil War. It was, of course, the motives of Southerners, taken collectively, that were attacked. Thaddeus Stevens even argued in December of 1865 that the Southern states should be reduced to territories as a means of cleansing their motives and understandings:

There they can learn the principles of freedom and the fruit of foul rebellion. . . . I know of no better place nor better occasion for the conquered rebels. . . . If we fail in this great duty now when we have the power, we shall deserve and receive the execration of history and of all future ages.

The formal Report of the Joint Committee on Reconstruction in June of 1866 also recalled the base motives of the South:

It must not be forgotten that the people of these states, without justification of excuse, rose in insurrection against the United States. . . . They continued this war for four years with the most determined and malignant spirit. . . .

Here, as in the case of the Federalists, the point is that opponents' *positions* were not made the objects of criticism, but the opponents' *motives* for holding their views were assaulted and treated as probably permanently debarring them from civil considerations.

Joseph McCarthy became noted for his attacks on individuals' motives and trustworthiness. His targets included even such prominent figures as General George Marshall, Secretary of State Dean Acheson, and Owen Lattimore, a noted specialist on Asian affairs in the State Department. McCarthy was especially sweeping and vitriolic: Professor Lattimore was "the top Soviet espionage agent" in the State Department, and President Truman was "a sonofabitch" who would let "red waters . . . lap at all our shores."[27] This sort of recklessness and character assassination probably contributed more than anything else to his ultimate censure by the Senate. McCarthy's attack on one of attorney Joseph Welch's aides was one of his most widely noticed uses of senatorial immunity to attack the characters of those who opposed him. His charge and Welch's reply (cited in a later section) occurred on national television during the 1954 "Army-McCarthy Hearings." Said McCarthy of a member of Welch's staff:

I think we should tell Mr. Welch that he has in his law firm a young man named Fisher whom he recommended incidentally to do work on this committee, who has been . . . a member of an organization which is named . . . as the legal bulwark for the Communist Party.

Attorney Welch's reply would win sympathy for his young aide and draw popular confidence away from McCarthy's integrity and general fairness. In January of 1954, the Gallup Poll showed a record high of 50

66

percent of the American people viewing McCarthy with some favor; 29 percent viewed him unfavorably, and 21 percent expressed no opinion. By the time the Army-McCarthy Hearings ended on June 17, 1954, McCarthy's standing in the Gallup Poll had dropped to 35 percent favorable and 49 percent unfavorable.[28] There seems little doubt that the opportunity to watch McCarthy's televised attacks on the character of individuals established in the minds of many people that he was too unrestrained and insinuative to be credible on the general subject of the threat of Communist influence in government and elsewhere.

In the cases I have described, moderate and balanced opinions ultimately curbed the influence of radical character assassins, but meanwhile radicals are often able to arouse *community actions* on behalf of the causes they so dogmatically espouse. Federalists encouraged tarring and feathering "Jacobin sympathizers." Radical Republicans set up puppet governments in the states they readmitted to the Union, installing local sympathizers as officers who also served as informants to the Freedmen's Bureau and even to the Congress. The McCarthyists incited the citizens of Boston to take action against their own public library.[29] Once organized, these people removed books from the shelves and instituted censorship.

On college campuses the picture was not much better. Those who admitted to being former Communists or left-wing radicals or took the Fifth Amendment before congressional committees were often fired, censured, or placed on probation even though Congress took no action against them. Harvard proved an exception. When Governor Christian Herter of Massachusetts asked Harvard President Nathan Pusey to fire physicist Wendell Furry because the professor had taken the Fifth Amendment before McCarthy's committee, Pusey refused, arguing, "There is now an especially urgent obligation upon our universities to preserve freedom of inquiry and freedom of teaching."

At the level of "community action," the end comes to justify the means. Radical elements are apt to become guilty of wide ranging repression, and others, such as college administrators and librarians, often cower before them. McCarthyism inspired twenty-six states to enact laws barring Communists from running for public office. Twenty-eight states passed laws denying state or local civil service jobs to Communists, and thirty-two states required teachers to take a loyalty oath. In eleven states, Communists were denied the right to meet in school buildings. Furthermore, many private meeting halls, including Madison Square Garden, refused to rent to groups tagged as communist by the Attorney General's list. Suspected Communists were denied low-income housing, and they could not obtain passports.[30]

Post Civil War Reconstruction laws contained numerous restraints on the freedom of former "traitors." Ultimately, radicals who receive reinforcement from the public become still more extreme: The Federalists finally succeeded in putting Hamilton, the head of their party, in command of the army; Radical Republicans tried to impeach the president; and McCarthyists carried on a "witch hunt" that destroyed the lives of government servants, writers, performers, professors, and members of the press corps.

OPPOSITION GROWS MORE INTENSE

In this country, at least, the tendency has been to judge radicals as "going too far." The beginning of the decline of radical movements has, not surprisingly, been correlated with *increased activity on the part of their opposition*. This usually takes the form of responsible persons within the system using freedom of expression to exert authority and to demonstrate leadership in the interest of restraint. As radicals' threats to their opponents increase, the opponents begin to act in systematic ways. When Jefferson and Madison wrote the Virginia and Kentucky Resolves, they were assuming this role as well as appealing for the preservation of the free marketplace of ideas. For his part, Jefferson invoked states' rights; then he spoke of the danger of increased presidential power; and finally, he closed with an argument for free speech and press. Madison argued that the new laws gave the president too much power. "The people not the government possess absolute power. . . . In the United States, the executive magistrates are not held to be infallible, nor the legislature to be omnipotent . . ." He concluded that freedom of expression was essential to the workings of democracy:

> The security of freedom of the press requires, that it should be exempt, not only from previous restraint by the executive, as in Great Britain, but from legislative restraint also; the Act will make us unfree because the people will be compelled to make their election between competitors, whose pretension they are not permitted, by the Act, equally to examine, to discuss, and to ascertain.

These three pillars—states' rights, limited presidential power, and free speech—were the supports of the Democratic-Republican counterattack on the Federalists, who had dominated political activity since the ratification of the Constitution in 1789.

Political leaders were not the only ones to take on Hamilton and the

Federalists. One of the strongest arguments that can be made for a free press can be drawn from the role that opposition papers played in rousing the public against the Alien and Sedition Acts. A chorus of protest arose.

Greenleaf's *New Daily Advertiser* published an attack on the Sedition Bill while the ink from the president's signature was still wet. On Wednesday, June 13, 1798, it said:

> If the constitution of the United States was not considered by the majority of the house of representatives as a mere dead letter, or a piece of musty parchment, they would never have ventured to bring in a bill so directly contravening one of the most essential articles of freedom, and as clearly defined as any other clause in the bill of rights, namely, liberty of speech, printing and writing, all of which will not merely be infringed, but wholly annihilated, should this nefarious bill pass into law.

Perhaps the most outspoken was the editor of the *Aurora*, which was published in Philadelphia. On July 3, 1798, he wrote:

> What is meant by defaming a law is beyond my comprehension. To laugh at the cut of a coat of a member of Congress will soon be treason; as I find it will be to give a Frenchman a dinner or a bed, as soon as this bill passes.

The *Boston Gazette* joined the battle on July 9, 1798:

> The Editor of the Aurora was [recently] arrested, on a warrant from Judge Peters of the Federal Circuit Court, on a charge of libelling the President, and the Executive Government in a manner tending to excite Sedition, and opposition to the laws, by sundry publications and republications. . . . The period is now at hand when it will be a question difficult to determine *whether there is more safety and liberty to be enjoyed at Constantinople or Philadelphia.*

Once the Sedition bill passed, Southern papers took up the call for its repeal. The *Norfolk Herald* of September 1, 1798, not only opposed the bills, but applauded mass action against them:

> The real friends to the liberties and happiness of America will rejoice at the decided part which the people of Virginia have taken against the *Alien* and *Sedition* bills. In the large and respectable

county of Goochland, the people met on Monday last to consult on the present crisis of American affairs, and adopted by almost an unanimous vote, Resolutions, expressive of their strongest disapprobation of the late acts of Congress and the President. There was a very full meeting consisting of about four hundred, of these not more than twenty or thirty were against the Resolutions.—They also voted instructions to their delegates in the state legislature, requesting them to move, in the next session of the Assembly, a Remonstrance to Congress, against the late obnoxious acts of government, or to support any other constitutional measure which may be deemed more effectual, to vindicate the liberties of Speech and the Press, and to restore the trial by jury.—BRAVO!

Artists, particularly poets and song writers, also saw the Alien and Sedition Acts as threats to freedom. They used their crafts to stir the public against the new restrictions. In fact, many scholars believe the election of 1800 was the first in which campaign songs were used to ask citizens to vote for a specific candidate. For example, in response to the rather martial lyrics of the Federalists and their standard campaign theme, "Yankee Doodle," the Jeffersonians sang of attacking "men in pow'r [who] cry 'sedition.' " Other lyrics praised Jefferson and the action he would take if he were elected:

> If you peace and freedom love,
> Act with circumspection,
> Ev'ry foe to these remove,
> At your next election,
> Choose for chief Columbia's son,
> The immortal Jefferson.
> He will ever-ever-ever-ever stand,
> Watching o'er your freedom.

After Jefferson's Inaugural, a lyricist wrote:

> Acting in a noble cause,
> He abolished cruel laws,
> Set the mind and body free,
> He's the son of liberty.

Perhaps the most devastating attack on the Federalists' repressive policies came in a poem placed in the *Boston Gazette*. It appeared on September 17, 1798, the day Benjamin Edes, the *Gazette*'s editor, resigned:

70

Since we are forbid to speak, or write
   A word that may our BETTERS bite,
I'll sit mumchance from morn to night;
   But pay it off with THINKING.
One word they ne'er shall fish from me
   For Master Rawle, or Charley Lee;
Yet, if they'll let my thoughts be free
   I'll pay them off with THINKING.
When George began his tyrant tricks,
   And Ropes about our neck would fix,
We boldly kicked against the Pricks
   Nor sat mum-chance, a THINKING.
We freely spoke, and freely thought,
   And freely told him what we sought.
Then freely seiz'd our swords, and fought
   Nor dreamed of silent THINKING.
If Hancock and great Washington,
   Had nothing said, and nothing done,
His race the tyrant would have run,
   Whilst we were mum a THINKING.
Had Dickenson not dar'd to write,
   Had common sense not spit his spite,
Our soldiers had not dar'd to fight,
   But set down mum, a THINKING.
We swore that thought and swords were free,
   And so the Press should ever be,
And that we fought for Liberty,
   Not Liberty of THINKING,
But Liberty to write or speak,
   And vengeance on our foes to wreak;
And not like mice, in cheese, to squeak,
   Or, sit down mum, a THINKING.
Again on Constitution Hill,
   We swore the sovereign people's will
Should never want a press or quill,
   Or tongue to speak as THINKING.
That still we're sovereign who'll deny?
   For though I dare not speak, Yet I
ONE SOVEREIGN RIGHT, will still enjoy
   The SOVEREIGN RIGHT OF THINKING.
                           AMERICANUS

Hamilton's political control crumbled over the French crisis.[31] American naval vessels won victories at sea, providing Adams with needed credibility and calming fears of an invasion. Next, Adams dismissed radicals McHenry and Pickering from the cabinet. By the summer of 1800, the Federalist Party was divided by preferences for one or the other of Hamilton or Adams. The public began to see in the Alien and Sedition Acts what Congressman Jonathan Livingston had predicted early in the debates over the Sedition Bill:

> The President alone is empowered to make the law, to fix in his mind what acts, what words, what thoughts or looks, shall constitute the crime contemplated by the bill. . . . He is not only authorized to make this law for his own conduct, but to vary it at pleasure, as every gust of passion, every cloud of suspicion, shall agitate or darken his mind.

The signing of the Franco-American Convention relieved the external pressure and revealed that Hamilton was at best mistaken, for an agreement *could* be reached with the French after all. The Jefferson-Burr ticket was elected in 1800, ending Hamilton's dreams of power and striking a blow from which the Federalist Party would not recover. In February of 1801, just days before Jefferson's Inaugural, Adams concluded a treaty with France, thus ending all pretense of a crisis. Upon assuming the presidency, Jefferson allowed the Alien and Sedition Laws to lapse during his first days in office.

In 1868, moderate Republicans and Democrats joined to restrain Radical Republicans. The seven Republicans who voted against the removal of President Andrew Johnson were protecting the social fabric of the country with renewed zeal. Senator Grimes of Iowa, who was carried into the Senate on a stretcher for the vote, put it this way: "I can not agree to destroy the harmonious working of the Constitution for the sake of getting rid of an unacceptable President."

Another example of the passions of the opposition came from the *Atlanta News,* "The radicalism of the Republican party must be met by the radicalism of white men." This quotation should remind us that one radical political campaign can set off another. One need only recall partisans on both sides of the Vietnam War issue in the late 1960s and early 1970s to see how such interaction has occurred in recent time.

As in the Alien-Sedition crisis, the press played a responsible role when it went after the excesses of Radical Republicans. The *New York Times* was a leader of rational sentiment when it said on March 3, 1868:

> [W]hat else are the heated appeals of party organs, the fervid exhortations of party orators, the instructions of party majorities in

State legislatures, and the resolutions of party meetings, but attempts to use the forms of the most solemn judicial proceeding known to our Constitution, for the purpose of accomplishing party ends and anticipating the results of next Fall's election? If President Johnson may thus be ejected from office,—not because he is guilty of the "crimes and misdemeanors" for which he has been impeached, but because he is deemed "unfit" of the place, and because the "country will be safer," in the Senate's judgment,—so may his successor: so may any President who shall come after him. And, under such a precedent, whenever the President shall belong to one party and the Congress to another, the former may be removed, and the Senate may appoint one of their number to take his place.

A month later, the *New York Times* issued another appeal for rational action:

[I]f the President is removed merely for a mistake, or because he is in the way of party triumphs, or from partisan hatreds, having committed no crime or misdemeanor in the opinion of the nation, when it read the testimony and arguments, *even then* the people will be calm, because they will fall back on justice, and know that wickedness and passion will be avenged. Then the perpetrators of injustice will lose all their *prestige,* and no other harm will come than a wound to a party which cannot rule but by passion. We take it for granted that, whatever the verdict, there is patriotism and intelligence enough left to the nation to see the right ultimately vindicated. What is *any party,* to the eye of the patriot, compared with the dominion of truth, and the integrity of institutions?

No doubt these sentiments helped to form moderated opinions in the population of which the Radicals were only a part.

When President Eisenhower, who had appeared with McCarthy in Wisconsin during the 1952 presidential campaign, spoke out against McCarthy in 1954, Eisenhower, too, was acting against an apparent aggressor. Here is an excerpt from his televised address to the nation:

[T]he greater is the need that we look at them, our anxieties, clearly face to face without fear like honest, straightforward Americans . . . so we do not fall prey to hysterical thinking. . . . First of all, this fear [of Communist subversion] has been greatly exaggerated as to numbers.[32]

But more dramatic was the televised assault launched by Joseph Welch in response to McCarthy's smear of one of Welch's aides. Welch, while on camera, provided the most dramatic moment of the Army-McCarthy Hearings:

> Until this moment, Senator, I think I never really gauged your cruelty or your recklessness. Fred Fisher is a young man who went to the Harvard Law School and came to my firm and is starting what looks to be a brilliant career with us. . . . It is, I regret to say, equally true that I fear he shall always bear a scar needlessly inflicted by you. If it were in my power to forgive you for your reckless cruelty, I would do so. I like to think I'm a gentle man, but your forgiveness will have to come from someone other than me. . . . Let us not assassinate this lad further, Senator, you've done enough. Have you no sense of decency, sir, at long last?

Welch then stalked from the hearing room, tears streaming down his face. The scene was played and replayed on television across the land. Public approval of McCarthy dropped markedly after the broadcast of this confrontation.

Long before McCarthy's vile tactics were obvious to the complacent nation, they were clear to opinion leaders in the media. The printed press assumed its historic role of guardian for the First Amendment, while at the same time uncovering the truth about Senator McCarthy. The truly encouraging fact from this period is that McCarthy was attacked not only early and often by the print media, but that even conservative Republican publications went after him.

For example, Republican Henry Luce's *Time* magazine printed this of McCarthy on October 22, 1951:

> The Reds in Government, if any, were safe. After nearly two years of tramping the nation and shouting that he was "rooting out the skunks," just how many Communists has Joe rooted out? The answer: none. At best, he might claim an assist on three minor and borderline cases which Government investigators had already spotted. . . . The public quite correctly, thought that someone must be to blame. Joe McCarthy went into the business of providing scapegoats. It was easier to string along with Joe's wild charges than to settle down to a sober examination of the chuckle-headed "liberalism," the false assumptions and the fatuous complacency that had endangered the security of the U.S. That he got a lot of help from the Administration spokesmen who still insist that nothing was wrong with U.S. policy helps to explain McCarthy's success—although it in no way excuses McCarthy. Joe, like all effective demagogues, found an area of emotion and exploited it.

74

No regard for fair play, no scruple for exact truth hampers Joe's political course. If his accusations destroy reputations, if they subvert the principle that a man is innocent until proven guilty he is oblivious. Joe, immersed in the joy of battle, does not even seem to realize the gravity of his own charges.

Almost a year later in Luce's September 8, 1952 issue of *Life* magazine, the warning was reissued:

If Mr. Truman & co. had not derided the issue of Communist infiltration of the U.S. government, it might never have gained currency. But the President did call the Hiss case a "red herring" and Secretary of State Dean Acheson did "refuse" to turn his back on Alger Hiss. So in 1950—a Congressional election year—another smart politician with an elastic conscience aimed low at an obvious target. The junior Senator from Wisconsin, Joe McCarthy, charged there were 205 persons, known by Secretary of State Dean Acheson to be Communists, who were still in the State Department. Joe never proved his charge, numerically or otherwise; instead he went on making more sensational accusations. . . . McCarthyism is a form of exaggerated campaign oratory; it is also abuse of the freedom of speech we enjoy in this country. Every single individual, including the editors of LIFE, who lapses from his highest sense of responsibility to truth, is guilty, in some degree, of McCarthyism. But we believe in free speech—we believe that the best cure for exaggeration and distortion is the counter attack which will be and *is* made against the exaggerations and distortions. Of this the history of McCarthyism is a superb example. No one has more energetically counterattacked than Senator Joe McCarthy. In fact, the very word McCarthyism is the cannon fire of the anti-McCarthyist.

McCarthy was opposed by the major newspapers of the time including the *New York Times,* the *Washington Post,* the *Christian Science Monitor,* the *St. Louis Post-Dispatch,* the *Baltimore Sun,* the *Chicago Daily News,* the *New York Herald-Tribune,* the *Kansas City Star,* the *Louisville Courier-Journal,* and even the *Milwaukee Journal.*

Individual journalists often proved to be modern day Thomas Coopers. For example, Anthony Lewis wrote a series of Pulitzer Prize winning articles in the *Washington Daily News* in July of 1954. They resulted in the reinstatement of Abraham Chasanow in the Navy after McCarthyists had had him removed.

The editorials and articles of the print media laid the groundwork for what would be transmitted by television, a newly emerging force in American society. The new medium attacked the monster that McCarthy had become by doing what the print media could not: television showed McCarthy and his tactics. The public did not like what is saw through the camera's eye.

Edward R. Murrow opened his *See It Now* broadcast of April 6, 1954 with: "Tonight's report consists *entirely* of certain remarks by Senator Joseph R. McCarthy. . . ." Murrow's earlier program of March 9 had shown McCarthy doing his worst. Then on the next program Murrow gave McCarthy equal time to reply. Both programs were carried at prime time in 36 major cities by the CBS television network. Murrow had said to the nation on March 9:

> Often operating as a one-man committee, [McCarthy] has travelled far, interviewed many, terrorized some, accused civilian and military leaders of the past administration of a great conspiracy to turn the country over to Communism, investigated and substantially demoralized the present State Department, made varying charges of espionage at Fort Monmouth. (The Army says it has been unable to find anything relating to espionage there.) He has interrogated a varied assortment of what he calls "Fifth Amendment Communists." Republican Senator Flanders of Vermont said of McCarthy today: "He dons war paint; he goes into his war dance; he emits his war whoops; he goes forth to battle and proudly returns with the scalp of a pink Army dentist." Other critics have accused the Senator of using the bull whip and smear. . . . Two of the staples of his diet are the investigators (protected by immunity) and the half truth. . . . His primary achievement has been in confusing the public mind as between internal and the external threat of Communism. We must not confuse dissent with disloyalty. We must remember always that accusation is not proof and that conviction depends upon evidence and due process of law. We will not walk in fear. . . . We will not be driven by fear into an age of unreason if we dig deep in our history and our doctrine, and remember that we are not descended from fearful men, not from men who feared to write, to speak, to associate and to defend causes which were for the moment unpopular. This is no time for men who oppose Senator McCarthy's methods to keep silent. . . . [H]e didn't create this situation of fear, he merely exploited it and rather successfully. Cassius was right, "The fault, dear Brutus is not in our stars, but in ourselves."

McCarthy chose to send a film of his remarks to CBS to rebut Murrow's charges of March 9. CBS played it unedited. Here are some excerpts that show just how well the audiovisual channel of national television worked:

[O]rdinarily, I would not take time out from the important work at hand to answer Murrow. However, in this case I feel justified in doing so because Murrow is a symbol, the leader and the cleverest of the jackal pack which is always found at the throat of anyone who dares to expose individual Communists and traitors. I am compelled by the facts to say to you that Mr. Edward R. Murrow, as far back as twenty years ago, was engaged in propaganda for Communist causes. For example, the Institute of International Education, of which he was the acting director, was chosen to act as a representative by a Soviet agency to do a job which would normally be done by the Russian Secret Police. Mr. Murrow sponsored a Communist school in Moscow. In the selection of American students and teachers who were to attend, Mr. Murrow's organization was known as Voks. V-O-K-S. Many of those selected were later exposed as Communist. Murrow's organization selected such notorious Communists as Isadore Bugin, David Zablodowsky. Incidentally, Zablodowsky was forced out of the United Nations, when my chief counsel presented his case to the grand jury and gave a picture of his Communist activities. Now, Mr. Murrow, by his own admission, was a member of the IWW—that's the Industrial Workers of the World—a terrorist organization cited as subversive by an attorney general of the United States, who stated that it was an organization which seeks (and I quote) "to alter the Government of the United States by unconstitutional means." Now, other government committees have had before them actors, screen writers, motion picture producers, and others who admitted Communist affiliations but pleaded youth or ignorance. Now, Murrow can hardly make the same plea. On March 9 of this year, Mr. Murrow, a trained reporter, who had travelled all over the world, who was the educational director of CBS, followed implicitly the Communist line as laid down in the last six months, laid down not only by the Communist Daily Worker, but by the Communist magazine. . . . Now, the question: why is it important to you, the people of America, to know why the Education Director and the Vice President of CBS so closely follows the Communist Party line? To answer that question we must turn back the pages of history. A little over a hundred years ago a little group of men in Europe considered to deliver the world to a new system, to Communism. . . . What do the Communists think of me and what do the Communists think of Mr. Murrow? One of us is on the side of the Communists; the other is against the Communists. . . . Here is a Communist *Daily Worker* of March 9, containing 7 articles and a principal editorial, all attacking McCarthy, and the same issue lists Mr. Murrow's program as—listen to this—"one of tonight's best bets on TV."

Here, as in later televised hearings, McCarthy's methods were more evident than on hustings. As viewers watched, often alone or with only family member's present, they watched dispassionately. McCarthy's shaky foundations of "fact" and his leaps in drawing inferences were more obvious in a "news program" than they were in heated political settings. Furthermore, he was attacking a very highly respected reporter-commentator and one who had weighed his own words carefully in criticizing McCarthy. The public had the choice of rejecting their most credible leaders—Henry Luce, Dwight Eisenhower, Harry Truman, Edward R. Murrow—or rejecting McCarthy. Increasingly, McCarthy stood alone until by the time of the televised Army Hearings, his strategies became too obvious and too well known to evoke respect.[33]

In each of the instances I have examined, opinion leaders stepped forward to protect the political system from being taken over by the radicals. The national media, whether newspapers, television, or artists, took on the obligation of protecting our most important rights, particularly freedom of expression. They did this not only by exposing the inaccuracies of the radicals but by revealing the radicals' methods in such a way that the public would understand the contradiction between the radicals' avowed goals and their practices. These steps were often taken at no small risk to the advocate, but such courage was critical in preventing radicals from infringing any further on basic civil liberties.

THE DECLINE AND FALL OF THE RADICAL SEGMENT

A radical party's political influence has usually lasted about four years in the United States. The movement is born when a radical group seeks support to fight a danger it has discovered. The word is spread to its members, and opinion leaders begin to emerge. Coalitions begin to be built. A significant number of people perceive that there is indeed a threat. The intensely interested are taken into the party. They become true believers, perhaps hard-core activists. As more public attention is drawn to the single issue of concern, legislation is introduced; it is at this point that opposition crystalizes.

Radicals who already have major influence in national government tend to initiate legislation early in their ascendancy. By 1798 the Federalists had already raised a large standing army and gained control

78

of it by pushing Hamilton to the position of acting commander. Then they passed the Alien and Sedition laws, set up a Department of the Navy, and armed merchant ships. Republicans had only limited power to govern prior to the election of 1866, but with a two-thirds majority following that election, the Radical Republicans passed the Civil Rights Bill, the Freedmen's Bureau Bill of 1866, and the Reconstruction Acts of 1867–1868, since they could override President Johnson's vetoes. Anti-communists in Congress were strong enough to pass the Subversive Activities Control Act in 1950, just as Senator McCarthy began his crusade. Less powerful radical groups can only propose where they cannot enact. In either case, however, it appears that at the point where radicals' schemes of *implementation* are made clear through enactments or proposals, these groups become most fully open to attack or, as in the case of the Populists, to partial cooptation by mainstream political groups.

The decline of radical groups who have power has been marked by flurries of desperate activity. President Adams, despite Hamilton's protests, began peace negotiations with France in Febraury of 1799.[34] When Adams sent envoys to France, Hamilton countered by expanding the army.[35] He used it the next month to crush Fries' Rebellion in Pennsylvania.[36] During the summer of 1799, Hamilton and the cabinet delayed the departure of the peace mission. They then attempted to convict Thomas Cooper, an anti-Federalist newspaper publisher, of sedition.[37] It was the last gasp of a desperate party.

Even though failure to remove President Johnson slowed the Radical Republican movement in 1868, they did succeed in nominating and electing General Grant President of the United States. Led by Charles Sumner in the Senate and Thaddeus Stevens in the House, they were instrumental in keeping Union troops in the South through the two terms of the Grant administration despite severe setbacks in the congressional elections of 1874 and 1876.

The McCarthyist collapse was more dramitic. To the end, McCarthy continued to claim there were Communists in the government, but his colleagues in the Senate grew impatient with his excesses. On July 30, 1954, a resolution censuring him was introduced in the Senate. It passed by a vote of 67 to 22.[38] His powers and authority—in decline since the televised Army Hearings—were thus further diminished. His death in 1957 left his now enfeebled "crusade" without a leader.

Radicals in American history have seemed more concerned with immediate threats than with long-term eventualities. This has frequently been their Achilles heel. Radicals often argue that we shall have no need to concern ourselves with our heritage or our long-range goals if we fail to cope with the crisis immediately before us. In the end, however, it has been precisely this attitude that has been attacked by the responsible elements in the society. In focusing so exclusively on the immediate, the radicals have revealed a near-sightedness that responsible people find pragmatically flawed and/or unconscionable. Moderates have successfully argued that abandonment of *constitutionally sanctioned* methods of dealing with problems presents a danger far greater than the danger described by the radicals. Thus, in the name of the Bill of Rights, Jefferson called on his countrymen to resist the Alien and Sedition Acts. In the name of due process and Union, Senator Grimes case his vote against removal of President Johnson, as did others among his colleagues. In the name of decency and individual freedom, Joseph Welch rebuked Joseph McCarthy, and in the name of freedom of expression and fair play, the Senate censured him.

Public support appears to begin to fade when people become aware that the rhetoric of radicals contradicts their actions and/or the sacred passages of the Constitution. Federalists were defeated by a free press and articulate Jeffersonians. They revealed that Federalist suppression of free speech was in conflict with the goals of liberty and internal tranquility. Jefferson, in his first inaugural in 1801, expressed the sentiments of what was by then the majority of the nation and the spirit of later responses to radicalism:

> Let us, then, fellow citizens, unite with one heart and one mind. Let us restore to social intercourse that harmony and affection without which liberty and life itself are but dreary things. And let us reflect that, having banished from our land that religious intolerance under which mankind so long bled and suffered, we have yet gained little if we countenance a political intolerance as despotic, as wicked, and capable of as bitter and bloody persecutions. . . . Every difference of opinion is not a difference of principle. We have called by different names brethren of the same principle. We are all Republicans, we are all Federalists. If there be any among us who would wish to dissolve this union or change its republican form, let them stand undisturbed as monuments of the safety with which error of opinion may be tolerated where reason is left free to combat it.

Perhaps no public figure has better expressed why stability and change reside together in the American environment of freedom of expression. In our time, presidents have shown similar leadership. Dwight Eisenhower,

80

delivering a commencement address at Dartmouth College on June 14, 1953, a year before the McCarthy hearings, attacked the Senator's excesses:

> Don't join the book burners. Don't think you are going to conceal faults by concealing evidence that they ever existed. Don't be afraid to go in your library. . . . How will we defeat communism unless we know what it is, and what it teaches; and why does it have such an appeal for men? . . . And even if they think ideas that are contrary to ours, their right to say them, their right to record them, and their right to have them at places where they are accessible to others is unquestioned. . . .

CONCLUSION

The three cases I have discussed illustrate a pattern of birth, growth and decline in radical movements. I believe this pattern, with certain variations, has been a general one in our history. When radicals have tried to combat perceived national dangers, defenders of constitutional procedures and personal liberties have also taken the field—at first in somewhat disorganized fashion. When radical movements have survived initial opposition, they have tended to respond with increased zeal. If prone to excess, their excesses increase, and this leads to increasingly coherent opposition, as in the cases I have reviewed.

Both radicals and their opponents tend to see themselves as "protecting" the establishment, and as long as the controversy remains one of *debate* it fits within the traditions of a free society. The controversies may be long lived. One might instance the activities of the Socialist party over the past century. However, if radicals move to *implement* policies in ways that would curtail the rights and freedoms of others, conserving forces begin to coalesce (1) to protect established freedoms and, perhaps, (2) to reform the establishment in ways that make radical changes less attractive or wholly unnecessary. If, as in the case of Populist radicalism, reform occurs before radical changes can be legislated, the radical movement is apt to die because its chief reasons for being have been coopted by those working within the established system. If, as with Radical Republicanism and to a lesser degree with McCarthyism, radicals succeed in imposing their wills through legislative, administrative, and/or procedural activities, conserving forces have usually sustained their persuasive pressure until a rhetorical situation favorable to constitutionalism is developed. It is a remarkable feature of American experience that situations favorable to forces safeguarding individual liberties *have* eventually developed and conserving forces have been able to preserve the *original, balanced, constitutional framework*. While an island of suppression, such as controls over "alien speakers," may be left behind for the Supreme Court to deal with, the mass of radical legislation is eventually swept away. My suggstion is that this has happened only because we have inherited personal freedom as a *legal* guarantee and have a profound and stable tradition of maintaining freedom of expression, religion, press, and political action at the pinnacle of our political values.

Radical parties tend to have hard cores of intense political alignment. Further, their concerns in this country have tended to be fairly narrow. Their targets have tended to be selective. This gives them cohesion and visibility, but it also renders them weak in the face of opposition that is more broadly based. Showing a broad political perspective was one of the major persuasive strategies that gave credibility to the conserving forces in the cases I have reviewed. Other major and minor instances from our history can easily be found: the various territorial compromises prior to 1860, the ending of Prohibition in the 1930s, alteration of the Neutrality Act in the 1940s, and moderation of anti-war spirit of the 1960s.

The three controversies I have examined in this chapter illustrate that even in a democratic republic with a heritage that can be traced to the Magna Carta, erosion of civil liberties is always *possible*. The instances of tensions between freedom and "protection" that I have cited are by no means the only ones in our hstory. On occasion, presidents, the Congress, and even the Supreme Court have circumscribed private citizens' rights to speak out and to live in freedom. In almost all of those cases, as in the three I have specifically examined, the tension between freedom and constraint arose between a perceived need to protect against some internal or external subversion and the need to maintain civil liberties. It is thus a continuing condition of American society that we will contest over *how much* and *what kind* of personal freedom may be exercised *where*. This is a built-in condition wherever the *first* social value is freedom to express.[39]

It is no doubt fortunate that contests between freedom and "protection" have tended to be settled ultimately by the majority's moderate judgments. Radicalism of left or right tends to be short sighted. It is thereby susceptible to (1) weakening by changes in events or by the majority's sheer boredom with the limited topics radicals tend to discuss; (2) weakening by the force of arguments and appeals that reflect longer and/or broader views and interests; (3) weakening by offering compromises and exceptions that mollify the concerns of the majority; and (4) the inherent difficulties radicals have in offering long-ranged outcomes that promise gratification for a full majority of the society.

The radicals I discussed in this chapter suffered from all four of these rhetorically disadvantaging forces. Moreover, as I have pointed out, they had the conceptual and rhetorical disadvantage of having to establish some value as a value *above freedom*. The radical Federalists had to place and keep national security and political power above the already enshrined value of freedom of expression. The Radical Republicans had to promulgate "racial equality" and "conquest" as higher values than equal freedom for all. McCarthy and those who supported him had to sustain a case that subversion was so ubiquitous that freedom of expression must be circumscribed. But with personal freedom clearly established in both law and tradition in our country, it has happily proved unfeasible to displace that value for any length of time.

NOTES

1. The Alien and Sedition Acts actually were four separate pieces of legislation: (1) the "Naturalization Act" of June 18, 1798, vol. I *Statutes at Large,* 566; (2) "An Act Concerning Aliens" of June 25, 1798, vol. I *Statutes at Large,* 570; (3) "An Act Respecting Alien Enemies" of July 6, 1798, vol. I *Statutes at Large,* 577; and (4) "The Sedition Act" of July 14, 1798, vol. I *Statues at Large,* 596. The Reconstruction Acts of 1867–69 can be found at Mar. 2, 1867, ch. 152, vol. 14 *Statutes at Large,* 28; Mar. 23, 1867, ch. 6, vol. 15 *Statutes at Large,* 2; July 19, 1867, ch. 30, vol. 15 *Statutes at Large,* 14; Mar. 11, 1868, ch. 25, vol. 15 *Statutes at Large,* 41; Dec. 22, 1869, ch. 3, vol. 16 *Statutes at Large,* 59. The text of the Subversive Activities Control Act of 1950 is at 18 U.S.C., Sec. 793, 1507; 22 U.S.C. Sec. 618; 50 U.S.C. Sec. 781–826 (1982).

2. See Gerald Malcolm Howat, general ed., *Dictionary of World History,* "Jacobin" (London: Thomas Nelson and Sons Limited, 1973), 757.

3. James D. Richardson, *A Compilation of the Messages and Papers of the Presidents, 1789–1897* (Washington, D.C.: GPO, 1897).

4. See *New York Times,* July 10, 1952. See also Herbert S. Parmet, *Eisenhower and the American Crusades* (New York: Macmillan Co., 1972), 95.

5. On February 1, 1799, the *Aurora* printed the Insurance Company of North America's figures for the last six months of 1798; American damages inflicted by French vessels were $260,000. Ironically, during the same period, British vessels inflicted damages of $280,000.

6. Thaddeus Stevens, a Radical Republican member of the House Ways and Means Committee, lost a nephew and the family iron works during the war. Revenge became an obsession for him.

7. Leonard W. Levy and Merrill D. Peterson, ed., *Major Crises in American History,* vol. I (New York: Harcourt, Brace and World, 1962), 200. Quotations

that follow from the House debate over the Alien and Sedition Acts are from this source unless otherwise noted.

8. Richard Hofstadter, *Great Issues in American History,* vol. II (New York: Random House, 1958), 36.

9. Waving a piece of paper, McCarthy startled his audience by charging that communists inside the State Department were responsible for American setbacks in the world, "I have here in my hand a list of 205." Robert A. Divine, *Since 1945: Politics and Diplomacy in Recent American History* (New York: John Wiley and Sons, Inc., 1975), 33.

10. Divine, *Since 1945,* 34.

11. Conservatives were merely one segment behind McCarthy. Catholics, with strong ties to traditionally anti-communist areas of Europe or countries that had become Russian satellites, were strong supporters of McCarthy in Wisconsin; thus, McCarthy enjoyed strong support from Poles and Czechs. He was also strong among East Coast Catholics including Irish and Italian Americans. Parmet, *Eisenhower,* 125.

12. This fact explains why the young Robert Kennedy became a committee staff member for Senator Joseph McCarthy.

13. Levy, *Major Crises,* 28. Long John Allen was one of those involved in the fisticuffs that broke out during this debate.

14. Hofstadter, *Great Issues,* 36.

15. Emile de Antonia and Daniel Talbot, *Point of Order* (New York: screenplay, 1964), 9.

16. These acts were directed primarily against anti-Federalist editors of French and English heritage, such as Thomas Cooper, Joseph Priestley, James Callender, Benjamin Bache, Count de Volney, and others. For further information on the Alien and Sedition Acts, see Frank Maloy Anderson, "The Enforcement of the Alien and Sedition Laws," *American Hist. Ass'n. Reports,* Annual Report for the Year 1912 (Washington, D.C.: American Historical Association, 1914) 113–26; Claude Gernade Bowers, *Jefferson and Hamilton* (St. Clair Shores, Mich.: Scholarly Press, 1925) ch. xvi–xvii. These Acts are reprinted in Henry S. Commager, *Documents of American History,* 9th ed. (Englewood Cliffs, N.J.: Prentice-Hall, 1973), 175–78.

17. This act is in force (U.S.C. Sec. 21–24, 1982) with only one substantive change: States no longer have the jurisdiction to deal with enemy aliens. In March, 1988, for example, the State Department denied a visa to Gerry Adams, a member of the British Parliament representing Belfast. He is also president of Provisional Sinn Fein, a legal political party in Northern Ireland with ties to the outlawed Irish Republican Army. The State Department argued that Adams was "involved with terrorist activities" and therefore, subject to exclusion under the Immigration and Nationality Act.

18. The Alien and Sedition Acts were never reviewed by the Supreme Court. Justice William J. Brennan, Jr., observed in *New York Times Co. v. Sullivan:* "Although the Sedition Act was never tested in this Court, the attack upon its validity has carried the day in the court of history. . . . Jefferson, as President, pardoned those who had been convicted and sentenced under the Act . . . stating: 'I discharged every person under punishment or prosecution under the sedition law, because I considered, and now consider, that law to be nullity. . . .' The invalidity of the Act has also been assumed by Justices of the

Court. Their views reflect a broad consensus that the Act, because of the constraint it imposed upon criticism of government and public officials, was inconsistent with the first Amendment" 376 U.S. 254, 276 (1963). See John Chester Miller, *Crises in Freedom: The Alien and Sedition Acts* (Boston: Little, Brown & Co., 1951), 193; William M. Malloy, "Annual Report for 1912" of the American Historical Association *reprinted in* House Document No. 933, 63rd Congress, 2nd Session, 115–16. The Sedition Act expired by its own terms on March 3, 1801, just before Jefferson's inauguration. He immediately pardoned all who had been convicted or who were awaiting trial under the Act. See Edward Gerard Hudon, *Freedom of Speech and Press in America* (Washington, D.C.: Public Affairs Press, 1963), 48. There appear to have been about 25 persons arrested under the law, with 15 or more being indicted. A shifting of the historical evidence indicates that only 10 or 11 cases came to trial. In 10 cases the accused was found to be guilty.

19. The fact that Federalists would actually jail a political opponent shows how strongly they acted when they felt threatened. Hamilton's grasp at control of the army was an example of the extra-legal maneuvering that can occur. See Smith, Freedom's Fetters (Ithaca, N.Y.: Cornell University Press, 1963), second ed., 185–86; Frank Luther Mott, *American Journalism: A History of Newspapers in the United States through 250 years: 1690–1940* (New York: Macmillan, 1949), 149.

20. In 1866, Congress voted to extend the appropriations of the Bureau and to strengthen it. Johnson vetoed the bill, but Congress overturned the veto. Richard Nelson Current, *The Essentials of American History* (New York: Alfred A. Knopf, 1976), 170.

21. Johnson would eventually succeed in getting rid of Stanton, but it would take him a year. Stanton barricaded himself in his office and issued a warrant for the arrest of his successor in February of 1868. The controversy was one of the major issues in the President's impeachment.

22. Current, *Essentials of American History,* 171.

23. See Poyntz Tyler, ed., *Immigration and the United States* (New York: H. W. Wilson Co., 1956). For President Truman's veto message, see *Documents of American History*, 578–82. See also Nat Hentoff, *The First Freedom* (New York: Delacorte Press, 1980), 137–38.

24. The Subversive Activities Control Act of 1950 was upheld by the Supreme Court in a 5–4 decision in 1961. See *Communist Party v. Subversive Activities Control Board*, 367 U.S. 1. In 1965 the Court reversed itself in *Albertson v. Subversive Control Board*, 381 U.S. 910.

25. Often the tone taken is highly moral or puritanical. The rationale for some of these methods is that they are required by the underhanded tactics of the opposition.

26. Levy, *Major Crises,* 199. By 1807 Dayton would become so frustrated at the ascendance of the Democratic-Republicans that he would join Burr in an attempt to overthrow the government.

27. Divine, *Since 1945,* 34, 42.

28. Ibid., 69–70.

29. Ironically, the first public burning of a book in America took place in Boston in 1650. Hentoff, *First Freedom,* 61.

30. See Parmet, *Eisenhower,* 226–46.

31. The growth of the standing army and the direct tax also contributed to the downfall of the Federalists.

32. "Radio and Television Address to the American People on the State of the Nation, April 5, 1954," *Public Papers of the Presidents: Dwight D. Eisenhower, 1954* (Washington, D.C.: GPO, 1960), 375–77.

33. We should not neglect the role artists played in rallying to defend their own and to alert the country to danger. Though Arthur Miller has steadfastly refused to confirm it, his play in four acts, *The Crucible,* implied an analogy between the Salem witch trials and McCarthy's investigations. Miller's play was first performed on January 22, 1953 at the Martin Beck Theatre in New York City. Miller was subsequently denied a passport by the State Department to see the Brussels premiere of the play. Nonetheless, the play met with critical success and gave artists an articulate vehicle by which to rally support. Miller was summoned before the House Un-American Activities Committee and eventually tried for contempt of Congress.

34. The parallel between Adams' level-headed approach to the French crisis and Eisenhower's approach to the Korean crisis is uncanny. Both men suffered severe criticism from the radicals in their own ranks.

35. In a letter to Theodore Sedgwick, Hamilton wrote that the militia of loyal states could not be counted on to restrain "a refractory and powerful State. . . . When a force has been collected, let them be drawn toward Virginia, for which there is an obvious pretext [that of strengthening border defenses in the Mississippi Valley], then let measures be taken to act upon the laws and put Virginia to the test of resistance." Hamilton to Theodore Sedgwick, Feb. 2, 1799, Henry Cabot Lodge, ed., *The Works of Alexander Hamilton* (New York: G. P. Putnam's Sons, 1903), 340–42, quoted in Stephen G. Kurtz, *The Presidency of John Adams: The Collapse of Federalism, 1795–1800* (Philadelphia: University of Pennsylvania Press, 1957), 356.

36. In March 1799, a group of angry Pennsylvania Germans led by Fries, a militia officer, organized an attempt to rescue some of their outspoken allies who had openly defied the direct tax imposed by the Federalists. Federal marshals were prevented from incarcerating the men, skirmishes broke out, and General McPherson's Pennsylvania army was rushed to the scene. Kurtz, 358.

37. Cooper defended himself when he came to trial in 1800. Judge Chase's handling of the case was prejudiced against Cooper. In his speech to the jury, Cooper said, "We have advanced so far on the road to despotism in this republican country that we dare not say our President is mistaken." Cooper was convicted, but eventually pardoned by Jefferson.

38. See U.S. Sen. Select Committee to Study Censure Charges, 83rd Cong. Hearings . . . pursuant to Sen. Resolution 301. The resolution stated in part "The Senator from Wisconsin, Mr. McCarthy, . . . acted contrary to senatorial ethics and tended to bring the Senate into dishonor and disrepute, to obstruct the constitutional processes of the Senate, and to impair its dignity; and such conduct is thereby condemned." *Documents of American History,* 601.

39. Notes from the Constitutional Convention in Philadelphia and reports from the ratification debates in the states show that these built-in tensions were recognized by friends and opponents of the new government. To the Federalists, the structural tensions were one of the virtues of the system because they helped provide a "balance of powers."

4

THE CONTEMPORARY ENVIRONMENT

To this point I have been discussing tensions between freedom and constraint in political persuasion that was largely carried on through print and voice. What I have said applies to our past and to our present insofar as these media of communication are concerned. But in the last two-thirds of this century our media of communication have multiplied and created new forms of communication and new tensions between freedom and constraint. Developments in the mass media of communication have given special prominence to problems of balancing freedom of expression with such other highly held democratic ideals as equality of opportunity, "truth," and "safety."[1] Conflicts among these ideals are seen prominently in (1) government's confused and inconsistent responses to different media of communication as they have developed, and (2) confused and confusing responses to changes in the character of political campaigning. A comparable but different conflict arises between (3) the ideal of freedom of expression and the ideals of maintaining "objectivity" or "truth" in public communication and assuring the "health" and "safety" of the citizenry.

The first of these tensions arises from a number of sources. Foremost among them is the fact that leadership in a democracy changes. Different approaches to regulation in general and legislation in particular are taken by different administrations, congresses, courts and even independent agencies.

Another cause of this first tension is the historic fear of new technology. Rulers have long been wary of technology that improves communication among their subjects and provides new ways by which dissident views can be spread. When Gutenberg introduced moveable type by printing Bibles in Mainz in 1456, local officials immediately placed restrictions on the new device. Charles VII of France sent Nicholas Jensen to find out what the new press could do. He became an apprentice to Gutenberg and assured Charles that the device was under strict watch he authorities. By 1486, civil authorities heeded the pleas of bishop Berthold von Henneberg to establish Commissions of Censorship in Frankfurt and Mainz for all published works. These restrictions eventually led to the collapse of the popular book fair in Frankfurt.

In 1476 the new press was introduced in England under the reign of Edward IV; ten years later, Henry VII restricted its use to prevent "forged tydings" and seditious documents. Henry VIII expanded the suppression by making sure that all presses were licensed and subject to prior restraint. By 1630 there were only twenty-three master printers and fifty-five presses in the Kingdom, all in London save two, and all directly responsible to and licensed by the crown.

In this century in the United States, every new technology of mass communications that has developed has been subject to regulation by the government. The legislative history of the 1934 Communication Act reveals that the restrictions imposed on radio and television were motivated by fear of the power of the new technology and by partisan ardor. In the 1920s, broadcasters had asked Secretary of Commerce Hoover to help them unscramble overlapping broadcast signals. Hoover's suggested legislation became the Radio Act of 1927, which established the Federal Radio Commission and required broadcasters to operate in "the public interest." This phrase allowed a Republican appointed Commission to review programming content when considering the renewal of broadcast licenses. In 1929, the Commission denied a request by a licensee, the Chicago Federation of Labor, to expand its program offerings. In 1931, the Commission went further; it denied a license renewal and based its decision on the content of programming provided.

In 1934, Democrats struck back when the Radio Act was rewritten as the Communications Act. It replaced the Radio Commission with a Federal Communications Commission and gave it power over telephone, telegraph, and television. Newspapers had generally supported Republican candidates for federal offices; New Deal Democrats wanted to make sure that radio and television were nonpartisan. So they strengthened the provisions of the law applying equal time for candidates and ballot issues. As we shall see, the new law provided the government and private groups with a way to harass and intimidate broadcasters.[2]

The second tension results from fear that political strategists can use new technologies with devastating effectiveness. Again, the fear that too much power will be placed in too few hands has led to many changes in our campaign laws. In chapter 2, I pointed out that election reform was the main goal of Progressives. In this and the next chapter I will show how those "reforms" led to changes in campaign practices.

The third tension derives from the human desire to find the "truth," while at the same time guaranteeing freedom of expression. The price of freedom is sometimes lies, distortions, or subjective judgments that fly in the face of "conventional wisdom."[3] Most legislators feel a need to eliminate falsehoods in order to protect the public. How far to go in promoting the "truth" and protecting the "well being" of the public is grist for the legislative mill. But often the legislation proposed to ensure "truth" and prevent deception strains the First Amendment.

The analysis that follows focuses on questions surrounding freedom of expression in the print and electronic media. Regulation of this freedom has been divided into three models by the government: The print model, which is the least restricted because of our First Amendment heritage; the common carrier model, which is the most restricted because of its monopoly status; and the electronic model, which falls somewhere in between. Over the last decade the courts and the Federal Communications Commission have moved to apply the print model to other media wherever feasible. For example, while cable television is a franchised monopoly in each market, the courts have given it as much protection in the area of pornography and obscenity as they have to print.[4] The courts have also struck down the requirement that cable companies "must carry" all local stations on the ground that cable operators are roughly akin to newspaper editors.[5] But the pervasive nature of radio and television have prevented those media from gaining the same rights.[6] The confusion resulting from the imposition of content controls on media of communication is the subject of the following pages.

FREEDOM OF EXPRESSION VERSUS REGULATION OF CHANNELS

No better example of the government's inconsistent and confused treatment of media exists than the difference in the ways print and electronic media have been regulated. The last serious attempt to regulate the content of a newspaper was swept away by a unanimous Supreme Court in 1974. In *Miami Herald v. Tornillo,* the Court held that equal space provisions written into Florida's law were unconstitutional.[7]

Some believe the circumstances of the case justified limits on the First Amendment protection of large newspapers. Pat Tornillo was running for public office in Miami; his opponent was endorsed by the *Miami Herald*. Tornillo invoked a little known state law passed in 1913 that required newspapers to give a right of reply to the opponents of those they endorsed. The *Herald* refused and lost the case unanimously in the

Florida State Supreme Court. The Court cited restrictions that had been placed on the electronic media as one of its rationales for upholding imposition of restrictions on the *Herald*.

The Florida Court found that the *Herald* was the only major daily newspaper in Miami,[8] that it owned several broadcasting outlets, and that Tornillo was involved in an election that was important to the community. Citing the U.S. Supreme Court's ruling of 1969, *Red Lion Broadcasting v. FCC* (reviewed below), the Florida Court ruled that the Miami *Herald* owed Tornillo equal space because of its endorsement of his opponent.

The U.S. Supreme Court never mentioned its *Red Lion* decision when it reversed the Florida Supreme Court and struck down the Florida law. It simply said that freedom of the press was inviolable. Thus, the *printed* press in America has strong protection from governmental interference.

Such protection has not been accorded the electronic media even when they serve the same purposes as newspapers. The reasons for this double standard can be traced back to the 1920s. As radio grew like Topsy, signals between stations began to interfere with one another and with naval operations. Some order had to be brought to the chaos. And so, in 1927, at the behest of Secretary of Commerce Hoover, Congress passed the Dill-White Radio Act which created the Federal Radio Commission, the forerunner of the Federal Communications Commission.

The new legislation required federal licensing of broadcasting stations and stipulated that stations must operate in the "public interest" and provide candidates for office equal opportunities for air time.[9] The law was first tested in 1929 when a radio station owned by the Chicago Federation of Labor was denied increased operating time because the Federal Radio Commission deemed its programming not in the public interest. This decision established the principle that an agency of the federal government could evaluate news, editorial content, and entertainment programming in order to determine whether a license to broadcast should be renewed. That power was used for the first time in 1931 when the Federal Radio Commission denied a license and justified its decision with an evaluation of the content of broadcast programming. The right of the government to regulate the content of broadcast programming has been the rule ever since.

In 1932, Congress tried to expand the equal opportunities rules to include public referenda, but the effort fell victim to a pocket veto by President Hoover. In 1934, the Democratic Congress revised the 1927 Act as the Communications Act, and gave strong authority to the new Federal Communications Commission (FCC). For example, in 1941, the

FCC handed down the *Mayflower* decision, ruling that the
Network would have its license renewed contingent upon its ag.
not to editorialize. The Commission said, "the broadcaster cannc
advocate."

In 1943, the National Broadcasting Company challenged the FCC's
program-content rules in the Supreme Court as a violation of the First
Amendment. But, particularly because NBC programmed 86 percent of
all nighttime broadcasting, the Supreme Court ruled against and reinforced the initial rationale for the legislation: That a scarcity of outlets
exists for broadcast programming, therefore, the government has a right
to license the electromagnetic spectrum and assess its use for qualities of
programming.[10]

In 1949, the FCC promulgated a policy that became known as the
"Fairness Doctrine." The policy effectively overturned the *Mayflower*
decision in that it encouraged editorializing but attempted, at the same
time, to avoid the dangers it believed inherent in overly partisan
programming. The Doctrine required coverage of controversial issues of
public importance and presentation of contrasting points of view on
those issues. Said the Commission:

> [T]he needs and interests of the general public with respect to
> programs devoted to news commentary and opinion can only be
> satisfied by making available to them for their consideration and
> acceptance or rejection . . . varying and conflicting views held by
> responsible elements in the community. And it is in the light of
> these basic concepts that the problems of insuring fairness in the
> presentation of news and opinion . . . must be considered.[11]

In 1959, Congress thought it codified the "Fairness Doctrine" into
federal law, making it a major measure of the performance of broadcast
stations.[12] That was the standard interpretation until the TRAC case of
1986 (discussed below).

In 1963 the Doctrine was expanded by the *Cullman* decision, which
"provides that a licensee cannot refuse to air an unpaid presentation
otherwise suitable for broadcast if: (1) the licensee has broadcast a
sponsored program which for the first time presents one side of a
controversial issue; (2) the licensee has not presented (or does not plan to
present) contrasting viewpoints . . . and (3) the licensee has been unable
to obtain paid sponsorship for the appropriate presentation of opposing
viewpoints."[13]

Another expansion of the Fairness Doctrine came with the implementation of the "personal attack" rule in 1962. It requires that when an attack is made on the "honesty, character, integrity or the like of personal qualities of an individual or group" during the broadcast of a controversial issue of public importance, the broadcaster must notify the attacked individual or group, provide a transcript of the attack, and offer a reasonable opportunity to respond over the broadcaster's facilities.[14]

The issue of controls over broadcasters came to a head in the *Red Lion Broadcasting* case, which centered on the constitutionality of the "personal attack" rule.[15] The circumstances of this case were similar to those of *Miami Herald*. Red Lion Broadcasting Company owned a small radio station, WGCB, in Red Lion, Pennsylvania, a town of fewer than six thousand persons. Listeners in the town were able to receive over twenty other radio signals in 1964, the time of this incident. They also had access to cable television, of which about half the households took advantage. There was, in short, no scarcity of electronic informational services in Red Lion. During the election of 1964, WGCB aired a five-minute syndicated editorial by the Reverend Billy James Hargis of the "Christian Crusade." In the editorial, Hargis attacked a member of the staff of the Democratic National Committee named Fred Cook. Neither Cook nor Hargis were members of the community of Red Lion, Pennsylvania.

Cook demanded time for a response to Hargis's editorial.[16] WGCB said that Cook would have to pay for his response time; the cost would be five dollars. Cook refused and the case wound up before the Supreme Court in 1969. The Court ruled in favor of Cook, sticking to the old argument that broadcasting frequencies on the electromagnetic spectrum are scarce, hence the use of the spectrum must be regulated to assure balance and fairness. As this case shows, the Fairness Doctrine provides various interest groups with a means by which to harass broadcasters with threats of demands for free time. Phyllis Schlafly, the head of the Eagle Forum, successfully used the Doctrine to keep editorials favoring the Equal Rights Amendment off the air. Ralph Nader, the consumer advocate, uses the Doctrine to keep editorials and advertisements inimical to his position off the air. Two chief difficulties broadcasters face are determining which groups meet the FCC's standard for qualifying as a "responsible element" in the community, and which issues are "controversial" and "important" to the community.

THE "THE SCARCITY RATIONALE"

Today, electronic media remain subject to governmental evaluation of the content of what is broadcast, and the *NBC* and *Red Lion* cases provide operant precedents. The printed media are free from such controls, and the *Miami Herald* case provides the operant precedent. The irony is that the number of television stations nearly equals the number of daily newspapers and that there are about eight times as many radio stations as there are sources in the other media. Yet television, radio, and even cable programmers can be subject to the Fairness Doctrine because they supposedly use "scarce" resources.[17]

There are many problems with the "scarcity rationale." First, it was clearly not a concern of the Founders when they drafted and submitted the First Amendment to the states for ratification. Only a handful of newspapers existed at that time.[18] They were expensive to produce and hence a scarce voice. Existing newspapers were highly partisan; there was generally no effort to print "balanced" reporting. Nonetheless, despite scarcity and partisanship, the press was formally protected from governmental intrusion. Furthermore, those who formed and adopted the First Amendment were fully aware that all presses had been licensed in England since the time of Henry VIII. They quite specifically *chose* not to follow this practice, demonstrating that they accepted neither scarcity nor partisanship as a ground for imposing controls on freedom of expression.

Second, "scarcity" is a relative term that provides government with a dangerous method of controlling the media. Judge Robert Bork understood this well in his recent decision in the *TRAC* case. He wrote:

It is certainly true that broadcast frequencies are scarce but it is unclear why that fact justifies content regulation of broadcasting in a way that would be intolerable if applied to the editorial process of the print media. All economic goods are scarce, not least the newsprint, ink, delivery trucks, computers, and other resources that go into the production and dissemination of print journalism. Not everyone who wishes to publish a newspaper, or even a pamphlet, may do so. Since scarcity is a universal fact, it can hardly explain regulation in one context and not another. . . . One might attempt to resolve the tension between [*Miami Herald*] and *Red Lion* on the ground that, while scarcity characterizes both print and broadcast media, the latter must be operating under conditions of greater "scarcity" than the former. This, however, is unpersuasive. There is nothing uniquely scarce about the broadcast spectrum.[19]

Bork recognized that today's media marketplace is characterized by great abundance and diversity. There are now 10,128 radio stations and 1,315 television stations.[20] Television reaches 98.2 percent of all U.S. households. Ninety-six percent of all households with television receive five or more stations; 71 percent of those households receive nine or more stations. Today, there are approximately 7,300 cable systems in the United States reaching forty million subscribers, 46 percent of the nation's television households.[21] Cable is now available to more than two-thirds of American homes and the percentage is growing weekly. Additionally, the Cable Communications Policy Act of 1984 allows communities to establish public, educational, and governmental access channels on their local cable systems. Besides ABC, CBS, NBC, and CNN, many local stations are using satellite transmissions to produce their own national news programs. Fifty stations have already formed a consortium that uses local satellite vans to transmit news from almost anywhere in the country for only fifteen dollars a minute. Group broadcast owners,[22] such as Westinghouse, Storer, and Taft, are not only developing alternate programming, they are developing strong news services. For example, Westinghouse has developed Newsfeed, which now serves at least eighty local stations and bypasses the networks.

Without reviewing the growth of radio, multi-point distribution systems, and satellite relays, I have said enough to show that there is no scarcity of diverse sources of news and opinion. The problem is trying to choose among all of the available sources.

In the *Miami Herald* case, the Supreme Court considered a newspaper reader sophisticated and intelligent enough to form his or her own opinion. In *Red Lion,* however, the radio listener was treated as one who must be protected by a governmental agency that assures "fairness." What makes this proposition especially suspect is that the newspaper reader and radio listener could be the same person, and the news they receive could very well come from the same source, say the AP or UPI wire. Furthermore, while the newspaper reader only has the choice of reading the paper or putting it aside, the radio listener has a plethora of stations to listen to, as well as the option of turning off the broadcast. It is therefore very odd that the scarcity rationale continues to be applied to the electronic media rather than to the print media. Such considerations forced Justice William O. Douglas to conclude:

> Television and Radio . . . are . . . included in the concept of press as used in the First Amendment and therefore are entitled to live under the laissez-faire regime which the First Amendment sanctions.[23]

94

THE BURDEN OF REGULATION

Abiding by the Fairness Doctrine on a case-by-case basis was one condition the government imposed on broadcasters in exchange for a license. When a station's license came up for renewal, a government agency examined the station's files to determine whether the broadcaster had been "fair" and "operating in the public interest" for the time the broadcaster has held the license. If there had been no complaints and the station had complied with technical and other rules, renewal was relatively automatic in the majority of cases. However, if a question was raised concerning whether, during the previous license term, the station had operated "in the public interest," a formal evidentiary hearing must be held, which is both costly and time consuming. According to a National Association of Broadcasters survey among 40 license renewal proceedings, the average case lasted eight years.[24] Radio stations spend an average of $600,000 and television stations $1.2 million for legal fees in contested cases. But the costs do not stop there. Stations must bear the cost of providing "public affairs" programming, which consistently draws the least audience and is therefore the hardest for which to find advertising. In certain instances they must also provide free time for responses.

Many "fairness complaints" were made but few were judged appropriate for hearing. In the three years from 1973 to 1976, 13,800 complaints were filed. That is an average of 1.3 complaints per station over a three year period. Less than eleven of these complaints resulted in any formal sanctions. Between 1980 and 1986, only twenty broadcasters were found to have violated the Fairness Doctrine, 132 additional cases went through a formal, serious hearing, and thousands were dismissed as frivolous or unworthy of review. On this evidence it is apparent that most complaints are groundless.[25] The complaint procedure did, however, harass stations because broadcasters had difficulty determining which specific complaints will be taken seriously by the FCC. For example, NBC and one of its local affiliates became embroiled in a fairness complaint concerning their broadcast of the miniseries "Holocaust." A Friedrich Berg filed a complaint, arguing that the April, 1978 "docudrama" was "generally anti-German and pro-Jewish." He demanded an opportunity to oppose and refute the "allegation of a German policy of Jewish extermination during World War II," which he contended was a controversial issue of public importance under the Fairness Doctrine. It was a year before the case was dismissed. I have also shown

95

that unlike their print brethren, broadcasters are subject to *both* libel laws and to the "personal attack" rule. The "personal attack" rule puts a broadcaster at risk for editorializing about public persons and groups. Under the circumstances, the electronic media are discouraged from making attacks on the public officials and the actions those officials take.

Government-imposed programming standards also lead to uniform, bland programming and to costs in terms of foregone business opportunities. Let me cite just one case of how the rules can work.

Simon Geller obtained a license to operate a daylight FM radio station from his apartment over the Whale-of-a-Wash laundromat in Gloucester, Massachusetts in 1961. He experimented with various formats and examined what was available to his listeners on other stations. Geller, who was the sole operator of the station, decided to play only classical music—no all-talk, no news, no accu-weather—just classical music. Geller's operating costs were covered by small donations from the public and six minutes of advertising by local businesses.

In 1977, the FCC felt obligated by the rules to delay his license renewal, despite the fact that there were at least thirty-five other stations in the Boston area available to Geller's listeners, including an all-news station. In 1982, the FCC decided to award Geller's license to Grandbanke Corporation, claiming that Grandbanke would better serve the public interest. Community groups immediately petitioned the FCC to reverse the decision. One group of five thousand argued that Geller's classical music provided a unique service to the public. The FCC denied the petitions, but the U.S. Court of Appeals ordered the FCC to reconsider the case. The Court noted that the FCC had silenced Geller's ideas and for that the public suffered. Finally, on December 17, 1985, the FCC reversed itself and renewed Geller's license. Grandbanke appealed the decision and lost in the U.S. Court of Appeals in late 1986. The legal expense on all sides was substantial.

Many stations, hearing about Geller's plight, conform to what they *believe* are the FCC's standards for "public interest" broadcasting. In such an environment, the diversity of the marketplace is lost to intimidation.

One of the unstated assumptions in regulating broadcasting is that five men and women who sit on the Federal Communications Commission are better judges of what people should see and hear about controversial issues than are those who make up the audience, or those who must compete for their attention.[26] Two important challenges of principle can be made against this assumption: (1) Is the listener's right to receive "balanced" programming *superior* to the right of a citizen to speak?

(2) Is regulation of content of any medium of communication appropriate in a pluralistic and free society? A third, more pragmatic objection to governmental regulation of broadcasting media is that the *threat* of penalties weighs most heavily on broadcasters who lack the resources with which to challenge "public interest violations." In fact, there is evidence that many broadcasters responded to the Fairness Doctrine by refusing to air anything controversial for fear of legal entanglements.[27]

Under the Fairness Doctrine, local stations often had trouble determining what a controversial issue was, how much time it should be given, and who in the community represented "responsible contrasting views." Even members of the FCC admit that the Doctrine was abused because of the arbitrary way its rules had been applied. James McKinney, former Chief of the Commission's Mass Media Bureau, described how a "fairness assessment" was made:

> We . . . sit down with tape recordings, video tapes of . . . what has been broadcast on a specific station. We compare that to newspapers [and] other public statements that are made in the community. We try to make a decision as to whether it is of public importance in that community, which may be 2000 miles away [from our offices in Washington, D.C.]. . . . When it comes down to the final analysis, we take out stop watches and we start counting the seconds and minutes that are devoted to one issue compared to the seconds and minutes that are devoted to the other side of the issue.[28]

Commissioner Mimi Dawson wrote in frustration, "It is virtually impossible for a broadcaster to read the [FCC's recent fairness decision] and know what its responsibilities are under the fairness doctrine."[29] In many cases, broadcasters have simply thrown up their hands and avoided controversial issues so that they will not have to endure the endless red tape of an FCC hearing, a court battle over access to their station, or worse, the loss of their license.

These financial threats hang over each and every television and radio station in this country, and many go to costly hearings before the FCC before they are resolved. It should, therefore, come as no surprise that many scholars who testified before hearings of the Senate Commerce Committee in 1982 and 1984 believed that existing rules had a chilling effect on the discussion of issues in the broadcasting media.

Defending against a "fairness complaint" is a sobering experience and indicates just how difficult insuring a "truth standard" and providing "contrasting views" can be. Consider the struggle of Eugene Wilken, former general manager of KREM-TV in Spokane, Washington. A complaint arose immediately following KREM's one-time airing of a sixty-second editorial endorsement of EXPO 74. Four people identifying themselves as representatives of an environmental group entered the station's offices and demanded air time to rebut the editorial. Wilken asked for proof that they represented some "responsible" group in the community. These "environmentalists" turned out to be a splinter group of eight neighbors who had broken off from the major environmental organization in the city. Wilken denied them access to the station's broadcast facility. They filed with the FCC. This seemingly minor confrontation snowballed into a major investigation during which KREM's staff was interviewed extensively by the FCC and KREM'S files were searched. After $20,000 in legal fees, 480 hours of executive time, a delay in license renewal and four years of investigations and delays, KREM was exonerated. However, Wilken's career was ruined.

The examples cited here and later in this chapter are not aberrations nor are they kept quiet. They are the source of the chill that blows across the entire broadcasting community. The current situation, which still includes a "personal attack" rule,[30] may be the reason that investigative reporting is more prominent in the print than in the electronic media. It surely explains the timid approach broadcasters take, compared to their print brethren, on issues of importance to the community or the nation.

But the "public interest" regulations also affect the print media. Those companies that own broadcast licenses, and most do, are targets for intimidation by the government or other parties. A 1969 memorandum from Jeb Magruder to Robert Haldemann proposed "an official monitoring system through the FCC" and documented that Nixon had ordered his staff to take "specific action relating to what could be considered unfair news coverage" twenty-one times in one month. In a secretly taped conservation with John Dean and Haldemann, Nixon advocated using the license renewal procedure at the FCC to intimidate the *Washington Post* through their television stations:

> *Nixon:* The main thing is the *Post* is going to have damnable, damnable problems out of this one. They have a television station—
> *Dean:* That's right, they do.
> *Nixon:* And they're going to have to get it renewed.

Of course, it was the *Post* that was doing the very investigating that would eventually lead to Nixon's downfall. Had Nixon convinced others on his staff to use the FCC's power against the *Post,* American history might have been different.

One of the greatest dangers posed by government control over the content of electronic communications lies ahead. This danger also reveals a way by which a revived Fairness Doctrine could be applied to the print media. Technology is rapidly blurring the traditional line between print and broadcast journalism. With the advent of cable, videotex, and teletext, and the electronic delivery of news and other information, distinctions may soon be impossible to discern. *USA Today* and the *Wall Street Journal* already use satellites to beam their copy across the country to various printers. Many other newspapers are allowing their columns to be carried over videotex systems. In the coming years, the courts and the Congress are going to have to face the difficult question of whether to extend the rights given to print to the electronic media or to impose the controls applied to electronics on the print media.

Perhaps that is why, in the summer of 1984, in *FCC v. League of Women Voters of California*, the Supreme Court in two footnotes questioned the wisdom of retaining the *Red Lion* precedent. Said the Court:

> We note that the FCC, observing that "if any substantial possibility exists that the [Fairness Doctrine] rules have impeded, rather than furthered, First Amendment objectives, repeal may be warranted on that ground alone," has tentatively concluded that the rules, by effectively chilling speech, do not serve the public interest, and has therefore proposed to repeal them. . . . As we recognized in *Red Lion*, however, were it to be shown by the Commission that the Fairness Doctrine "has the effect of reducing rather than enhancing" speech, we would then be forced to reconsider the constitutional basis of our decision in that case.[31]

The Court went on to observe that the "scarcity of spectrum" rationale for the controls imposed by the government has been severely eroded. Given the explosion of electronic outlets such as cable, direct satellite broadcasts, and microwave signals, it is difficult to maintain that the electronic media should not be accorded parity with the print media. For that and other reasons mentioned above, the FCC repealed the Fairness Doctrine on August 4, 1987. The action was immediately challenged in court and legislation was introduced to codify the Doctrine. That legislation was vetoed by President Reagan. In November of 1987, Senator Ernest Hollings rewrote the codification bill to include a tax penalty on broadcasters found guilty of "fairness" violations. Again he was defeated. The Fairness Doctrine legislation supported in both Houses did not include the tax provision; but it too was stripped from the massive Continuing Resolution of December 22, 1987, when President Reagan threatened to veto the entire bill unless the "fairness provision" was removed. Thus, while we await the decision of the courts, there is no Fairness Doctrine in effect at this time.

The latest communication technology to come under government control is *remote sensing*. This satellite technology not only allows for better weather reports, it permits better coverage of wars, fires, earthquakes, and other apocalyptic events, such as the meltdown at Chernobyl. The proliferation of satellites that can take better and better pictures is astounding. The Earth Observation Satellite Company (EOSAT), a private group, is planning on launching a satellite capable of producing pictures with fifteen-meter resolution; the French launched one that can produce pictures of objects smaller than ten meters. What's more, the turn around time on these pictures is getting shorter. It used to take days; now, for some pictures, it takes hours. Satellite-based news gathering is revolutionizing the information age.

The Land Remote-Sensing Commercialization Act of 1984 ("LANDSAT") provides the guidelines for satellite use. It authorizes the Department of Commerce to license any private party, including a news organization, to construct, launch and operate a remote sensing system. But LANDSAT also puts barriers in front of news organizations in the form of national security regulations. They are being implemented in part by the National Oceanic and Atmospheric Administration (NOAA), which has the authority to define "national security and international obligations."

Tension developed between the First Amendment rights of the press to obtain information via remote sensing, and national security interests that must be protected by the government. The questions were, what First Amendment standards govern remote sensing, and how will NOAA write and incorporate them to serve the national interest?

To answer these questions, one can examine case law and legislative prcedent. Since the law allows one to build and launch a satellite, it is not government property and should not be subject to government access rules. Since the United States does not own outer space, the government should not be able to interfere there. Furthermore, the United States has adhered for nearly three decades to the "open skies" policy, which states that no nation is entitled to control or prevent remote sensing of its own territory. In fact, Congress endorsed that policy when it adopted LANDSAT.

But the Department of Defense proposed that certain "limitations on access" that apply to government property, documents and information be applied to remote sensing via satellite. That meant that remote sensing could be limited in the same way access to government property, documents and information is limited. One would apply on a case by case basis and the information obtained would be subject to prior restraint. That violates the First Amendment, which, if it prohibits anything, certainly prohibits prior restraint.

The other problem here was that the Departments of Defense and State proposed standards for information gathering that were too ambiguous. Because ambiguous standards can be applied arbitrarily and capriciously, the courts have ruled that they violate the First Amendment. NOAA had to determine whether considerations of national security were strong enough to justify curtailing First Amendment rights. And they had to spell out those determinations in some detail so that they could not be applied arbitrarily or capriciously. For example, they could have said, as media representatives recommended, that "a serious and immediate threat to distinct and compelling national security and foreign policy interests would allow the curtailment of remote sensing." Such language would have allowed the Department of Defense to interrupt satellite transmission if a U.S. task force was moving to counter a specific threat or answer a terrorist attack. Such language would have allowed the courts and the media to determine if any threat was "serious, immediate and concerned distinct and compelling interests." While those words are open to interpretation, as are virtually all laws and regulations, when taken together the terms do identify some standards to be met and so mitigate against arbitrary bases for determining when interference is appropriate.

The Defense Department responded to this requested language by arguing that such wording would "limit unnecessarily the ability of the Secretary of Defense to fashion license requirements that take into account future events."[32] The State Department was similarly concerned with limitations on its power to prevent access. The Department said:

> . . . we are skeptical that the proposed revisions serve to elucidate the applicable legal standard, or strengthen the legal protections available to applicants or licensees. We are concerned that the revisions could be used to argue that NOAA intended to change the prevailing legal standard, hold the government to a particular procedure or require a certain content in making a foreign policy objection.[33]

But the legal precedent required that the government articulate a "particular procedure" concerning "a certain content" to determine access denials. Later in its reply, the State Department argued that many events capable of being sensed by remote means have impact on national security. "Even weather information may be deemed to have national security implications." Then in what has to be a semi-Freudian slip it continued, ". . . we would advise against any regulations that could cloud the authority necessary to protect the foreign policy and national security interests of the United States."

One problem with this debate is that it focuses on United States' satellites and the use of them by the American media. But other countries, France, for example, have the same technology. The Soviet Union is perfectly capable of intercepting transmissions on these foreign satellites. Thus, it is entirely possible if the rules were written too broadly, that the Soviets could be aware of events that our media has been precluded from knowing. Like the citizens of Frankfurt in the eighteenth century, we would be unable to receive information that was readily available in other parts of the world. Certainly, national security should be taken into account; the preamble to the Constitution mentions the "common defense," which was a topic of discussion throughout the debates over forming a new nation. But the courts have consistently held, when balancing one part of the Constitution against another, that limitations on our freedoms must be specifically defined and not subject to abuse. To date, NOAA has not prevented any news organization from using data obtained from remote-sensing.

FREEDOM OF EXPRESSION VERSUS EQUALITY OF POLITICAL OPPORTUNITY

In its 1964 decision in *Sullivan v. New York Times* the Supreme Court endorsed "the principle that debate on public issues should be uninhibited, robust, and wide open." I have already shown how the doubtless meritorious value of *fairness* has both infringed and blunted full and free discussion in the electronic media. The equally meritorious value of *equality of opportunity* has like effects, especially on political persuasion. In the first place, every attempt to *equalize* opportunities for free expression will inevitably *restrict* someone's freedom to express—to persuade. This has been the effect of restrictions derived from the 1934 Communications Act and of legislation governing political campaigning. The 1934 Act has been so interpreted by the FCC and the Courts that coverage of political candidates' debate and advertising has become restricted.

The law says that a station must provide "equal opportunities" for

102

appearances by all bona fide candidates for public office, including write-ins. Thus, if a station wishes to sponsor a debate between the Democrat and Republican running for Senate, it must also provide comparable time for others who have filed for the office, no matter what the size of their following or the legitimacy of their effort. For example, in the 1984 New Hampshire presidential primary, there were twenty-two candidates who paid the $1,000 filing fee to run. These "candidates" included a mechanical robot!

The application of equal-opportunity rules can result in strange happenings. In 1974, KOOL-TV in Phoenix, Arizona offered all qualified candidates in the upcoming gubernatorial election a free five-minute program in which they would be interviewed by a reporter from the station. KOOL hoped to serve the public in this way, thereby fulfilling its obligation to operate in the public interest. Soon, however, a Mr. Russ Shaw requested equal time since he had filed as a write-in candidate for governor. Under current broadcast regulations, KOOL had to comply. Then Mr. Shaw demanded that KOOL bill him as "Wonderful Russ Shaw," which KOOL discovered they also had to do. Mr. Shaw's platform included "freedom for all prisoners . . . free food and gas for the people who vote for me. . . . No taxes . . . secession from the Union." During his interview, "Wonderful Russ" stated that one of his first acts as governor would be to "blast California off into the ocean and turn Arizona into a seaport community." When asked to list his qualifications, Mr. Shaw told viewers that he had served as President of the Wickenburg Clown Club for several years and was tell-monitor of his third grade class for over two months.

Luckily, in 1975 with the Aspen Rules, and again in 1983, the FCC made it easier for a station to cover debates, no matter who participated, as long as the debate is put on the air live and in its entirety. In 1984, half the television stations in the country offered time for debates, a major increase over the number offering to cover debates in years when the FCC did not suspend the rules. In those years, many broadcasters simply avoided the problem of accommodating multiple candidates by refusing to sponsor forums or debates involving candidates. This procedure greatly enhanced the chances of the incumbents, because it deprived challengers, who are generally less well known, of the opportunity to get air time.

A different section of the 1934 Act applies to advertising by candidates. The Equal Access Rule requires that a broadcaster must make advertising time available to candidates for *federal* office. Furthermore, comparable air time must be made available to candidates for the same ven if a request from one comes in much later than the others, en if that means that the broadcaster must cancel normal ising to make room. During the campaign season this advertising must be made available at the lowest unit rate the station charges for any advertising. In 1970, the FCC held that when a station sells time to supporters of or spokespersons for a candidate during a political campaign, it would not be reasonable for the broadcaster to refuse to sell time to authorized spokespersons for the candidate's opponents.[34] Under the circumstances, it behooves broadcasters to sell as little advertising time as is allowed under the law. Again, a well-intentioned law clearly works to curtail freedom of expression in political campaigns.

Third, the 1934 Act and subsequent amendments have made it difficult for stations to editorialize during campaigns. The Political Editorial rule provides that if a station broadcasts an editorial endorsing or opposing a candidate for office, the candidates for the same office who are not endorsed or who are opposed must be sent notification of the editorial, a script of the editorial, *and* given an offer to air a reply.[35] Failure to take these steps can result in sanctions that affect the station's license renewal.

These restrictions on the broadcasting of political campaign persuasion work to close down the marketplace of ideas. Given that technology makes possible the proliferation of channels for expression, and given the importance of freedom of expression in our nation, the burden of proving that regulations are necessary ought, in every case, to fall on those proposing them rather than on those seeking to have them removed.

RESTRICTIONS ON THE CAMPAIGN

Beyond these rules concerning news coverage and advertising over the air in a campaign, are a host of restrictions placed on the management of the campaign itself. In an effort to create a level playing field for candidates and supporters of ballot propositions, and to reduce influence peddling, the government has placed restrictions on campaign spending and advertising.

The Supreme Court has clearly established that Congress has the right to regulate federal elections as long as the rules do not violate the Constitution.[36] In 1974, following abuses revealed in the Watergate Hearings, Congress tightened restrictions on raising and spending campaign contributions. These restrictions were added to the Federal Corrupt Practices Act of 1925 and the Federal Election Campaign Act of 1971. Along with requiring full disclosure of contributions to a federal campaign, the new rules limited individual contributions to $1,000 per election, prohibited corporate contributions, and established that employees could contribute to a campaign only by forming political action committees (PACs), which could make maximum contributions of $5,000 per candidate per election. No individual would be allowed to give more than $25,000 overall to candidates, groups, and parties during a single year. The new law also carefully monitored and limited what a political party could contribute to its candidates and what corporations or unions could "contribute in kind"—equipment, services, travel, and the like. Further, the law provided for public financing of presidential nominating conventions and for matching funds to help pay for presidential primary and general election campaigns. In return for accepting matching funds, presidential candidates were limited in how much they could spend overall.

The goal of those supporting the new rules was to provide more parity between rich and poor candidates and between those with large corporate backing and those without. The laws were quickly challenged in the courts by persons who argued that the rules infringed on freedom of expression because the more money a campaign has at its disposal, the more media it can buy to communicate its message.

The case challenging the new laws was brought by Senator James L. Buckley, a conservative Republican from New York, and Eugene J. McCarthy, a liberal Democrat and former Senator from Minnesota. The Supreme Court, in a curious decision, ruled that the restrictions on contributions were constitutional but that the spending limitations were not.[37] The former, said the Court, were appropriate ways of controlling undue influence in a campaign; the latter, however, restricted freedom of expression. This decision sent politicians scrambling for ways by which they could raise money in small amounts, but gather enough contributions to meet their campaign needs.

As I will show in the next chapter, politicians quickly adapted to the new rules. The Republican Party has become the party of the small donor by using very sophisticated direct mail campaigns that build huge lists of supporters nationally but stay within the letter of the law. The result is that in first 18 months of the 1986 election cycle the National Republican Senatorial Committee raised $59.6 million compared to $6.8 million raised by its Democratic counterpart.[38]

Political action committees (PACs) through which employees can shift money to campaigns have grown in number from 600 in 1974 to over 4,500 in 1988. Of these about 3,000 contributed to federal elections. PAC contributors, including union and corporate members, number over four million, and total donations in 1986 reached $125 million. Over the past four election cycles (1980–86), about one-third of all federal campaign funds came from PACs.[39]

PACs started by employees of a company or union members are different from so-called "independent PACs." Independent PACs are issue oriented and generally collect funds under the federal rules to support candidates with similar views and/or "educate" the public on certain issues. Norman Lear's People for the American Way, for example, was created in part to combat the persuasion of the Moral Majority. A millionaire in California created his own independent PAC and ran $1 million worth of advertisements against Senator Percy of Illinois in 1984. It was perfectly legal as long as he did not "coordinate" his activity with Percy's opponent, Paul Simon. Simon won in a very close contest.

Since the federal rules allow the creation of independent PACs, many presidential candidates-to-be establish PACs as a way to generate funds that do *not* count toward their presidential campaigns. These "educational PACs" may also house future campaign staffs, pay the candidate's travel expenses, and provide valuable research for the impending campaign under the guise of educating voters on certain issues. George Bush established The Fund for America's Future three years before he announced his candidacy for president. Bob Dole took the same step with Campaign America PAC. The Fund for America's Future, according to Federal Election Commission (FEC) records, received $285,000 during the first six months of 1987 from individuals who also donated $80,000 to Bush's presidential campaign. Campaign America during the same period received $244,000 from persons who also contributed $82,000 to the Dole presidential campaign. Thus, independent PACs can be used to advance a presidential campaign, which clearly was not the intent of those who wrote and passed the federal election law.

Once a candidate formally declares his candidacy, contributions to his campaign and spending by the campaign are carefully monitored by the Federal Election Commission. The rules are not difficult to circumvent. For example, in 1988 campaigns were allowed to spend no more than $770,000 in the Iowa caucuses and $460,400 in the New Hampshire primary. But certain campaign activities can be exempted from those limits. For example, if direct mail or campaign advertising includes an appeal for funds, it is considered fundraising and does not count toward the limit. Television advertisements broadcast into Iowa from Omaha and into New Hampshire from Boston are counted toward the spending ceilings in Nebraska and Massachusetts. Interstate travel does not count against the limit. And the pay of staff members must only be counted

106

toward the state limit if he or she stays in the state for four days. Staffers simply leave the state for a day, for example, by registering motel across the state line, every three and a half days so their pay will not be counted toward the total spending limit for a given state. These are legal ways to defeat the purpose of the federal election laws in presidential campaigns. Most critics contend that a law so easily circumvented should be reformed because it penalizes the campaign that abides by the spirit of the law while rewarding the campaign that takes advantage of the loopholes.

As politicians, particularly incumbents, adapt to the new system, new restrictions have been proposed. Senators have introduced bills that would make the openings and closings in federal campaign commercials uniform, that would require candidates to appear in their commercials, and that would force stations airing "negative ads" to grant free response time to attacked candidates.

Barry Goldwater, former Republican Senator from Arizona, and David Boren, Democratic Senator from Oklahoma, introduced legislation in 1986 that would have limited how much money a candidate can receive from PACs. They proposed $100,000 for House candidates and a varying amount ($175,000 to $750,000) for Senate candidates, depending on the population of the candidate's state.[40] A single PAC could give no more than $3,000 to a candidate, whereas the current level is $5,000 for a primary and $5,000 for the general election.

Similar legislation was reintroduced in the 100th Congress, along with a bill to provide for taxpayers' financing of Senate general elections. To qualify for funding under these measures, a candidate must, within seven days of qualifying for the general election ballot: agree to a specified expenditure limit ($600,000, plus 25 cents multiplied by the state's voting-age population); agree to limit use of personal and family funds to $20,000; certify that a threshold of $250,000 or 20 percent of the spending limit, which ever is lower, has been raised from individuals in amounts of $250 or less, with 80 percent of the funds coming from the candidate's home state; agree not to raise funds from private sources in excess of the threshold amount. An "eligible" candidate would be entitled to receive: taxpayers' funding equal to the expenditure limit, less the qualifying threshold; the lowest unit rate for television advertising, as under current law, but no longer would this apply to non-participants; additional taxpayers' funding would be provided equal to independent groups' spending in excess of $25,000; additional taxpayers' funding equal to the expenditure limit if the opponent is a nonparticipating candidate who exceeds the limit. Since the majority of Republican reforms were not included in the legislation, Republican senators mounted a successful filibuster and defeated it.

The actual and proposed regulations on political campaigning have come under considerable criticism, chiefly on the grounds that the right to political expression, not equality of financing, is the first and most sacred of our political rights.[41] In a dissent from the *Buckley* decision, Justice Blackmun wrote that the Court could not make a distinction between contributions and expenditures on the basis of which was more vital to freedom of expression. Chief Justice Burger said in his dissent: "Contributions and expenditures are two sides of the same First Amendment coin. . . ." One person's contribution is another person's expenditure.

These opinions bring before us once again our constant tension between freedom of expression and other values such as equality of opportunity. Indeed, if there is a correlation between campaign funds and campaign persuasion, as would-be regulators certainly imply, tampering with financial freedom in political campaigning becomes tampering with freedom of expression. This is all the more obvious when we face the fact that dollars given to political campaigns no longer represent corporations and unions; they represent *individuals* who participate in campaigns by giving to their favorite candidates directly or through PACs. The contribution is an expression of support; limiting the contributions of individuals limits their expression of support; and limitations are easily circumvented, particularly in the case of "independent PACs." Political action committees provide a way for citizens to participate in the political process and give some weight to that participation by joining together with others who have similar interests. Over 4.5 million people contributed to PACs in the 1986 election cycle. As long as contributions must be fully, promptly, and publicly disclosed, as they are now, it seems anti-democratic to limit a citizen's participation in the political process by reducing what he or she can contribute.

FREEDOM OF EXPRESSION VERSUS "TRUTH" AND "SAFETY"

In 1942 the Supreme Court ruled in *Valentine v. Chrestensen* that "commercial speech" did not enjoy the same protection as political speech. "Commercial speech" is defined by the Court as that which seeks to do "no more than solicit a commercial transaction." A tension arises from the phrase "no more than." Many corporations discuss only their products in their advertising. In other cases they do "more than solicit a commercial transaction" by talking about the health benefits of their

108

products. So, beginning in 1975, the Supreme Court began to r
has become known as the "commercial speech doctrine."

The Court has now extended First Amendment rights to cor
speech under certain circumstances. In *Bigelow v. Virginia,*[42]
preme Court asserted that commercial speech should be protected by the
First Amendment. The Court argued that to take advertising information
away from consumers is patronizing at best and unhealthy at worst. The
Court went further in 1976 in *Virginia State Board of Pharmacy v.
Virginia Citizens Council:* "[P]eople will perceive their own best interests
if only they are well enough informed, and . . . the best means to that
end is to open channels of communication rather than close them. . . .
As to the particular consumer's interest in the free flow of commercial
information, that interest may be as keen, if not keener by far, than his
interest in the day's most urgent political debate."[43] Finally, in *Central
Hudson Gas v. Public Service Commission,*[44] the Court said that
commercial speech could be limited only if it was found to be misleading,
false, or related to illegal activity. *In re RMJ,*[45] reaffirmed this position,
establishing a standard where the degree of regulation allowed is
proportional to the degree of deception or the need of the government to
advance an overwhelming public interest. Clearly, any attempt to ban
advertising would now have to meet the strict tests that the Supreme
Court has set for regulation.

The waters were muddied, however, in the summer of 1986, when a
five-to-four majority of the Court argued against protecting advertising
of lawful commercial transactions. In *Posadas v. Tourism Co. of Puerto
Rico*[46], the Court upheld a restriction on advertising casino gambling in
Puerto Rico.

For several reasons, this case must be distinguished from the line of
cases I have reviewed to this point. First, the decision by Justice
Rehnquist reaffirms that restrictions on commercial speech cannot be
sustained unless they "directly advance" a substantial government
interest and that interest cannot be served and/or achieved by "less
restrictive" means. Second, casino gambling is illegal in most of the
United States and subject to severe restrictions even in Puerto Rico.
Therefore, in this unique case, imposing a ban on advertising can be
interpreted as an extension of that government's policy to discourage its
citizens from taking advantage of a service the government means to
provide only to tourists. Clearly, there is no analogy here with advertising broadly available legal products. Cigarettes, for example, are a legal
product; their sale is legal in all states. And they are available to all adults
within the population.

Finally, *Posadas* must be read in the context of Puerto Rico's economic development legislation with its "unique cultural and legal history"[47] and its political relationship to the United States, to use the language of the Court. The ban in Puerto Rico applied only to commercials addressed to citizens of Puerto Rico. The decision did not ban advertisements addressed to tourists, even though the advertisements could be overheard or read by locals, which in fact they were. In short, the Puerto Rican law made circumvention of the ban quite simple; it is a "porous" law and therefore, less harmful, according to Justice Rhenquist, than an absolute ban.

Since the landmark ruling in *Virginia Pharmacy* in 1976, no *blanket ban* on commercial speech has been held to be legitimate except where that speech was found to be deceptive or related to unlawful activity. The operant legal principle was stated in *First National Bank v. Bellotti,* "[T]he people in our democracy are entrusted with the responsibility for judging and evaluating the relative merits of conflicting arguments."[48] This principle is now widely applied in judging the legitimacy of commercial speech; it represents a relaxation of paternal regulations established between 1942 and 1975. As I have shown, however, it is a movement of thought that has not yet informed legislative policies concerning broadcast speech, nor does it uniformly hold in all quarters concerning commercial speech.

The older limitations on commercial speech rested on a shaky distinction between two markets: one market for ideas and one for goods.[49] Justice Brennan's dissent from the *Posadas* decision said, "I see no reason why commercial speech should be afforded less protection than other types of speech where . . . the government seeks to suppress commercial speech in order to deprive consumers of accurate information concerning lawful activity." The qualifications of even the majority's *Posadas* decision reflect the Court's agreement, at least in principle, with Brennan's observation. It is also clear from the newspapers protected by the First Amendment in 1791 that those who composed and passed the amendment made no distinction between commercial and political speech.[50]

All informed persons know that although the legal position I have just reviewed is reasonably clear, freedom of commercial expression is by no means free from attack. There have been and continue to be those who would remove commercial information inviting viewers and readers to pursue happiness in this or that legal way. In 1975, *Bigelow v. Virginia* legalized advertising by abortion clinics. In 1976, *Virginia Pharmacy* legalized advertising prescription drug prices. In 1977, *Carey v. Popula-*

110

tion Services legalized advertising contraceptives. But our general situation remains odd. Abortions, drug prices, and contraceptives can be advertised *generally,* but cigars, cigarettes and pipe tobacco can be advertised in some media but not others. Arguments are made that these latter items have been scientifically demonstrated to be harmful to one's health and so commercial speech concerning them needs to be restricted. But, then, what products would be safe from restrictions? What of products containing caffeine, sodium, cholesterol? The widespread fear of AIDS has brought to the fore the issue of whether *televised* advertising of condoms is appropriate.

The fundamental fact is, however: short of insuring freedom of expression everywhere, on all subjects, American society is destined to continue to be involved in complicated and convoluted arguments about what can and cannot be freely discussed, and where. In commerce as elsewhere, the guarantee of freedom of expression carries its inevitable "price tag"—freedom to contend for restraints on freedom of expression.

The complicated consideration of what commercial speech is and how it is protected was even more confused by the fact that the FCC ruled that such advertising triggered the Fairness Doctrine. Lee Iacocca was free to talk about the virtues of his American cars and their Japanese engines. But if Iacocca wanted to spend the sixty seconds his company bought arguing in favor of mandatory seat belt laws, he would effectively be precluded from doing so because stations or networks running the advertisements would face "fairness complaints" and be forced to defend their decision before the FCC or would have to capitulate to requests for free time for those with contrasting views. In this case, that would mean giving time to Ralph Nader to explain why air bags are better than seat belts and to the Libertarian Party to explain why the government has no right to order you to wear seat belts in your own car.[51]

If the hypothetical example seems absurd, reality bordered on insanity in application of the Doctrine up to its repeal in 1987. For example, in 1986 W. R. Grace and Company tried to air advertisements arguing against government waste and the deficit. The advertisements featured a courtroom set in the next century where a senior citizen is on the witness stand being grilled by an adolescent prosecutor in front of a jury of children. "Didn't you know what your deficits would do" to our future? he is asked. The old witness, dressed in rags, as are the jurors, withers under this attack and begs forgiveness. While some independent stations ran this advertisement, the networks found it too controversial. Finally, ABC relented and agreed to run the advertisement after 11:30 PM; then

111

CBS said they would run it if wording that referred to a constitutional amendment to balance the budget were removed.

Mobil Oil offered to pay for the response time of those wishing to present contrasting views to their advertisements dealing with public issues. The networks turned Mobil down because they would be put in the position of having to decide who should be chosen to respond to Mobil, a position fraught with litigious possibilities.

With all this confusion engendered by the application of the Fairness Doctrine to advertising about issues, one would have thought that Congress would work to untangle the mess. Instead, the Congress has moved to broaden the application of the Fairness Doctrine and to insist that certain kinds of commercial speech be banned altogether. The most dangerous proposals would ban the advertising of certain legal products that some members believe are harmful to the health of citizens.

When, if ever, personal health can be said to constitute an "overriding governmental interest" seems likely to become the next major "line of battle" in the ever-running contest between freedom of expression and other "first" values. The Court has ruled that commercial speech is protected most of the time. But beer, wine, and tobacco advertising has come under scrutiny in recent sessions of Congress. Congress has been discussing proposals to restrict advertising of these "harmful" products[52] without banning the products themselves. For example, HR 2657 would eliminate taxes on the product as a deductible business expense for advertisers of alcoholic beverages. Will there be a decision declaring "personal wellness" an overriding governmental interest, and, if so, could the range of subjects covered by that judgment ever be determined? The First Amendment to the Constitution is unqualified. My object in this chapter has been to show what confusions and anomalies arise from attempting to qualify it.

CONCLUSION

There are some generalizations to be drawn from these tensions in our system. First, those who govern tend to fear new technology and to impose regulations on it. The printed press was afforded protection in America because it had played an important role in developing a consensus in favor of revolution, had been suppressed by English monarchs, and was familiar to the Founders. The electronic media of mass communication enjoy no such history. Their introduction as radio in 1906 and as commercial television in the 1930s scared legislators in much the same way the invention of moveable type in 1456 scared the Germanic princes. Supreme Court Justice William Brennan explained this phenomenon when he addressed the graduating class at Brandeis University in 1986:

> Rulers always have and always will find it dangerous to their security to permit people to think, believe, talk, write, assemble and particularly to criticize the government as they please. But the language of the First Amendment indicates that the founders weighed the risks involved in such freedoms and deliberately chose to stake this Government's security and life upon preserving the liberty to discuss public affairs intact and untouchable by Government.

Second, in this environment the ideal of freedom of expression is pitted against (1) channel-specific administrative regulation, (2) equal political opportunity, and (3) efforts to keep content "pure" and "true" in order to "protect" the citizenry in the marketplace. Our problem is how to resolve these tensions between praiseworthy ideals. Because freedom of expression is the foundation of all other rights, I believe it is desirable to apply the full rights of the printed press to all other media of mass communication on the ground that the original regulations of electronic channels are anachronistic and steadily becoming more so.

Without free speech, truth and safety may not be discovered or retained. They emerge from and are refined by the competition of the open marketplace. Further, the ideals of "truth" and "safety" must be given a lower priority than freedom to express because if they are not they will corrupt the freedom we have. In chapter 2, I showed that those who believe they have the "truth" can be very dangerous and are usually highly intolerant of challenges to their authority and intolerant of other "truths." In chapter 3, I illustrated how those who believe they should protect the "internal security" of the country often trample over the rights of those they are supposedly protecting. While freedom of expression is expensive, it is undoubtedly worth the price because it ensures so many other liberties.

Because of controls on the electronic media, we do not live in the environment suggested by the Founders. That circumstance can change if the Supreme Court overturns the controls over content or the Congress returns to the ideals of the Founders. Meanwhile, the marketplace for ideas remains large and active if crimped here and there. It is to political persuasion in that marketplace that I now turn my attention.

113

NOTES

1. This latter value was elevated by Progressives in the first part of this century and by consumer advocates in the latter part. But it can be traced back to the Preamble of the Constitution where the following goals are set: ". . . insure domestic tranquility, [and] promote the general welfare. . . ."

2. The Constitutionality of the Fairness Doctrine, which was derived from the "public interest" standard, was challenged in a recent case at the U.S. Court Appeals in the District of Columbia. During oral arguments on September 13, 1988, intervenors presented evidence that members of the administrations of Presidents Franklin Roosevelt, John Kennedy, Lyndon Johnson, Richard Nixon and Ronald Reagan had used the content control provisions of the Communications Act to intimidate broadcasters. See *Meredith Corp. v. FCC*, 809 F.2d (D.C. Cir. 1988); Judge Bazelon, "FCC Regulation of the Telecommunication Press," *Duke Law Journal* (1975), 213, 214, 235, 247–48.

3. See Lee C. Bollinger, *The Tolerant Society* (New York: Oxford University Press, 1986). Professor Bollinger's thesis is that distasteful and even harmful speech should be permitted in order to ensure a tolerant society.

4. See *Jones v. Wilkinson*, 800 F. 2d 989 (10th Cir. 1986). The decision was summarily affirmed by the Supreme Court.

5. See *Quincy Cable TV, Inc. v. FCC*, 768 F. 2d 1434, 1452 (10th Cir. 1985). The Supreme Court denied *certiorari* on appeal of this decision.

6. See *FCC v. Pacifica Foundation*, 438 U.S. 726 (1978).

7. *Miami Herald Publishing Co., v. Tornillo*, 418 U.S. 241. 258 (1974). There has been regulation of Wall Street trade newspapers and investment newsletters. This regulation is imposed by the Securities and Exchange Commission in the name of protecting consumers. Several courts have overturned these regulations while others have held them valid.

8. There are a few weeklies and one Spanish daily.

9. The new law also required that no speech be censored unless it was "obscene, indecent, or profane." That rule was upheld in *FCC v. Pacifica Foundation*, 438 U.S. 726, (1978), the famous "seven dirty words" case.

10. *National Broadcasting Co. v. United States*, 319 U.S. 190, 215–16 (1943).

11. *Editorializing by Broadcast Licensees*, 13 FCC 1246, (1949).

12. Congress was attempting to clarify the equal time provisions of section 315 of the Communication Act when Senator William Proxmire offered an amendment the intent of which was to codify the Fairness Doctrine. Proxmire, Democrat of Wisconsin, changed his mind after seeing its effects. For years he has tried but failed to get the law repealed. In 1983 a new grouping of bipartisan support developed in favor of repeal. Its most prominent members include Senators Barry Goldwater and Bob Packwood, Governor Mario Cuomo of New York, and President Reagan. In 1986, the U.S. Court of Appeals in the *TRAC* case (see later in this chapter) declared that the Fairness Doctrine had not been codified, only the FCC's authority to implement it. The FCC on August 4, 1987 repealed the Doctrine. Their decision has been appealed. Arguments were heard before the U.S. Court of Appeals on September 13, 1988. On February 10, 1989, the court ruled 3–0 upholding the FCC's decision to repeal the Fairness Doctrine.

13. FCC, *Inquiry into Section 73.1910 of Commission's Rules and Regulations Concerning Alternatives to the Fairness Doctrine,* Aug. 4, 1987, 51. See also

114

Cullman Broadcasting Co., 40 FCC 576 (1963). The Cullman rule was repealed on August 4, 1987 along with the Fairness Doctrine. Rulings on the appeal to the U.S. Court of Appeals are pending.

14. *Memorandum Opinion and Order in Docket No. 16574,* 8 FCC 2d 721 (1967); *Clayton W. Mapoles,* 40 FCC 510 (1962); *Times-Mirror Broadcasting Co.,* 40 FCC 531 (1962).

15. 395 U.S. 367 (1969).

16. It has since been learned that Cook selected Red Lion's station in order to intimidate small stations across the country in an effort to keep right-wing attacks on the Johnson Administration off the air. Edward R. Murrow's producer, Fred Friendly, discovered that Cook had been working with Democratic Party officials in a campaign to suppress right-wing opinion on radio by means of the Fairness Doctrine. This plan began in the Kennedy Administration and was carried on by Lyndon Johnson. See David Kelly and Roger Donway, *Laissez Parler: Freedom in the Electronic Media* (Bowling Green, Ohio: Bowling Green University Center for Social Policy and Philosophy, 1983), 32. Fred Friendly also indicted other administrations for coercion. He points out that the Kennedy Administration sought to undermine opposition from right-wing groups to the proposed test ban treaty by inundating radio stations that broadcast anti-treaty statements with demands for response time. See *The Good Guys, The Bad Guys and the First Amendment* (New York: Random House, 1976), 32–35.

17. I say "can be" because the *TRAC* decision of 1986 leaves the matter in the hands of the FCC. And on August 4, 1987, the FCC repealed the Fairness Doctrine, including the Cullman rule, *but* excluding the "personal attack" rule. This does not resolve the matter, however, since a future FCC could reimpose the Doctrine. That is why groups on both sides of this issue are supporting efforts to obtain a definitive ruling from the Supreme Court that either reaffirms or overturns the *Red Lion* decision.

18. Eight daily and 70 weekly newspapers were published in 1791.

19. *Telecommunication Research and Action Center v. FCC,* No. 85-1160, Slip. Op. at 15, 16, n.4 (D.C. Cir. Sept. 19, 1986), petition for rehearing *en banc* denied, Dec. 16, 1986.

20. This does not count the rapidly growing number of low power television stations that stood at nearly 400 in August of 1987.

21. See *Broadcasting/Cablecasting Yearbook* D-3, 1986.

22. Current rules allow a single person or corporate entity to own no more than twelve television stations, twelve FM radio stations, and twelve AM radio stations. However, with respect to television, the combined national audience may not exceed 25 percent. Minorities are given special considerations under these rules as are owners of UHF stations. No one has taken full advantage of this rule. Even when the old rule of seven, seven, and seven from each category was in effect, only one, Roy Park, owned a full allotment of 21 stations.

23. *CBS v. Democratic National Committee,* 412 U.S. 94, 161 (1973), concurring opinion. See also Thomas G. Krattenmaker and L. A. Powe, Jr., "The Fairness Doctrine Today: A Constitutional Curiosity and an Impossible Dream," *Duke Law Journal* (Vol. 85, no. 1, 1985) 151–76.

24. Congress is considering legislation to reform the comparative renewal process. One of the problems with the process is that competing applications for a single station are considered at the same time as the current licensee is evaluated. Competitors can be bought off by one another and often are.

115

Furthermore, if one or more of the competitors do not like the outcome at the FCC, they are free to appeal the whole process in court.

25. For a full reading on the comments of scholars, broadcasters and other expert witnesses with regard to this and other points in this section, I recommend, *Freedom of Expression Act of 1983: Hearing before the Senate Committee on Commerce, Science and Transportation,* 98th Congress, 2nd Session, 1984.

26. For example, the FCC assumes that operating in the public interest means broadcasting the news on a regular basis and providing public affairs and other non-entertainment programming beyond those broadcasts. Why having *all* stations broadcast news to the exclusion of other programming is in the public interest has not been addressed by the FCC. In most markets, all-news stations are ranked very high in listeners' ratings. In 1986, for example, all-news radio formats ranked second in San Francisco and Philadelphia, fourth in Detroit, and third in Dallas. Where all-news stations were not in the top five of the ratings, hourly news and all-talk formats were. Since most news programming makes money, it is unnecessary to require that it be carried. A survey conducted by Professor Vernon Stone, Director of the School of Journalism, Southern Illinois University in 1983 revealed that 85 percent of all stations reported that news either pays for itself or makes a profit. In a follow-up survey published in 1984, Stone found that radio deregulation had "caused no change in news or public affairs staffing or programming at the great majority of stations." See *RTNDA Communicator* (May, 1985) 14.

27. Testimony before the Senate Commerce Committee Hearings in 1984 (op. cit.) revealed that broadcasters have refused to show documentaries for fear of legal action, and they have given in to demands for responses to Presidential speeches. Nonetheless, under legislation introduced by Senator Hollings in late 1987, a broadcaster who was found to have violated the Fairness Doctrine would pay a higher tax on the transfer of the station when it was sold. The legislation was defeated in a conference committee of the Congress but the legislative exercise was not lost on broadcasters. See also Timothy B. Dyk, "Full First Amendment Freedom for Broadcasters: The Industry as Eliza on the Ice and Congress as the Friendly Overseer," *Yale Journal on Regulation* (Vol. 5, no. 2, 1988), 299–329.

28. *Fairness Report,* 58 Rad. Reg. 2d (P&F) (1985) at 1175 n.174.

29. Dissent in *Complaint of Syracuse Peace Council against Television Station WTVH,* 99 FCC 2d 1389, 57 Rad. Reg. 2d (P&F), 519 (1984) at 10.

30. While writing this chapter, I met with the General Counsel of the FCC, Diane Killory. She informed me that the FCC intended to repeal the "personal attack rule" as soon as possible, perhaps by the fall of 1988.

31. 104 S. Ct. 3106, 3117, n.12 (1984).

32. See letter from M. Craig Alderman, Jr., Deputy Under Secretary of Defense, to Mr. Thomas N. Pyke, Jr., NOAA (January 22, 1987), Docket No. 51191–5191 in response to National Oceanic and Atmospheric Administration, *Notice of Proposed Rulemaking,* 51 Federal Register 9971 (Mar. 24, 1986).

33. *Ibid.* See letter of Richard J. Smith, Principal Deputy Assistant Secretary of State (Dec. 29, 1986).

34. See *Nicholas Zapple,* 23 FCC 2d 707, 1970.

35. 104 S. Ct. 3106, 3117, n.12 (1984). This rule parallels the "personal attack" rule which grew out of the Fairness Doctrine.

116

36. For a detailed look at the case law surrounding the issues treated in this section see, Senator Bob Packwood, "Campaign Finance, Communication and the First Amendment," *Hastings Constitutional Law Quarterly* vol. 10, #3 (Spring, 1983), 745–62.

37. See *Buckley v. Valeo*, 424 U.S. 1 (1976).

38. By the end of the 1986 campaign, the Senatorial Committee had raised over $90 million, an all-time high for a two-year period for any political committee. Nonetheless, the Republican Party lost control of the Senate. In 1988 the Democrats closed the gap some, but Republicans still raised much more.

39. In the 1986 election cycle, two political action committees led all others in contributions and topped the one million dollar mark. They were the Realtors PAC, which gave $1.4 million by Labor Day and the National Education Association PAC, which had contributed $1 million by Labor Day. These PACs and others were free to contribute right up to election and after. So their total contributions for 1986 were undoubtedly higher than these Labor Day reports.

40. If the candidate had a primary, he or she would be allowed another $25,000 in PAC money.

41. PACs are diverse and controlled by employees, not corporations; they contribute on average only 20 percent of the total funds raised in a Senate campaign. Yet Senators seek to restrict PACs whereas there is no effort to restrict honoraria that come directly to Senators, not their campaigns, and directly from corporations or unions, not their employees or members. If PACs have an undue influence on the political process, then honoraria constitute a more concentrated influence on the same process. To restrict the lesser danger, if there is one, and ignore the larger is hypocritical and bad policy-making.

42. 421 U.S. 809 (1975).

43. 425 U.S. 748, 763, 770 (1976).

44. 447 U.S. 557, 571 (1980).

45. 455 U.S. 191, 203 (1982).

46. 54 U.S.L.W. 4956 (U.S. July 1, 1986).

47. 54 U.S.L.W. at 4959 n.6.

48. 434 U.S. 765, 791 (1978).

49. R. H. Coase, "The Economics of the First Amendment: The Market for Goods and the Market for Ideas," 64 *American Economic Review* 384, 385 (May, 1974).

50. I invite the reader to examine newspapers of 1789 to 1791. You will find that advertising is usually featured more prominently than current events.

51. Those seeking free time are supposed to demonstrate that they do not have the money for paid advertising. Nader accomplishes this by operating a nonprofit organization which spends its advertising budget on the print media.

52. Medical evidence indicates that even one cigarette is harmful to the smoker and those around him or her, but that people who have a drink or two a day are healthier than those who abstain. Thus, to end alcohol consumption might reduce deaths on our highways but would increase deaths elsewhere. One further point, there is no evidence that restricting or eliminating the advertising of alcohol would result in less consumption of alcohol. Prohibition often encourages consumption.

5

PERSUASION IN POLITICAL CAMPAIGNS

Leadership *emerges* in democracies: it is neither inherited nor arbitrarily assigned. As long as there is freedom of expression, leader-spokespersons can come from almost any segment of the population. In recent times, Abbie Hoffman rose through the ranks of young radicals; Lee Iaccoca came from the auto industry to speak on national issues; and ministers ranging from Jesse Jackson on the left to Pat Robertson on the right have tried to seize the mantle of political leadership. Emergence of leaders and would-be leaders is contingent on the right of *every citizen* to address public issues. It is also contingent on freedom of access to the media of mass communication. As I have shown in the preceding chapters, these freedoms have been difficult to protect, and access to the media of communication remains an imperfectly sustained ideal.

Political leadership is, of course, not the only kind of leadership dependent on the exercise of free speech and effective use of the media of mass communication, but it is paradigmatic of how leadership is attained in free societies, and it is a selective process in which all citizens are principal participants. I shall look at presidential political campaigns, for here we can see most clearly the tensions that arise among the ideal of complete freedom of expression, the ideal of equality of opportunity, and the enormous array of strategies of political persuasion that is available to those who aspire to national leadership. Because these values and possibilities clash, there is at least a perceived danger that the arsenal of weapons and strategies can become a threat to the freedoms of all.

As I showed in chapter 4, we already have restrictions on candidates' use of the media of communication and proposals have been made to control certain persuasive strategies such as "negative advertising." In contests for national leadership, as elsewhere, we see a contest of values—a contest between freedom to express on the one hand and such other democratic ideals as equality, fairness, truthfulness, and rights of privacy.

119

There are but two general directions in which a society such as ours can go in this contest. We can censor political campaigns and restrict their resources and activities, as Congress has already done. Or we can adopt freedom to express as the highest social value and undertake to understand the system of political campaigning so well that we neutralize "abuses." I am an advocate of the latter course. Restrictions on political campaigning have been circumvented each time regulations have been instituted. New communicative technologies are so sophisticated and ubiquitous that it is impossible to prevent "black markets" of communication—created by campaigners, cliques, government, or foreign powers. For example, many campaigns are now sending "candidate videos" directly to voters to be played on their VCRs. These are, in effect, unregulated campaign commercials. Most importantly, every regulation that restricts expression constrains what Justice Oliver Wendell Holmes called the "free marketplace of ideas." This marketplace is the only one in which the generality of voters can secure information about candidates, their characters, and their positions, if any, on issues. Finally, we need to recognize that, in many cases, the political marketplace is self-correcting. As we shall see, parties, candidates, and the media are so competitive with one another that little escapes the eyes of professionals, who then pass the results of their scrutiny on to the public.

With these circumstances in mind, I shall look first at the environment contemporary candidates face, then turn to how they deal with the American voting public, and finally, examine specific weapons that have evolved in modern campaigns.

THE BASIC ENVIRONMENT

Most presidential campaigning occurs within the context of major party politics; in fact, within the context of two-party politics. Third parties are generally short-lived, issue oriented, and/or swallowed by the major parties (see chapters 2 and 3). Major parties are interested in issues in themselves *and* as a means to advance the party. Obtaining power, particularly the presidency, is an overriding goal. Thus, they are concerned with establishing and maintaining a party apparatus capable of producing electoral victories.

The spectrum of "mainstream" political opinion in the United States runs roughly from "liberal" through "independent" to "conservative." At each end of this continuum lie what most Americans consider the "extremists." At least since Franklin Roosevelt, the Democratic party has occupied the "liberal" portion of the continuum and the Republican

120

party the "conservative" portion. Within each party, however, there are also "liberal" and "conservative" wings that vie with each other for control of the party's machinery and positions on matters of public policy. Within each major party, then, there are tensions or "pulls" between the party's political right and political left.

When one turns from opinions within the major parties to opinions held by the totality of voters in the United States, the source of a different kind of tension for political persuaders emerges. Political analysts attribute the outcomes of the most recent American elections to swings of sentiment among middle-class Americans. Theodore White observed in 1964 that ". . . there is in America neither a conservative nor a liberal majority, but two dogmatic extremes which vie for a vast uncertain middle ground which can be tilted one way or another by events, by leadership, by campaign practice, by impact."[1] White's comment is appropriate to campaigns going back as far as 1860, and as contemporary as 1988, where the word "liberal" became a major focal point.

Neither political party has majority support today. The voters are divided roughly into thirds, with almost as many people calling themselves "independents" as call themselves Democrats or Republicans. The candidates of the major parties, after a four-year fight to win their parties' nomination, must turn around and demonstrate that they are not really the darlings of the special interest groups that make up their parties but are, in fact, middle-of-the-roaders ready to protect the interests of the independent voter. The independents, together with the candidate's partisan 40 percent, will provide the victory.

Few modern candidates receive less than 40 percent of the votes cast. Senator Barry Goldwater received roughly that amount in 1964, even though he was considered the most conservative major party candidate of this century. Senator George McGovern also received 40 percent of the vote in 1972, even though he was considered the most liberal major party candidate since William Jennings Bryan. So the game is to capture the 20 percent of the voters in the middle. Candidates believe that their party supporters will remain loyal while each candidate gears his or her rhetoric to the task of putting together a larger coalition.

Idealists, particularly people new to politics, often complain about candidates' broadened appeals. In 1964, Barry Goldwater did the unthinkable and strategically unworkable by refusing to adapt. George McGovern, on the other hand, did try to unite a Democratic majority behind his candidacy by abandoning stands he had taken earlier in the primaries. He appeared hypocritical to many voters and alienated his most idealistic supporters at the same time. While Goldwater retained his

121

intense supporters, he lost the broad middle. When McGovern reached for the middle, he diminished the intensity of his core support.

The cases of political persuasion that I have reviewed in early chapters of this book suggest that ideologies and ideologues have not endured in the United States. Ultimately they have been defeated or their most practical ideas have been co-opted by more pragmatic political entities. For reasons I have just pointed out, individual candidates are forced into similarly moderated positions. The result is that in modern presidential campaigning there is always tension between the kinds of rhetoric and claims that were necessary to recruit ardent supporters and win primary elections and the kinds of moderated rhetoric and claims that are necessary to win general elections. While seeking the nomination, a presidential candidate must portray him- or herself as "different" on specific points and issues in order to stand apart from the pack of other candidates. But the "independents" who must be won over in the general election tend to be pragmatists rather than followers of partisan creeds. Therefore, each party's candidate must identify with "the people" more than with "the party" while seeking victory in the general election. There usually is, and pragmatically there must be, a shift from partisan doctrines that build intense support to themes associated with expediency and feasibility that build broad support. The shift creates tensions within parties, among political strategists, and between the candidates themselves.

Perhaps the most successful recent candidate at overcoming these tensions was Jimmy Carter in the 1976 election. In 1975, Carter began by calling himself a conservative but "responsible" alternative to George Wallace. This accomplished two things. It separated Carter from the other Democratic candidates, most of whom were new liberals like Representative Morris Udall, or old guard liberals, like Senator Henry Jackson. Once George Wallace was out of the race, Carter had the conservative side of the Democratic spectrum to himself. The Southerners and conservatives in the Democratic party did not constitute a majority of its membership, but they gave Carter enough votes to win in the early primaries because his opponents divided the liberal vote. Carter also spent a good deal of time playing up his Southern roots, which also made him seem unique. Further, time and time again, he argued that he was outside of Washington and, therefore, unlike the politicians of the Watergate era; he was uncorrupted, competent, and ready to provide new leadership.

Once Carter won the nomination, he moved quickly to seize the middle ground in order to keep the grand umbrella of the Democratic

122

Party intact. To do this, Carter had to avoid addressing specific issues. In fact, when he had addressed specific issues in the primary campaign, he had often gotten into deep trouble. For example, in a speech in Pittsburgh, Carter advocated a neighborhood program to maintain "ethnic purity." Some accused him of racism. In fact, Carter lost four of the last five primaries of 1976. So in the general election, Carter stuck to such generalities as competence, honesty, and evangelical morality.

What undid the Carter strategy was President Ford's challenge to debate the issues. The Gallup Poll taken immediately after the Democratic Convention put Carter 33 percentage points ahead of Ford. Thus, Ford had little to lose and much to gain from a debate. Moreover, as the challenger, Carter could hardly refuse to debate. After the Republican Convention, which culminated with Ford's acceptance speech containing the challenge to a series of debates, Ford closed the gap with Carter to 13 percentage points. And after the first debate Ford closed to within four percentage points. Carter's coalition was coming apart. According to White House tracking polls, conservatives, particularly in the Deep South and Midwest, began to see that on the issues, Ford was much more their man than Carter. Had Ford not blundered in the second debate, or had Dole not offended sensibilities in the vice presidential debate, Ford might have defeated Carter. The fact is that the last Gallup Poll taken showed Ford ahead by one percent. Carter eked out a victory, his coalition strategy unraveling even as he took the oath of office.

To sum up, the focus of modern presidential campaigns is narrowed to the tasks of retaining party loyalty (the faithful 40 percent) and gaining a majority of the middle 20 percent of voters, the "swing vote." This is why candidates spend so much time and money on devices that can win only relatively few voters. Presidential campaigning is thus partly shaped by the need to respond to standard party issues and partly shaped by the need to reflect the issues and values of the *middle majority*. That shaping is strategically creative if it takes advantage of new technologies and is inventive in adapting to campaign laws such as those I reviewed in chapter 4.

RESPONDING TO PUBLIC OPINION

How does a candidate retain his or her values, yet get close enough to the voters' psyches to be effective at building a majority?

The human psyche is a fascinating collection of drives, values, sensed data, and imagination. As I pointed out in the chapter on philosophical confrontation, preachers in Colonial America addressed their sermons to what they believed were the dominant constituents of the listeners' psyches. They began by adapting to the "understanding," hoping it would move the "will" to cause the converting experience. Later, the evangelicals appealed to the "emotions" to move the "will," and their rhetoric was dramatically different from that of their Puritan predecessors.

Political persuaders also have to adapt to voters' psyches. Most political and rhetorical advisors now believe that at the core of the human psyche are drives such as hunger, sex, and survival. These drives are socialized, becoming expressed in such cultural values as love, family life, and financial success. When these values are applied to what we see, smell, taste, hear, and otherwise experience, judgments are made, and these judgments result in the formation of attitudes on various questions. In short, the contemporary understanding is that attitudes express value judgments about the data we sense as those data are perceived in relation to our core of beliefs.

In rhetorical application, the closer a statement comes to the core, the more likely it is to be examined by voters. Thus, questions about the price of nuclear power in Seattle are less likely to affect a citizen in Miami than are questions about Florida sales taxes. Local taxes affect the Miamian's income and therefore his or her ability to provide food, clothing, and shelter to the family. If, however, a toxic waste dump is found in the Miamian's yard, that threat, being nearer and more urgent, will dominate the voter's critical faculties.

There are a number of measures of how important an issue is to a voter. One measure is *depth:* Does the issue touch the voter at the level of opinion, value, or drive? Another is *distance:* How far from the voter is the problem? A third is *time:* Is the problem urgent or can it be put off?

The best political figures understand these principles well. Franklin Roosevelt seldom raised an issue without tying it closely to the human needs of his audience. Ronald Reagan, who has great admiration for FDR, uses the same technique. He has taught Republicans to talk about inflation in terms of the price of groceries, not in terms of abstract percentages. When he talks about deficits, he builds images in the mind so that we can picture the astronomical numbers; he then personalizes the results of deficits by giving human examples that make the problem seem immediate and close.

In his 1972 campaign for the presidency, George McGovern, who was far behind from the beginning, tried desperately to tie his campaign to values with which voters could identify. He addressed many issues from a base in morality:

Corruption: "These are the kind of tactics of disruption which made it impossible to carry on a national political dialogue and that is what I despise."[2] "Americans are a fair and moral people. They're going to reject those un-American and unethical tactics."[3]
Vietnam: "[P]eace is not at hand. It is not even in sight. . . ." [later in the day] "I've never heard a statement more sickening than Kissingers's."[4]
Defense: "It was immoral for us to spend so much on defense when there were needy and hungry so ever present."
Welfare: "I have consistently held to the principle that we replace a welfare system that is unfair both to those who pay for it and to those it seeks to serve."[5]

McGovern's reference to and demand for egalitarian reform pervaded his rhetoric. He spent a good deal of energy portraying Nixon as an elitist and a defender of wealthy special interest groups:

Mr. Nixon chose a course that robbed you to reward the rich. . . . The major preoccuption of the Nixon Price Commission has been to protect corporations, not to prevent inflation. . . . Mr. Nixon's campaign is bankrolled by those so rich that they can give millions. . . .[6]
There is a depletion allowance for oil wells, but no depletion for the farmer who feeds us or the worker who serves us all.[7]

Behind most of McGovern's rhetoric were the premises of a Puritan-like morality. His speeches were at times punctuated by scripture from the Old Testament, as on October 19, 1972: "I want us to claim the promise of Isaiah, 'The people shall be righteous and they shall inherit the land.' "[8] In accepting the Democratic nomination, he stated: "In Scripture and in the music of our children, we are told: 'To everything there is a season, and a time to every purpose under heaven.' And for America, the time has come at last."[9]

It was no accident that McGovern spoke of the president's moral leadership, of leading the people out of the "wilderness," and of "trust between those who elect and those who are elected."[10] He argued that some original purpose had been betrayed and that Nixon symbolized that betrayal:

We see now when the President's most important advisor announced that peace had come, it was a deception. . . .[11] We are confronted, in short, with both a moral and constitutional crisis of

125

unprecedented dimension. . . . A free society might never recover from a sustained assault on its most basic institutions. And one can only ask, if this has happened in four years, to what lengths would the same leadership go in another four years. . . .[12]

McGovern's attempts to build a majority with appeals to moral values failed for a number of reasons. First, many of his observations seemed unrelated to the drives of the voters he needed to win. His appeals were almost always metaphysical, beyond the levels of action with which middle-class voters could easily associate political leadership. Second, incumbents have a natural advantage in most campaigns, and McGovern was unable to break through Nixon's advantage with arguments and appeals that were so general. Third, McGovern was perceived as a representative of the political left rather than of the center. His moral appeals were aimed at solving that problem; but for reasons I have just given, they were unlikely to "convert" centrists. Fourth, by focusing on political actions, Nixon was able to neutralize McGovern's generalized moral appeals.

President Nixon's rhetoric reflected the wishes of the middle class. Few presidential campaigns have adapted to the issues and values of the great middle majority more effectively than Nixon's campaign in 1972. In that campaign he developed a view of the "American way of life":

I have found hard evidence of something I always believed—that despite our vast diversity of races, of ethnic origins and of faiths, when you get down to the basics, we are still one America. . . . And the basics are the same in every part of the country. They are the same for the Polish-American, the Italian-American, and the Mexican-American, the steel worker, the farmer.[13]

Earlier in the campaign, he had said:

The rights of each minority must be vigorously defended—and each minority must be protected in the opportunity to have its opinion become accepted as the majority view.[14]

There can be little doubt that Nixon was playing to diverse ethnic groups, some of whom had little love for the others. The use of ethnic appeals was an attempt to bring blue collar voters into the Republican party—a group that Senator Muskie, as a vice presidential nominee, and George Wallace, as a third party nominee, had successfully wooed in the 1968 race.

126

Because Nixon appeared to be concerned with making the government work and with protecting the governmental structure during crisis, his persuasion was much more pragmatic than McGovern's, and therefore more appealing to centrist voters. Furthermore, Nixon's references to crime, busing, and national security, along with his appeal to ethnic groups, was the first such concerted appeal by the national Republican Party since the 1920s. This may partially explain why in cities with 500,000 inhabitants or more, Nixon ran 8 percentage points ahead of his 1968 totals. In cities of 250,000 to 500,000, he ran 16 percentage points ahead of McGovern and his own totals for 1968. In the suburbs, Nixon was able to add former Wallace and Humphrey voters to his 1968 plurality so that he did much better in these areas than ever before.[15]

Nixon took a pragmatic approach to the issues that were uppermost in the voters' minds. To do this seems to be critical in national campaigning. In 1976, for example, Carter moralized, but he took the extra step of associating his evangelical views with specific public needs and desires. His opponent, Gerald Ford, campaigned blandly on the issues and ran behind until he tied those issues to specific human needs and added a patriotic component to his rhetoric. Ford's full strategy first emerged in the bicentennial speeches for the Declaration of Independence, and then forcefully in his acceptance of the Republican nomination. What are a campaigner's specific rhetorical options for getting his or her propositions "down to earth"? There are two broad considerations that yield a variety of specific options: adaptation by contrast and use of incumbency.[16]

ADAPTATION BY CONTRAST

As it has been throughout our history, appeal for centrist votes remains a major feature of modern campaigning. In some campaigns adaptation to the great middle can be enhanced by contrast. Presidential persuasion is often successful when contrasts between candidates can be highlighted. The move is not always possible, but there are numerous cases where it has proved decisive. What works best is to find means of emphasizing contrasts where a candidate's positions identify him or her with the *centrist* majority and his or her opponent with one end of the spectrum of opinion. In the 1988 presidential campaign that strategy was consciously adopted by George Bush as he repeatedly insisted that Michael Dukakis was an "eastern liberal," whereas Bush presented himself as a moderate conservative.

In 1979, George Wallace visted one of my classes at the University of

Alabama in Birmingham to give a lecture. The Governor was genial and a genius at explaining politics to the undergraduates. For instance, when asked what newspapers he read, Wallace responded that he began his day with the *New York Times* and the *Wall Street Journal*. A shocked freshman from rural Alabama said, "Governor, I thought you hated those Northern papers." The Governor looked at the boy and smiled. "Son, you've got to know what the enemy is saying if you're going to beat him."

Later I asked Wallace about his 1968 race for the presidency. That was the campaign in which Wallace said that there was "not a dime's worth of difference between the Republican and Democratic nominee for president."[17] When I asked him why he made that his theme, he said that people don't convert to religions close to their own. "When they convert, they want it to be a big leap. I tried to give them the feeling that voting for me would really be doing something different." As a third-party candidate, Wallace received almost 13 percent of the votes.

Why in 1960 did Nixon run as the "me too" candidate? Why in 1968 was he unable to differentiate himself on policy from Humphrey? And why in 1972 did he push McGovern so far to the left that a majority of virtually every major constituency voted for Nixon?

The answer lies in the issues of the time and Nixon's clever manipulation of them. In 1960 he was insecure in Kennedy's presence, did not enjoy a solid lead in the polls, and was intent on making the Republican Party the party of the middle. His strategy failed because when voters perceive that there is little difference between the candidates on the issues, they tend to vote on the basis of image. Kennedy won in 1960 by only 112,000 votes, indicating what a difficult time the voters had deciding between these candidates, and indicating too that a strategy of major contrasts was not possible for either candidate.

In 1968, with a big lead following the conventions, Nixon decided to contrast his candidacy with Humphrey's and lock up the landslide that the polls were predicting. Several things went wrong. First, Wallace continued to chip away at Nixon's conservative flank in the South and in key pockets in other parts of the country. Second, Humphrey's choice of Edmund Muskie as a running mate proved effective. Muskie brought blue collar and other conservative Democrats outside the South back into the party by election time. He convinced them that they would be throwing their votes away by voting for Wallace and helping Nixon get elected. Third, a Democrat was sitting in the White House at the time of the election. And when Johnson halted the bombing of North Vietnam, it looked to many voters as if a step toward ending the war was being taken. Nixon's portrayal of himself as the peace candidate in contrast

128

with Humphrey as the war candidate was undone. Leftists came back to the Democratic Party and nearly gave Humphrey the election. Fourth, Nixon refused to debate Humphrey, which appeared cowardly to some and unfair to others.

None of these conditions afflicted Nixon in 1972; as we know only too well, he was in control of his own destiny. At last he was able to launch a full scale model of the rhetoric of contrast and make it work. First, the advertising of "Democrats for Nixon," headed by former Governor John Connally of Texas, focused on McGovern's contradictions and vacillations. The Connally group relied essentially on attacks that Hubert Humphrey had made on McGovern during Humphrey's futile attempt to win the California primary.[18]

Second, McGovern himself had erred seriously by selecting Senator Thomas Eagleton for Vice President. The man McGovern chose as his running mate could not stand up to press scrutiny and the public reaction to the revelation that Eagleton had undergone shock therapy. McGovern withdrew his "1000 percent" backing of Eagleton and opened himself to tremendous criticism. The issue of credibility, supposedly the Archilles' heel of the "old Nixon," was the ruin of the new McGovern.[19]

Third, Nixon had consolidated his support and was ready to make sure it did not defect. By June, 1972, the month of the Watergate break-in, the public approved Nixon's position over McGovern's on fifteen out of sixteen major issues.[20] Thus, Nixon could say on July 27, "The issues that divide the opposition and this administration are so wide—in fact the clearest choice in this century—that we must campaign on the issues." Having already won the issues, Nixon could agree with his opponent's desire to discuss the issues of the campaign. It offered an opportunity to shove McGovern as far away from the majority positions as possible.[21] In his 1984 acceptance of the nomination, Reagan echoed Nixon: "America is presented with the clearest political choice of half a century." This is not to say that Reagan ran only on the issues. He did not. But it is to say that the incumbents' strategies were similar in terms of adapting to the polls on issues. Vice President Bush, the quasi-incumbent of the 1988 race, used the same strategy in his acceptance speech. Near the end, he contrasted his positions on such issues as gun control, national defense, taxes, the death penalty, abortion, and the Pledge of Allegiance with those of his opponent. Each issue was set out as a separate sentence in his text and each was punctuated by applause from the assembled Republican delegates. This tactic was one of the reasons Dukakis's seventeen point lead in the polls disappeared after the Republican Convention.

Contrasts between presidential candidates can be produced and emphasized by "programming" as well. National party conventions can be rendered persuasive by being staged to highlight contrasts. Nixon was ready to stress the differences between his conception of America and McGovern's by the time of the Republican Convention. The convention was therefore managed to emphasize the contrast. The Republican Convention was orderly. The GOP youths were clean cut and disciplined; the women were proper and formal; the schedule was followed to the minute. The speeches were planned to acclaim the Nixon administration, condemn the opposing ticket, and appeal to Democrats to join the mainstream.

Once again, the similarities between Nixon's 1972 convention and Reagan's in 1984 are notable. Both were scripted and highly orchestrated. Both used speakers to praise the incumbent and attack the opposition. And both built toward an acceptance speech that would emphasize *contrast* rhetorically for the purpose of portraying opponents as not really serious contenders.[22]

In his introduction of Nixon, Agnew supported the crucial themes. He could be positive: "Our mission is to create a climate in which all Americans can live their lives in dignity and security, in peace and honor." Or he could be negative: ". . . in the name of reform, the practice of pitting the most publicized minorities against the least publicized continues. . . . A quota system, regardless of its avowed intent, has no place in a free society."

Nixon in 1972 and Reagan in 1984 came forward at the perfectly orchestrated moment. They rationalized the cruder appeals made earlier into centrist values. They praised the youth attending the Republican Conventions, contrasting them to those at the "other one." They attacked quotas, implying that they would turn America into chaos, just as they had turned the "other party" into chaos. Said Nixon in 1972: "Six weeks ago our opponents in their convention rejected many of the great principles of the Democratic party. To those millions who have been driven out of your home in the Democratic party we say—come home—not to another party but to the great principles we Americans believe in together." Reagan put it this way in 1984: "I began political life as a Democrat. . . . Did I leave the Democratic Party or did the leadership of that Party leave not just me but millions of patriotic Democrats[?] As Democratic leaders have taken their Party further and further away from its first principles, it's no surprise that so many responsible Democrats feel that our platform is closer to their views. And we welcome them to our side."

Nixon associated McGovern with radicalism even as he denied doing

130

it: "The choice in this election is not between radical change and no change. The choice is between change that works and change that won't work." (This had been the theme of the Nixon biography for television shown earlier in the convention; Reagan also used a televised biography in 1984.) Said Reagan, "The choices this year . . . are between two different visions . . . two fundamentally different ways of governing." Neither Nixon nor Reagan would talk about "what's wrong with America." No, they would point to the prosperity they had provided and ridicule the proposals of their opponents. Each man listed the accomplishments of his administration. Both concluded sections of their speeches by portraying their opponents as weak in contrast to their own strength: "Let us reject the policies of those who whine and whimper about our frustration and call upon us to turn inward," said Nixon. Reagan argued that the Democrats presented a vision of "pessimism, fear and limits."

During the campaign that followed the conventions, the rhetoric of contrast continued. Nixon's rare campaign speeches were limited to thirty minutes and given much fanfare. More important, he spoke on key issues to reinforce his perceived ability to handle problems. In his Labor Day speech, he labeled McGovern part of the "welfare ethic," while identifying himself with the "work ethic." McGovern never recovered from Nixon's labeling because middle America could reformulate all they knew about McGovern into a consistent image based on Nixon's descriptions.

Reagan had a harder time. At first Mondale's announcement that he would raise taxes, his historic selection of a female vice presidential candidate, and his appointment of Bert Lance as Party Chair helped Reagan contrast his campaign to Mondale's and move further ahead in the polls. But Reagan's strategy came undone in the first debate with Mondale. There was contrast, but nearly all the wrong way. Mondale appeared sharper, crisper, more aggressive. But by the second debate, Reagan was back in stride. He was witty, warm, relaxed, and less muddled in endless statistics. Mondale seemed defensive and tired.

Where constrasts can be established in campaigning, candidates gain advantage or suffer disadvantage in news coverage. Conflict sells papers; harmony rarely does. Consequently, if candidates clearly differ on an issue, news correspondents and commentators will tend to focus on the contrast of views, often exaggerating the differences and helping the candidate who has taken the more popular stand. As the primary contests of 1988 were being launched in 1987, Representative Richard Gephardt of Missouri deliberately separated himself from the five other announced Democratic candidates vying for their party's nomination. In debate with them he stressed his distinctive demand for stiffer trade sanctions against countries undercutting American producers in world markets. Senator Albert Gore of Tennessee set himself apart by stressing his Southern background and strong record on defense. News reporters played up these distinctions and pronounced that Gephardt was specially positioning himself to win labor votes and Gore was looking forward to the primary elections in Southern states. While Gephardt succeeded in winning the Iowa caucuses and Gore did very well in Southern primaries, neither man achieved broad enough support to win the nomination. However, the rhetoric of contrast did win them attention above that given to their fellow debaters. And, of course, to the extent that their statements in the debate were emphasized by the news media, the contributions of the other four candidates were overshadowed. Gephardt's strong showing in the Iowa caucuses and Gore's strong showing on "Super Tuesday" may have resulted from this strategy.

INCUMBENCY AND POLITICAL PERSUASION

Where contrast is not a strong resource in presidential rhetoric, the advantages of incumbency become especially important—if, of course, the incumbent has built a decent record. Incumbency *can be* a built-in conservative factor in political persuasion. Incumbents not only have a past record to conserve, their positions in office greatly enhance their access to the media of mass communication. Their official functions become "news" whereas challengers must face the tensions associated with *creating* occasions that will gain them attention from those controlling the media of mass communication.

Almost all statistical analyses of recent elections for Congress or state offices show a strong trend in favor of incumbents. Part of the reason is that office holders have to be "upset" if change is to occur. Then such cultural commonplaces as "Why change horses . . . ," "Stick with what you've got . . . ," and "You have to beat the champion to become one . . ." reflect voters' attitudes in many political races. Beyond a challenger's burden of demonstrating why the incumbent should be tossed out, incumbency gives the holder additional resources to keep challengers at bay—a public position and forum, a record of activity in office, and some sort of political organization already in existence. For such reasons, those in power tend to stay in power, and this phenomenon is a moderating influence and a stabilizing force in our system.

Somewhat oddly, however, a number of recent presidents have been

132

unable to retain the office despite the huge arsenal of power the office offers. This does not mean that presidential incumbency cannot be a positive influence. Since 1960, Richard Nixon, Lyndon Johnson, and Ronald Reagan have won reelection. But only Nixon and Reagan have won two consecutive elections. Each used incumbency to his advantage, and it is useful to focus on the reelection campaigns of 1972 and 1984 to discover the nature of presidential incumbency as a persuasive resource.

Nixon and Reagan began the persuasive process for reelection immediately after they were elected to their first terms. The first public appeals came in their Inaugural addresses. The Inaugural is the first chance a new president has to consolidate support and to confirm his position. It is his opportunity to set a tone and demonstrate a style. The pragmatic dynamism of FDR first emerged in his 1933 Inaugural Address, after he had run a very conservative campaign. John Kennedy was perceived as akin to royalty after his highly stylized Inaugural Address. These speeches were, of course, transmitted to the nation, their impact was thereby greatly enhanced. A free press guarantees public access, now live access, to most major presidential speeches. Thus, the channels of communication become particularly valuable to the incumbent.

Other speeches, such as the State of the Union Address, give the president additional chances to reinforce his leadership in voters' minds. Press conferences, two-edged swords for Eisenhower and Reagan, were the places where Kennedy and Nixon performed best. Their ratings in the polls, in Nixon's case even in the depths of the Watergate crisis, rose after nationally televised press conferences. An advantage of the incumbent is that these opportunities are of his own making. In each case, he controls most of the variables. The incumbent can cultivate a relationship with a single reporter or group of reporters by granting exclusive interviews. He can sit and answer questions in a relaxed setting or put out his own propaganda film and challenge the networks to use it, as Ronald Reagan did at the 1984 Republican Convention. He can sign legislation at arranged forums or veto legislation in private. He even has some leeway when it comes to releasing the funding of projects. He can choose the medium, the setting, and the time he wishes to speak, thereby controlling the size and composition of his audience. In short, the necessities of responding to public opinion provide opportunities to shape it.

Incumbents have many other powers by which they can display leadership. For example, Nixon and Reagan used Supreme Court nominations to win over segments of the voting public. Nixon's nomination of conservative and Southern justices raised his ratings in the South. Reagan's nomination of the first woman to the Supreme Court helped

133

close the "gender gap" in Republican polls. And presidents can take action to solve problems. Nixon's initiation of wage and price controls at just the moment when Democratic leaders were calling for them partially defused what was then the most pervasive issue in American society, the faltering economy. The cease fire in Israel and the trips to China and Russia seemed to thaw the Cold War even as Nixon punished North Vietnam with renewed attempts at economic strangulation. Reagan's economic reforms and his response to the Grenada crisis buoyed his popularity.

The incumbent also has powerful *surrogates* he can use to defend his position. These surrogates, appointed by the president himself, are given special credibility by their rank. Traditionally, in reelection campaigns, the vice president serves as the hardest working defender of the regime. He is often assigned to do the dirty work in the campaign. Nixon in 1956, Agnew in 1972, and Bush in 1984 were classic models of this strategy. Each emerged from the campaign tarnished, but each served his leader well by drawing fire as the president spoke to higher concerns.

Nixon's use of surrogates in 1972 was particularly effective. Agnew became the antagonist of McGovern and other surrogates attacked where they could. Melvin Laird, Secretary of Defense, accused Mc-Govern of favoring "unconditional surrender" in Vietnam. Clark Mac-Gregor, director of the Nixon campaign, claimed McGovern's proposals would result in a "doubling of the income tax for the average worker."[23] Attorney General Richard Kleindienst claimed McGovern was using "hysterical campaign rhetoric" over the Watergate affair.[24] But it was Agnew who focused the attack. He claimed that McGovern's amnesty proposal "would tear the country apart."[25] "The people aren't buying [McGovern's] charges that the President has wrecked the economy. . . . They know that by every indicator the economy is healthy. . . ."[26] Agnew accused McGovern of advocating "busing of school children over great distances to achieve an arbitrary racial balance."[27] While Mc-Govern was doing battle with Agnew and the other surrogates, Nixon could devote himself to policy rhetoric, taking the high road and sounding ever more presidential.

Reagan's use of surrogates in 1984 was less effective. Because he faced his opponent in two debates, it was difficult for Reagan to assign major attacks on Mondale to his vice president, who campaigned as hard as Agnew had in 1972. Nonetheless, every president leads an army into battle. Its troops are government officials of standing with the public. For example, the Reagan campaign asked Cabinet members to campaign for at least fifteen days during the 1984 election. The challenger has fewer

134

resources in persons—perhaps a House Speaker, some Senators and governors, but no member of the Executive Branch.

With the authority of office, each president has opportunity to "rise above" partisanship on such presidential rhetorical occasions as the Inaugural Address, State of the Union addresses, budget addresses, and many ceremonial occasions. With these opportunities, an incumbent can build his ethos as a *national* leader well before the opposition has chosen its challenger. If these opportunities are effectively used, the opponent, when he or she is finally chosen, will tend to appear a partisanly narrow aspirant while the president keeps "the affirmative" on the "high road" of policy making and policy defense.

Of course, whether the advantages of incumbency really operate in a reelection campaign depends on having a "good record" from which to appeal for continuance. The advantages of incumbency are *potential* advantages; events and mistakes can overwhelm them. Johnson's incumbency was ruined by the Vietnam War. Ford had too brief a time to build a record of his own. Carter compromised his prospects by complaining more than he acted and by having a drastic action for recovery of the hostages in Iran dramatically fail. An incumbent at any level of politics must be able to invest his or her special persuasive opportunities with leaderly deeds as well as words.

THE SYSTEM

In our political system, *voters* are the final arbiters of persuasive strategies in politics. The complexities of our political system impose considerable burdens on voters and these burdens make it difficult to persuade them and contribute to low turnouts in elections.

THE VOTERS' BURDEN

Less than two weeks after the reelection of President Reagan in 1984, columnists began speculating on who would be the presidential nominees in 1988. Having participated in presidential campaigns, I know with certainty that before the voters had gone to bed on election night the lieutenants of George Bush, Jack Kemp, Bob Dole, Pierre du Pont, Pat Robertson, Bill Bradley, Gary Hart, Joe Biden, Richard Gephardt, and others were plotting the strategies they hoped would take them through straw votes, delegate caucuses, and primaries.

That is only one of the many reasons why Americans are inundated with campaign persuasion. Another is that we have so many elections and so many things on which to vote. California is a somewhat extreme example of the burden we have put on voters. Every four years, as in other states, Californians vote for president, but in even numbered years they vote for state-wide posts such as governor, and for federal Representatives. In addition, there are votes for state senators, state assemblymen, members of the county, city, and/or school boards. And because California, like Wisconsin, Oregon, Louisiana, and a number of other states, was "reformed" by zealous Progressives, the electorate votes in spring primaries to nominate party members to be voted on for offices in November. Furthermore, in either the June primary or the November general election, Californians may face up to thirty ballot propositions (written in legalese) that could alter their taxes, their constitution, or even their state's borders.

As I showed in chapter 2, Progressives believed in "direct democracy" and instituted such measures as the *recall,* whereby voters can remove an official from office, the *referendum,* whereby the state legislature can ask the voters to decide an issue, and the *initiative,* whereby, through petitioning, an issue can be taken out of the hands of the state legislature and put on the ballot. According to the Citizens Research Foundation, $45.6 million was spent on ballot measures in twelve states during the 1983–84 election cycle. California has had some particularly wild propositions in the past. Some have been frivolous, but others have changed history. One of the most important examples of the latter was Proposition 13. It was approved by voters in 1978 and limited how much property tax a citizen would have to pay to the state.[28] In November of 1986, Californians voted on whether to quarantine AIDS victims. That election was further complicated by the fact that the law also provided for a referendum on whether to retain Rose Bird as Chief Justice of their Supreme Court.[29] The voters threw her and several of her colleagues off the bench. In the fall of 1988, Californians faced five initiatives related to auto insurance alone.

During the six months leading up to an election in an even numbered year, Californians are deluged with candidates' advertising and face an avalanche of advertising about issues. By election day, most voters are not only fed up, they are filled up, with campaign rhetoric. They have four choices when facing such a profusion of persuasion: (1) They can try to listen to and understand it all, in which case they are apt to suffer semantic overload. (2) They can ignore it all, and either vote "no" on every proposition, or boycott the polls, which many do. (3) They can vote for the top of the ticket and ignore the rest. Or (4) they can sift and sort the information they receive in an attempt to live up to their

136

responsibilities as citizens. We should not, then, be surprised that under these conditions the turnout of voters has diminished, as has loyalty to party. In 1900, for example, in 96 percent of congressional districts, the majority of voters did *not* split their tickets when they voted for the presidential and House nominees. In 1984, 45 percent of the districts had split majorities. For the last decade, polls have indicated that about one-third of the voters do not identify themselves with either party.

To overcome these problems, campaigners have developed a sophisticated set of tools.

POLL DATA AS THE GUIDING FORCE

How does a candidate get a citizen to cast a favorable vote? How does the candidate motivate voters and achieve a majority? The key is understanding the audience, and this requires information that can only be secured through thorough analysis, and that means extensive polling.

Polling represents one of the major costs in a political campaign. Polling guides most of the decisions in a campaign because polling is about voters and about what they believe. The more a candidate knows about voters, the more he or she can adjust to the voters' wants and needs and/or find the common ground necessary to build a winning coalition. More important, poll data guide the candidate in choosing the strategies and devices he or she will use in a given campaign.

About eighteen months before a run for Congress and three years before a run for president, candidates usually conduct a *benchmark* survey. It is called a "benchmark" because it establishes early levels of support, positions of the voters on issues, the image of the incumbent, and the image of the opponent(s) at that date. In most responsible campaigns, the benchmark survey is repeated six months before the election to determine what alteration has occurred respecting issues and images. In presidential campaigns, benchmarks have been taken monthly with parts of them being conducted daily.

Benchmark surveys are expensive because to administer just one questionnaire takes about forty-five minutes. In a state the size of Oregon, a pollster needs to reach 600 voters to obtain a reliable sample. Pollsters will tell you it takes at least a thousand people to be relatively accurate (plus or minus 3 percent) in California. In a natural campaign, fifteen hundred to two thousand voters are used; pollsters claim that number gives them enough samples in major segments of the audience to provide accurate (plus or minus 3 percent) information. Others dispute this claim, particularly when attention is focused on small cells within the

137

audience. My own experience indicates that a sample of two thousand produces remarkably accurate information.[30]

The benchmark survey is divided into several sections. Usually, the poll begins with questioning on the *issues* of the day. The object of this section of the poll is to determine issues on which the campaign will build its credibility and differentiate itself from opposing campaigns. The questions about issues also help to set an "issue agenda" for the campaign. Respondents are asked: "What do you think is the most important problem facing the nation? Our state? Our city?" This section of the survey is also used to test the salience of issues, particularly those on which the candidate has already taken a stand. For example, the interviewer might ask, "Are you more or less likely to support a candidate who favors federal funding of abortions?"

The next section of a benchmark survey attempts to define the *image* of the incumbent. The information obtained is compared with past surveys to discover his or her current vulnerability in reference to specific issues and the candidate's general standing with the public. "Unassisted name identification" is one of the key indices in this section. The question is, when only the name of the incumbent is given, can the respondent identify what office the person holds. The more voters who can do that, all other things being equal, the more likely the incumbent is to win, unless of course the name identification has been gained by scandal or some other problem.

Vulnerabilities and strengths are established by asking open ended questions, such as "What do you like most about the incumbent?" and "What do you like least?" Respondents' actual comments are recorded, sorted by the computers, and handed over to the campaign directors. These direct quotations are referred to as "verbatims."

Finally, in the section dealing with the incumbent, benchmark pollsters often test for specific characteristics, such as honesty, fairness, and humanity. The pollster is looking for strengths and weaknesses in order to locate a suitable rhetorical stance for the campaign, and he or she is also trying to refine an image of the incumbent that media advisors can use in campaign commercials.

The third section of the benchmark survey repeats the foregoing set of questions for the *challenger*(s). These levels of support can be referred to later to determine what progress has been made in the campaign in reference to increasing name identification, support on specific issues, and indices of values important to the voting public.

The fourth section of the benchmark survey is used to establish the *ballot strength* of each candidate. The first question normally establishes the strength of the incumbent in isolation: "Do you believe Senator Heinz deserves reelection, or that it is time for a new person to represent your state in the Senate?" This question is purposely worded in a direct and frank manner. Most political consultants say that if the incumbent scores less than 50 percent on this question, he or she is in some trouble. The second question poses a "head to head match up": "If the election were held today, would you be more likely to vote for John Heinz or Carroll Arnold for United States Senator?" Like other questions forcing a comparison, this one can be asked again later in the campaign to determine whether there has been a change in voters' sentiments over time. (Pollsters refer to such changes as "movement"; change consistently in favor of one candidate is called "momentum.")

The final section of the benchmark survey establishes the *demographics* of the voting population. It asks for party membership, ideological leaning (liberal, moderate, conservative), age, education, sex, race, career, ethnicity, religion, and political activity. The information obtained in the earlier sections of the benchmark poll will be cross-referenced with these categories to provide additional information useful in targeting campaign advertisements to specific audiences, scheduling appearances by the candidate, and taking positions on the issues before different groups. Pollsters refer to these cross-referenced groups as "cross tabs." For example, the position of working women on the question of a nuclear freeze is a "cross tab," as is the position of black voters on abortion. "Working women" forms one cell for tabulation and those taking a position on a nuclear freeze forms another cell for tabulation. The pollster then "pulls" all the working women out of the nuclear freeze cell to construct the cross tabulation.

Once the poll data from a benchmark survey are analyzed, the candidate and the staff can begin to work out a strategy. What are the most important issues to the voters? What is the candidate's stand on those issues? Should that stand be altered? Which issues should be discussed before which groups? Where would local appearances by the candidate be most likely to solidify or build support? What kinds of issues and themes should advertising develop? In what media should these advertisements be placed? The basic question is, of course, "How can we be most persuasive?"

As a campaign continues, other polls will be taken. A *follow up* poll can be taken on any section of the benchmark poll to see if any movement has taken place. A *brush fire* poll can be taken when an issue unforeseen in the benchmark survey emerges, for example, a scandal or a serious crisis.

139

Other than the benchmark poll, the most useful device is the *tracking* poll. Each day a certain sample of voters is asked the "head to head" question: "If the election were held today would you vote for X or Y?" At the end of five days, the first day's sample is dropped and a sixth day's sample of voters is mixed in. Retaining a progressively additive five-day poll of voters continues until election day and projects a picture of which way the campaign is going. Presidential candidates usually start tracking right after they receive the nomination. In 1976, for example, Jimmy Carter tracked his lead over President Ford from the end of the Democratic Convention to election day. He watched his lead slip from 33 percent the day after the Democratic Convention to 13 percent the day after the Republican Convention to 2 percent following the first presidential debate.[31] Here was clear movement with the momentum going to Ford. But Carter rebounded in polls after the second presidential debate, which fell to near even after the third and stayed that way until election day.

In the Packwood Senate race in 1980, we noticed in our tracking poll that we were gaining support in rural Oregon in the last week of the campaign, but losing support in Portland where our opponent had just run some advertisements. We immediately ordered volunteers into the Portland area to increase the campaign's presence and energize turnout efforts there. On election day, Packwood ran well in Portland, particularly in Multnomah County, which makes up one-third of Portland, where he received seven thousand more votes than Ronald Reagan. Our efforts had apparently reduced the opponent's margin of victory in that heavily Democratic county.

Tracking polls can be very dangerous. They should be used to determine *trends* and never be stopped before election day. The newsmedia, with the exception of CBS News, learned this lesson the hard way during the 1988 New Hampshire primary. For the first time, the media tried to use tracking polls to measure the swings in voter preference in New Hampshire. When Bush placed third in the Iowa caucuses, his popularity plummeted in New Hampshire in media tracking polls. The same polls showed Dole pulling even with Bush, or as in the case of Gallup, moving into a strong lead. Only the CBS-*New York Times* poll caught the countertrend that began on the Saturday night before the primary and after the Republican debate in which Bush acquitted himself well and Dole was sarcastic. Barry Goldwater, the patron saint of conservatism, endorsed Bush over the same weekend. And the Bush campaign released a new commercial that attacked Dole for "straddling" on the issue of whether taxes should be raised. While some polls began to

140

reveal a shift from Dole back to Bush, only the CBS poll predicted the Bush victory.

Poll data guide campaigners and help them adapt to their audiences and to changing situations. With the help of "cross-tab" data, a candidate can judge which parts of his or her message need to be directed to particular regions, neighborhoods, ethnic groups, and other segments of the total audience. Poll data enable candidates to change or mask their positions on issues, thereby concealing the candidate's actual stand. The data are also frequently used in devising commercials, perhaps to make the candidate more attractive than he or she actually is. Shifting positions, masking issues, and "playing to" specific audiences in special ways tend to occur in the closing days of the campaign. If voters are unaware of these possibilities, they may be misled concerning the candidates. Once more, we have the familiar problem: If candidates are free to communicate as they (and their managers) choose, the result may be misrepresentation. In the absence of regulation on matters of content and style, only the alertness of citizens and the "correctives" supplied by the press and opposing candidates can "keep the record straight." While Thomas Jefferson could not foresee the technological changes that would take place in campaigning in America, he did realize that "here we are not afraid to follow truth wherever it may lead, nor to tolerate any error so long as reason is left free to combat it."

DIRECT MAIL, VOTER REGISTRATION, AND TARGETING

There are a number of special demands to be met and problems to be solved because the strategies of using the mails, registering voters, and targeting special audiences impose constraints as well as opportunities for political communication. Each process and medium creates tensions between what campaigners would like to say and what *can* be said effectively given the opportunities and limitations of the media of communication. The problem of dealing with campaign reforms and the generalized need to appeal to 51 percent of the electorate have led to a new art of *dictamen,* political letter writing. If you have not received a solicitation through the mail from a candidate, a supporter of a ballot proposition, a national party, you have at least received one from a national subscription service or a direct mail seller. Why is so much money put into mass mailings? And why have they become an institutionalized part of our system of political persuasion? Consider a hypothetical example.

Imagine you have to sell a new Mercedes Benz to someone in an audience of one thousand people, and that you have twenty minutes to do it with *all* of them listening.[32] Imagine further that one quarter of the audience is composed of single, working women, one quarter are housewives, one quarter are blue collar, working males, and the last quarter are Hispanic males over the age of sixty-five.

Obviously, you are faced with difficult choices. If you adapt to one group, the other three can be alienated. If you adapt your remarks to all four groups, that is, the least common denominator, your speech will be mush. If only, like the apostles after the visitation of the Holy Ghost, you could speak with one voice but be heard in several.

That is the problem facing politicians. The more people to which one has to appeal to form the 51 percent necessary for victory, the more difficult the task of persuasion—presidential candidates having the toughest time of all.

The solution that has been developed for this kind of problem is "targeting." Targeting is a procedure by which segments of a total audience can be appealed to separately. Some targeting has gone on since the beginning of campaigns. One famous example occurred in the Illinois senate campaign of 1858. Stephen A. Douglas referred to Abraham Lincoln as "spotty" because Lincoln adapted his treatment of slavery to the locale or spot in which he was speaking. In the age of pervasive electronic and printed media, candidates can be even more selective. They can identify radio stations whose listeners are mostly young, or elderly, or made up of some other specialized group within a single community. They can then create messages adapted to those special groups and present them on the selected stations. The same tactic can be used in the printed media. Readers of the *New York Daily News* can be addressed differently from readers of the *New York Times*. Readers of physical fitness magazines can be addressed apart from readers of agricultural magazines, and so on.

Until recently, precise, effective, and relatively inexpensive methods of targeting national but specialized audiences were not available to political campaigners. Then came Watergate and the campaign reforms of 1974. The new Federal Election Laws limited the amount of money each contributor could give to $1,000 per election, with primaries counted as "elections." Republican operatives set about to find a way to generate millions of dollars from donors giving small amounts. A major solution was to send letters to voters asking for funds. This apparently simple system is actually expensive and easily overtaxed, but with refinements it has proved a very effective means of political communication and fund raising.

142

The first step in making targeted appeals effective is to determine one's targets. Poll data will reveal which voters are likely to be most favorably impressed by a given party, candidate, and/or position on issues. Once these classes of persons have been identified, a frequent next move is to buy mailing lists selectively. If, for example, I were George Bush, I might try to buy mailing lists from selected mail-order firms that solicit middle-aged, upwardly mobile consumers. L. L. Bean and Eddie Bauer provide such lists. Another method of targeting is to identify the geographic areas where polls show likely supporters live. Using a reverse telephone directory, one can then call or write to the people in these areas. Telephone calls from phone banks manned by campaign volunteers or paid callers can yield sympathetic voters and more volunteers. Moreover, computer software is available to place calls automatically into preset neighborhoods, saving the callers an enormous amount of time. They need only push one button to register the response, and then a new call is automatically dialed.

In direct-mail communication, once lists are compiled, letters are sent asking for support. This step is called "prospecting," and it has several purposes. Even if the addressee fails to respond, he or she actually reads the letter, particularly if it looks authentic: that is, is hand addressed, with a real (metered) stamp, and a signature that doesn't appear to have been printed by a machine. Computers are capable of doing all of these things, including merging names and addresses into a form letter, placing the first name of the recipient into the letter at relevant points, and even adding a personal "P.S." about the street or neighborhood. If the letter is read, some persuasion takes place, and the letter may be worth its cost for that reason alone.

Political experts judge a mailing a success if 6 percent or more of addresses respond with a donation. A response of 3 or 4 percent is often enough to pay for the cost of the mailing. All of those who respond are added to a separate master list, called a "house file." This group will be mailed to again and again because those who give once are likely to give again.

After several "prospecting" mailbags, a "house file" can grow to enormous size, manageable only by sophisticated computer programs. The National Republican Senatorial Committee, where I served as Deputy Director for the 1982 election cycle, had a "house file" of millions of names and addresses. Letters to these addressees generate a profit by producing many small donations that more than compensate for the cost of production and mailing.

In 1980, the reelection campaign of Senator Packwood raised over

$700,000 with one letter signed by Gloria Steinem. The cost of production and mailing was over $300,000, so our net was much lower than our gross. Our experience was a typical one. Half of the money raised in direct mail projects is eaten up by cost because it is a high volume business.

In presidential campaigns, the net amount raised can be higher. According to Federal Election Commission reports, the Bush campaign in 1988 became the most successful in history in terms of fundraising by putting together a tiered effort. By May, the campaign had raised $22 million by persuading 100,000 individuals to give an average of $211 a piece.[33] Four million dollars was raised by direct mail exclusively.

Aside from obtaining lists and building the "house file," there is the very important rhetorical task of composing the letter. The more specialized the audience, the more specific and effective the letter can be. By using the new nine-digit zip code, together with specialized information from polling, one can produce a very specialized appeal to a limited audience. But a special audience, say of single men with an income over $30,000, can be huge in number if one's appeal is national.

I will not catalog the long list of rhetorical ploys used in letters to solicit funds for political campaigns. Instead, allow me to use one letter from the Republican National Committee for a quick illustration. The letter was mailed on May 22, 1987 to the RNC "house file" by Frank Fahrenkopf, Chairman; the letter appears to be hand typed and signed, though close examination reveals that it is computer generated and the signature is photographed. At the top of the letter, the word "CRITICAL" appears in red letters.

The letter pretends to seek the donor's help with a survey; this is known as the "come on" in the carnival business. It reads, "I am calling upon you and other RNC members in good standing to help us revise our data bank of political information by completing the Survey and returning it to me by June 12." A few paragraphs later, the letter contains questions that are designed to excite partisanship: "Do you want *your* tax dollars to be used to reelect liberals like Ted Kennedy, Howard Metzenbaum and Alan Cranston? They're trying to destroy the gains we made in Party registration when President Reagan ran in 1980 and 1984. Mr. ——— [here the name of the addressee appeared for the first time], I need to know how you feel about these and other critical national developments."

Page two of the letter moves to an appeal for a contribution: "Since you've already been contributing so generously this year, I really wish I could tell you that we're on or ahead of schedule in our fundraising so far this year. But one look at the ledger books and I can see immediately that we've raised only 34% of our 1987 budget." Five paragraphs later, the pitch is made: "I just hope I'm right in having the faith that you'll understand how critically the RNC needs your financial support once again." Finally, after the signature, comes a postscript asking that the attached survey be filled out and returned by June 12. Obviously, the writer's hope is that a check will be enclosed with the survey.

Many political consultants argue that there is no substitute for personal contact. They argue that while computerized telephone banks are effective in prospecting, they are even more effective when used on the "house file." A computer calls the "house file" number, and then calls up data about the contributor on a screen in front of the caller. The caller knows when and how much the contributor gave the first time around. As the person called answers questions, the caller can punch the information into the computer and store it. Programs even allow callers to enter credit card numbers so that contributions can be made immediately and/or monthly.

Perhaps more important than its help in fund raising is the impact technological persuasion is having on voter registration and turnout at elections. In 1984, a major registration battle developed between the Republican and Democratic parties. Jesse Jackson fired the first salvo, using the traditional method of giving a speech at a campaign stop and then walking people to the registrar to get them on the rolls as voters. He was particularly successful in the South and on college campuses, but his action set off a strong reaction in the Republican party. Using telephone banks and specially developed computer programs, the Republicans registered persons with Republican sympathies who were most likely to vote on election day. Their lists were formed from census data, insurance records, car registration data, precinct voting histories, phone books, and anything else that would help the list maker locate a likely Republican voter. The callers used a form with a tree of questions likely to identify a Republican voter—a wrong answer to any of the questions would result in a terminated interview. The Republicans spent $10 million on this project, and focused it on key states, such as New Jersey, Connecticut, and North Carolina, where they expected the outcome to be close.

Not to be outdone, the Democratic National Committee bought the services of the Claritas Corporation which has "geocoded" all thirty-five thousand zip codes in the country. From these "geocodes" Claritas claims to have created forty "clusters" ranging from "home ownership" to "race." Claritas has given the clusters colorful nicknames. The "blue-blood estates" cluster represents such elite areas as Montecito in

California and River Oaks in Houston. The "sharecropper" cluster shows up mainly in the rural South and is predominantly black. The Democratic National Committee clustered their mailing lists using the geocoded zipcodes. This allowed them to identify likely donors and voters. But most important, it allowed the Democrats to tailor their appeals to unique clusters. Thus, their persuasion became more effective.

As Newton once said, for every action there is an equal reaction. When the Republicans learned about Claritas, which was put together by Republican consultants in the first place, they not only borrowed it, they went to another computer company, CACI, and refined the system. CACI broke voters into much more refined and smaller clusters for the Republicans. The CACI clusters usually contained no more than 275 households. A more specific targeting system had never been devised for use at the national level. On election day 1984, the Republicans reaped the reward of their diligence. They had registered about the same number of people as the Democrats had, but about twice as many newly registered Republicans voted as did newly registered Democrats.

The persuasive impact of the "personal" touch in direct mail and on the turnout of voters has yet to be gauged effectively. Raw vote totals and polls only hint at its impact. But given the technological war in which the two major parties are engaged, it seems likely that these programs have been effective in raising money and in getting voters to turn out for each party. The practices I have just described will almost certainly be continued and further refined in the future.

In recent years in the United States, the winning candidate in a presidential election has rarely received more than 55 percent of the total vote cast. This means that our national elections are normally closely contested and that the advantages gained from accurate polling, effective interpretation of poll data, direct-mail solicitation, and well designed appeals for a strong turnout of voters can spell the difference between victory and defeat. We should not, however, overlook the fact that each of these resources and requirements of campaigning limits and directs the exercise of freedom of expression in campaigns. No national candidate is wholly free to speak his or her mind because each interpretation of public opinion and each channel of communication restricts what it appears appropriate to say even though the channel and analysis of audiences allow the candidate and his supporters to reach more people more efficiently.

Several observations deserve to be made about the modern techniques of campaigning that I have described. First, the technological revolution in the conduct of political persuasion came about in considerable part because of laws passed to "reform" elections by equalizing opportunities to finance political campaigns. Initially, at least, the Republicans outdid the Democrats in using these techniques for fund raising and registering targeted voters. But, second, the technological advantage of one party for one election cycle becomes the property of the other party by the next election, so the new technologies encouraged by "reform" seem unlikely to generate monopolistic domination of the public arena by either major political party. For example, in the 1986 election, the Democrats outdid the Republicans in turning out newly registered voters, thereby reversing the results of 1984. Third, the new developments in campaigning seem likely to put minor political parties at further disadvantage because initiating sophisticated, far-reaching campaign programs requires huge investments of money and personnel. Fourth, a question that cannot yet be answered is whether at some point computer-dominated, "personalized" contact will become distasteful to contributors and voters. Only the future can tell us this. Fifth, throughout our history, freedom of expression has had to allow the freedom to propose and support suppression. Will extensive use of technological techniques in political communication breed attempts to control the use of computerized technologies as the emergence of broadcasting brought about new controls? To a degree this is already happening. In political affairs, we are not now free to spend entirely as we choose. Legislation has been introduced in the 100th Congress to impose controls over the format and content of political advertisements. Will we continue to be free to refine political campaigning technologically as new possibilities appear? These are points of tension the new technologies of political communication clearly invoke.

MANIPULATING THE MEDIA

In chapter 4, I discussed the tensions arising from the fact that political candidates' use of the airwaves is significantly restricted by the Communications Act of 1934. Rules that are not applied to powerful newspapers are applied to radio and television coverage of campaigns and to the broadcaster's right to put advertising on the air. But candidates are not without their own weapons by which to gain some control over the media that report on them. Their ability to manipulate the media somewhat balances the media's sometimes inadvertent distortion of the news. In the next pages I want to examine some of the common ways in which candidates use the media to shape perceptions.

147

POLITICAL COMMERCIALS

Political commercials are as old as political campaigning but new technologies allow different kinds of persuasion. Historically, political commercials were first handbills, then newspaper articles and advertisements, then billboards, and now the electronic media swell opportunities to persuade by means of commercials. Each option had advantages and limits. Handbills are useful for listing positions on issues and the qualifications of candidates, but they are difficult to distribute widely. It is even more difficult to insure that voters will read handbills and billboards when these are placed before them. Billboards help voters to identify candidates, and campaigners often use billboards to raise the enthusiasm of campaign workers. Newspaper advertising is useful in spelling out positions on issues, but voters also rely on editorial pages for that and ignore the advertisements. Furthermore, since more and more cities are becoming single-newspaper towns, it is becoming difficult to target audiences through newspapers.[34]

Radio and television advertising have more impact than print because it can add the humanity of a voice and with television, the reality of a picture. Radio and television advertising is immediate and hard to avoid without the bother of switching channels, punching the mute button, or walking out of the room where the radio or television set is located. Electronic advertising is costly, but a great advantage is that it can be targeted to specific audiences that watch certain programs.[35]

One of the most difficult tasks facing the presidential campaigns of 1988 was how to target television advertising for "Super Tuesday" across twenty primary and caucus states. The relative worth of each state in terms of voters, delegates, and press coverage had to be weighed against the commitment of funds and effort by other campaigns. The result was a highly complicated bidding war. Governor Michael Dukakis, for example, made an advertisement for working men in the South that was shown in such cities as Baltimore and Birmingham, and later used in Chicago. This section of the text featuring Thomas McIntyre, Vice President of the Bricklayer's International Union, reveals why the advertisement was put on the air in blue collar areas:

> I've known Mike a long time, and I gotta say Dukakis is not your shot'n'beer kinda guy. . . . But working people around here love him. . . . You want somebody to drink with? Call your buddy. You care about your job? Vote for Mike Dukakis.

By "Super Tuesday" Dukakis had put advertisements on the air in cities neglected by his opponents in an attempt to take advantage of "open

148

markets." These included Seattle and Charlotte. This kind of targeting is worth more than entering a market crowded with the advertisements of other candidates.

While "Super Tuesday" presented campaigns with the nightmare of placing advertising in twenty states and several media, the problem was further complicated by the number of media markets within each state and the share of the state market each local area (ADI) represented. For example, Texas is divided into nineteen local markets (ADIs) by the Arbitron rating service to help advertisers place commercials and secure a targeted share of the market. Voters in Dallas differ from voters in McAllen or Odessa. And voters in Dallas who listen to country music on the radio differ from voters who watch *Miami Vice* on television. Furthermore, because of campaign spending limits, presidential campaigns could spend no more than $3.8 million in Texas. Under these circumstances, targeting of campaign messages became a crucial rhetorical task in each campaign.

As new technologies have been developed by the media for covering campaigns, makers of political advertisements have quickly mastered and used them to make candidates appear more attractive than they would in person or if they were appearing on radio or television live. In short, the sophistication of political commercials is directly correlated with the sophistication of the technologies used to create and transmit them.

Presidential campaigns in 1988 proved innovative with new technology. First, many campaigns produced a twenty minute video cassette that was then lent to a supporter or local organizer. The supporter would then invite friends and potential workers or contributors to his or her home to view the presentation over coffee, drinks or dinner. The object was to personalize an impersonal medium. This tactic also took advantage of video cassette recorders available in almost every neighborhood in the country.

The second technique took advantage of satellites. The candidate could be interviewed or give an address in one location and have it transmitted to a satellite and then retransmitted to another location thousands of miles away. The second location could be a cable system hungry to fill empty access channel space, a gathering of supporters in a hotel, or a major fundraising dinner in a facility equipped with a receiving dish. These "uplink" operations were first developed by the Republican Conference of the U.S. Senate in 1980 and can function interactively, allowing viewers to ask the candidate a question. The "uplink" system allows the campaign to patch together its own "network" at very low cost and to adapt its message to very specific audiences.

149

We ought to note, too, that political commercials often entertain as well as inform and persuade. Talking cows that criticized the introduction of outside, conservative money into the Montana Senate race in 1982 are said to have helped reelect John Melcher. Snooping bloodhounds searching for the vacationing incumbent are said to have provided the margin of victory for the challenger in Kentucky's 1984 Senate race. Sometimes a political commercial takes on the patina of informing about the issues, while it is really persuading the viewer to a certain point of view or selling the viewer on the assets of a given candidate. At other times, commercials woo voters by ridiculing the opposition. That may be why so much money is allocated to advertising on television. The National Association of Broadcasters found that in 1986 House races .8 percent or $1.6 million of all campaign funds were spent on billboards, 4.8 percent or $10.2 million on radio, 5.8 percent or $12.3 million on newspaper advertising, and 10.9 percent or $23.1 million on television. In 1986 Senate races, .12 percent or $227,440 was spend on billboard advertising, .51 percent or $968,219 was spent on newspaper advertising, .6 percent or $1.1 million on radio, and 33.09 percent or $62.7 million on television.[36]

Radio and television commercials are clearly among the most potent weapons available to a candidate where freedom of expression abounds, and opportunities for such persuasion have multiplied swiftly.

The resources and ways of using electronic media for political persuasion have grown steadily as the technology has advanced. As television provided a larger and larger audience, campaigners began to use it more often and more effectively. Microwave technology was first developed during World War I, but it was not until the 1930s that television was thought to be a viable commercial medium. In 1946 there were only seven thousand privately owned television sets in America, and there were only ten television stations. However, by 1950, there were four million privately owned television sets, three major networks, and a number of independent stations. The first coast-to-coast televised programming took place in 1952 with Edward R. Murrow's *See It Now*. Walter Cronkite gave the first extensive televised coverage to a presidential campaign in the same year. And it was also in 1952 that the first television commercial for a presidential candidate appeared. Using George Gallup as a consultant, the Eisenhower team wrote, produced, and broadcast "The Man from Abilene," a commercial that touted Eisenhower's patriotic roots and his war record. Clark Gable became the first actor to give a televised presidential endorsement when NBC broadcast an Eisenhower rally late in the 1952 campaign.

By 1960, forty-four million homes had television. The networks covered the national nominating conventions from gavel to gavel, producing the largest audience in history to see and hear acceptance speeches by major party candidates. Presidential debates were telecast for the first time during the 1960 campaign, and the Kennedy forces used computers to divide American voters into more than 450 categories, then placed different commercials selectively to achieve the most impact.

History was made on September 2nd, 1963, when CBS expanded its fifteen-minute evening news program to thirty minutes. By the end of that year, polls indicated that more people received their news from television than from any other source. One suspects that the assassination of President Kennedy and the coverage that followed firmly established television as the place to see the news first.

The 1964 presidential campaign brought a new factor into campaigning. That was the first year in which nationally televised "negative" commercials were aired. Generally, a "negative" advertisement is one that attacks an opponent instead of praising the candidate issuing the commercial. On October 7, 1964, a commercial paid for by Democrats was shown on NBC. The commercial depicted a small girl in a white dress picking the petals off a daisy. Her voice was followed by a male voice that completed a 10–9–8–7–6–5–4–3–2–1 countdown. Then a nuclear explosion was shown. Yet another voice was then heard; it was the voice of Lyndon Johnson asking Americans to be sure they knew who and what they were voting for. The advertisement was aired only twice and was then pulled off the air because of the controversy it created.

The Johnson forces ran two other negative advertisements in the same campaign. One depicted a Social Security card being ripped up and implied that if Goldwater were elected, he would do away with the Social Security system. Another showed the East Coast being sawed off the continent. This was in response to a Goldwater remark that severing the East Coast would improve the country. Negative advertising had arrived and has been used in campaigns ever since.

The problem with negative advertising is knowing how far to go. In 1968, Nixon's advertisement attacking Humphrey ran only once. It counterposed a happy Humphrey addressing the Democratic Convention against the rioting that was going on all around the Convention site. In 1972, Nixon's attacks on the changing positions of George McGovern were more effective. These advertisements cited several position changes while a two-faced picture of McGovern flipped back and forth. The Democrats responded with an advertisement that began with the words "Agnew for Vice President," followed by hilarious laughing. Finally, a voice cut in, saying, "This would be funny if it weren't so serious."

In the 1980 campaign, the National Conservative Political Action

151

Committee (NCPAC) entered a number of races as an "independent voice" on the side of conservative Republicans. They did this by airing negative advertisements that examined the voting records of Democratic incumbents. In some cases these advertisements misrepresented the votes of the Democrats. The advertisements often resulted in sympathy for the Democrats, and in at least South Dakota and Iowa, Republican candidates for the Senate asked NCPAC to get out of the state and the race.

A problem with the NCPAC advertisements and others like them is that they are one of the reasons voters become anesthetized to any advertisements that purport to analyze the voting records of candidates. Polling shows that voters believe the data have been made up or badly distorted and will not change their allegiances on the basis of information contained in negative advertisements unless that information is confirmed by another source. Furthermore, in an age of inundation, voters tend to be attracted to advertisements that get their attention. Accordingly, *campaigners have begun to back away from issue advertising and concentrate on humorous, image-building, and positive commercials.*

Political advertisements are built out of information provided by pollsters and crafted to use most of the means of persuasion available. For example, if poll data reveal that voters do not have a "warm feeling" for a given candidate, media consultants will provide advertising that shows the candidate playing with children, petting dogs, or shaking hands with constituents. If poll data indicate that voters think a candidate is shallow, you can expect a set of advertisements showing the well-coached candidate addressing issues the voters are concerned about. If there are no issues to address, or if they are complex, you are likely to see and hear advertisements that tickle your fancy in an attempt to win your vote.

The emergence of negative televised advertising and the complaints about it illustrate that popular reactions "regulate" political rhetoric without there being any imposed controls. The Johnson forces withdrew their nuclear explosion advertisement because people found it "unfair" and even "vicious." The NCPAC advertising drew attention to its misrepresentations, and some smart candidates got NCPAC out of their campaigns entirely. How-far-you-can-go in a commercial is clearly determined by *the marketplace of ideas.* In politics at least, and in the examples I have reviewed, technological possibilities prove to be self-regulative. The historic American insistence on *moderation* and *fairness* is a sufficient control over excess in campaign communication, whether it be a negative commercial or the use of a computerized phone bank.

Moderation and fairness have long combatted political excess. Por-

152

trayals of Andrew Jackson and Abraham Lincoln as crude, frontier buffoons did not undercut their political futures—and the cases are still remembered and cited as "excesses." That Goldwater was unfairly represented as a nuclear war hawk in 1964 is similarly remembered as an instance of unfairness, and it surely helped Goldwater to earn the bipartisan respect he did not have before he was attacked. And portrayals of Ronald Reagan as ignorant or senile seemed to have little effect on his general popularity as President.

The Founders of the Republic insisted repeatedly that all *authority* in government rests ultimately with "the people." *The Federalist Papers* and James Wilson's sterling defense of the Constitution in the face of Pennsylvanians' charges that an autocracy was being created are among the evidences of this creed. Americans have tried to improve on this principle by removing some of what the Founders' thought of as "indirect representation," and by instituting new safeguards against abuse. The franchise has been widely expanded, first to the non-propertied, then to racial minorities, then to women, then to any citizen eighteen years or older. The system has been made more direct by Progressive reforms, and more accountable by campaign "fair practice" acts and fundraising limitations.

Yet, the system is not without its problems. Some complain that too few eligible voters exercise their rights. Those who do vote face overly complicated ballots and too many elections. Voters, some claim, are confused by distorted information and slick appeals that come to them through the mail, over the phone, and in the form of radio and television advertisements. For these reasons, there is no shortage of regulatory legislation introduced in Congress and in state legislatures every session.

As I have shown, the political marketplace in the United States has regulated itself fairly well. Even nonvoters stabilize the system. Non-voters exercise their freedom by staying away from the polls, and by their action they further stabilize the system. To the extent that they are ignorant of the issues of the candidates, as a good many surveys suggest, their absence from the polls does not skew the results with an uninformed vote. By staying away from the polls, a good many nonvoters are registering their opinions that there is little difference between candidates or that election of any of the candidates will make little difference in the nonvoters' lives or in the country as a whole. It may be that spokespersons for the democratic system should argue that *part* of openness is the right not to vote. Moreover, more effective and more stable democracies are not achieved in countries with very high turnouts of voters. Those who would hope for a turnout of voters constituting, say, 90 percent of

153

those eligible to vote would almost double the number of people who vote. On the basis of experience elsewhere, this would easily lead to creation of at least one more major party. Reformers ought to ponder with care the implications of strong multiparty systems. Neither greater stability nor more responsive legislation seem to be produced by such systems.

As a native Californian, I have sympathy for those who argue that voters have been overburdened by Progressive reforms. That problem could be solved by several simply reforms: (1) end referendums and initiatives, and return those powers to state legislatures;[37] (2) extend the terms of members of the House to four years and the Senate to eight years and have congressional elections only in presidential election years. The first reform could be achieved by the people of those states that now allow referendums and initiatives. The second requires a constitutional amendment that has not yet even cleared the Congress.[38] Even without such reforms, the evidence suggests that voters have survived, even in California, because, in the end, they rarely endorse radical or destabilizing propositions.

Finally, it is clear that voters have a low degree of tolerance for negative advertising, phone banks, and direct-mail solicitation. Statistics from the 1986 races make the point most strongly. In six of the costliest Senate races, the bigger spender used the new technologies most but nonetheless lost. Senator Alan Cranston, the incumbent Democrat, beat Representative Ed Zschau in the most expensive race of 1986, even though Zschau spent more money. Governor Bob Graham of Florida defeated the incumbent Republican, Paula Hawkins, even though she outspent him. In North Carolina, Georgia, and Alabama, the losing Republican incumbents outspent their Democratic opponents by large amounts. Republican Representative Henson Moore lost to Democratic Representative Jim Breaux for the open seat in Louisiana even though Moore massively outspent Breaux. In each of these races, there were, of course, other factors involved, but they do not mitigate the fact that contemporary voters are less influenced by modern technology than many political consultants would have their candidates believe.

Part of the reason for this is that the print and electronic media have done a fairly extensive job of informing the public about new political technology. Since Watergate, stories on political strategy and technology have been the stock in trade of journalism in election years. Thus, the guarantee of freedom of expression once again provides a natural corrective by making sure that even its most potent political weapons are exposed for voters to evaluate.

154

In recent elections, poll data have indicated that the influence of news media have grown while the influence of paid political advertising has dwindled. Political advertisements are declining in persuasive appeal.[39] Apparently because the advertisements are often trite, voters have learned to block them out or treat them as they do commercials for products. Accordingly, despite some cyncism about televised news and printed editorials, the voters turn to the news media to learn about candidates. This has come to mean that if candidates can manipulate the news media, they can then influence voters more effectively than they can through paid commercials. But manipulation may imply distortion, and that fact produces a healthy cynicism on the part of journalists when they cover political persuaders. It is appropriate to turn from political commercials to the relationship between the political persuaders and the news media.

THE CAMPAIGN STAFF AND THE MEDIA

Manipulation of the media is and has been a common political practice. Press secretaries, advance men, and schedulers all work to gain favorable coverage for their employers. These days the process is called "spin control" or "putting the right spin" on a story. This often means involving their candidates in unique events that the media will find interesting enough to cover and then telling the media how to write the story. But the tactic can backfire. Wendell Wilkie spoke from atop manure piles in 1940, and he got wide coverage until a farmer yelled out that Wilkie was standing on his speech. Other famous "news" events have included Eisenhower going home to Abilene, Stevenson displaying a hole in his shoe, John Kennedy sailing off Hyannis, Gerald Ford hitting spectators with golf balls, Jimmy Carter fighting off a swimming rabbit, and Ronald Reagan chopping wood. Such events, as well as news conferences, debates and speeches, are standard fare. After each of the 1988 primary and campaign debates, for example, staffs of the various candidates flooded the press with favorable impressions of how their candidate performed.

At the 1988 Republican Convention, the Bush campaign asked me and three others to write talking points for surrogates who were to appear on television news programs or before delegate caucuses. At 1 AM, each morning we were given the "line of the day" or theme that was to guide our writing for the next session. On a rotating basis, one of the four writers was assigned the task of staying up late and writing a "generic" speech. For example, the "line of the day" for Monday, August 15, 1988

155

was "Ronald Reagan and George Bush inherited an economy in decline and a weak nation losing its stature in the world. They took bold action to make America great again." The "line" for Thursday, August 18 was "George Bush has the strength and the stability, the values and the vision, to lead America into the 1990s as we prepare for the challenges and opportunities of the 21st century." Specific talking points on the deficit, taxes, family values, foreign policy and a host of other issues were spun around this theme by the rest of us for specific surrogates. This unified effort to drive home one major point every day of the convention worked remarkably well with the exception of Wednesday when Dan Quayle was selected as the Vice Presidential nominee. Each night monitors reported that the major networks, CNN, and most newspapers had picked up the "line of the day" and used it in reports. Ed Bradley of CBS even held up one of the "line of the day" sheets and read it to viewers to make the point that the convention was heavily scripted. The Bush campaign was delighted, believing that viewers would remember the message on the sheet, but not Bradley's criticism.

The strategy of *bad-mouthing your chances* is a little more sophisticated. The object here is to lower the press's expectations so far that if the candidate does at all well, the results will be declared newsworthy and the candidate's message will receive greater currency.

This strategy catapulted George McGovern into the lead in the presidential primary campaign in 1972. In New Hampshire, McGovern was rightfully pictured as an underdog. His opponent, Senator Edmund Muskie, had a big lead in the polls, and he was well known since he came from the neighboring state of Maine. McGovern's staff saw this as an opportunity to play on their candidate's very poor showing in national polls so that any *gain* in New Hampshire would appear to be a dramatic victory.[40] An intensive effort was made to run up the vote for McGovern. McGovern spent more than $200,000 and had the aid of an army of student volunteers. In the final days of the primary, Senator Muskie, the front runner, was forced to tears, some claim, by the Manchester *Union Leader's* attacks on his wife. Weakness was presumably conveyed to the electorate of New Hampshire by news coverage of his weeping. With this fortuitous help, McGovern got 38 percent of the vote to Muskie's 47 percent, which seems unimpressive; but the news media hailed the vote as a moral victory for McGovern. The strategy of bad mouthing had worked perfectly—with some unexpected help.

After placing sixth with 6 percent of the vote in Florida, and fourth with 1 percent in Illinois, McGovern won first place in the Wisconsin primary with only 30 percent of the vote. McGovern carefully picked the primaries where he would risk time and effort, and the press continued to forgive his losses and to praise his wins. McGovern's staff claimed there was only enough time and energy for the crucial primaries. The staff called losses ahead of time and trumpeted victories after the fact. The news media followed suit.

In 1976 White House spokespersons for President Ford were instructed to bad mouth Ford's chances of beating Ronald Reagan in the New Hampshire primary. They knew that presidents who had narrowly won that primary had been portrayed as losers by the news media and eliminated from the campaign. But Ronald Reagan was too clever for them. He began bad-mouthing his prospects too. The press releases coming from each camp implied that neither candidate was going to win the New Hampshire primary. Then Reagan's campaign manager for New Hampshire, a former governor of the state, predicted a Reagan victory. The media pounced on the statement. On election night Ford won an extremely close race, which normally would have severely damaged the chances of an incumbent president. But because Reagan's surrogate had predicted victory, his narrow loss was pictured in the press as a devastating defeat.

In the 1984 primaries, the same strategy was used by a desperate Walter Mondale on what came to be known as "Super Tuesday." Mondale had been upset by Senator Hart in New Hampshire and Maine. Momentum had shifted to Hart both in terms of voters' sentiment and speculation by the press. On "Super Tuesday" there would be nine primaries; Hart was expected to knock Mondale out of the race. Mondale's strategists quickly decided to bad-mouth their chances. In light of Hart's momentum, any victory would be astonishing, they claimed. On primary night, Hart scored a massive victory by almost any objective measure. He won seven of the nine primaries and demonstrated national appeal by winning in Massachusetts, Florida, and several western states. Mondale won in Alabama, and barely survived in Georgia where he was heavily favored because of Jimmy Carter's endorsement. Despite these results, most news media portrayed "Super Tuesday" as a draw; some even suggested it was the start of a Mondale comeback.

In 1988 the tactic was again evident. With the help of the news media's inaccurate tracking polls, George Bush was able to lower expectations so far in the New Hampshire primary that most pundits thought he was going to lose. When he won by eight percentage points, the press portrayed the victory as a substantial turnaround. The week before, Bob Dole had easily won the Iowa caucuses and all polls predicted the victory. But you would not know it from his comments leading up to election.

157

Said Dole, a few days before the event, "It's an uphill battle, but we're going to do the best we can." Dole's Iowa state chairman, Senator Grassley, echoed the candidate, "It's always been an uphill battle."[41]

Effects of bad-mouthing can be enhanced if a press secretary can reveal poll data that lower the expectations of the press. Momentum can be enhanced if poll data reveal a trend of gains by a candidate. Suppression of poll data that show a big lead can prevent campaign workers from becoming complacent. On the other hand, the same data can be shown to contributors and major fund raisers to "prove" that the candidate is going to win. (Donors love to be on the winning side; often they see their contributions as bets.) For all these reasons, bad-mouthing is generally saved for the news media and the volunteers, while its counterpart, "hyping" or exaggerating, is used to solicit contributions. Regardless of what you call it, the process is rhetorical, and one that the public ought to understand.

But why does it work if the media are as cynical, dogged, and immersed in campaign strategy as are the campaign managers? I will explore this question in depth in the next chapter, but for now, let me point out that the need to file copy or to get a story on the air means that reporters are predisposed to unique stories, and these are easily managed. If a candidate is set up to do something unique, the "unique" gets covered and gains free space. If the press—always committed to prodding political people to talk during campaigns—can be convinced that even a candidate's *supporters* take a dim view of his or her chances, the press will treat any decent showing as an "unusual" achievement. If they had a more sophisticated view of what "news" is, they wouldn't so treat it, but neither would they be able to please editors and producers who seek easily understood, short stories. It's the word "story" that is important. Unless an event has dramatic and narrative elements, it is not appealing to editors and producers. Ironically, this rather simpleminded definition of "news" makes manipulation of journalists possible despite their fears of being manipulated.

There are other routine manipulations that go on all the time. For example, the *timing* of party, committee, and other kinds of press releases is quite normally scheduled to fit or miss reporters' deadlines. "Bad news" for the campaign, such as high unemployment or inflation rates, is frequently released at times when other news is occupying reporters' attention or at the end of a week when part of the media's audience is about to leave on vacation.

The old-as-the-hills ploy of inserting catchy phrases and striking images into releases often gets more attention for a story than it deserves.

The equivalent in a speech or press conference is what reporters call a "sound bite." It is a quick moment or phrase or clause that catches attention and provides a moment of interesting coverage. Not infrequently, reports of an extended presentation focus on a "catch line" or a "blooper" at the expense of a full account.

Once more, reporters' and editors' eagerness for the unusual makes them susceptible to this kind of manipulation and it also leads them frequently to distort the realities of political persuasion. Therefore, political persuaders work hard to create labels and catch phrases that can give quick, persuasive characterizations to their enterprises. The "New Deal" was followed by a series of "Deal" slogans until it was hard to think of any more possibilities along that line. Hence, we have recently had "Crusades," until that term became overworked. "The New Frontier" seems to have worked better for John Kennedy than "A New Beginning" did for Ronald Reagan.[42] In any case, the entire business of sloganeering is an attempt both to manipulate the media into propagandizing for a party and rallying one's own troops in a campaign. Creating slogans takes advantage of the "folkways" of news gathering and dissemination of news.

Reporters choose to cover what they cover. They are second-guessed by assignment chiefs, editors, and publishers. They are rewarded both inside their organizations and by their industry for producing interesting stories and getting them right. When they uncover spectacular stories with national implications, such as the Watergate affair, reporters' rewards can be truly impressive. When journalists err or fail to find "news" of interest, they are punished in salary, in advancement, and they lose credibility. Beyond this, journalistic organizations are subject to libel laws, public ridicule, inter- and intra-industry criticism, and peer pressures. These are checks that balance the constitutional guarantee of freedom to write and speak. The checks place serious responsibilities on journalists, and at the same time they put limits on manipulation of the media in American political persuasion.

CONCLUSION

Several trends can be seen in political persuasion in this country. First and foremost, party loyalty has been eroding. At present either major party can count on about 40 percent of the vote and must compete against others for a majority of the middle 20 percent. As I have emphasized, adapting to this situation requires parties and candidates to moderate partisan appeals and move toward the middle of the political

159

spectrum. This necessity in turn tends to moderate proposals and platforms and increases the stability of the political system.

The tools persuaders have developed to measure and appeal to the views of the political middle are more sophisticated with each election. These tools are necessary because the overburdened voter is hard to reach, let alone convert to one political position over another. On the other hand, if the tools become too obvious, bothersome, or are otherwise abused, voters recoil, proving once again that the open marketplace of ideas contains its own correctives.

It is also clear than when confronted with a choice between pragmatic persuasion and moralistic persuasion, voters judge moralistic candidates more critically. If a morality-mongering candidate ever compromises one of his or her moral positions to gain votes, that candidate will be accused of being either wishy-washy or hypocritical. Since they commit themselves to no all-encompassing positions beyond solving individual problems, the pragmatists open themselves only minimally to such moral evaluations. Ronald Reagan may provide a compromised exception to this rule, for certainly his rhetoric is shot full of moral phrasing. However, his status as an exception is mitigated in two ways. While his rhetorical tone is at times moral, his action, particularly his legislative record, tends to be pragmatic. Second, when Reagan's action has been perceived to be in conflict with his moral tone, as in the case of the trading of arms for hostages or his administration's dealing with General Noriega, his popularity has fallen. Thus, Reagan may be less an exception to this principle than some would think.

Despite their specific differences, recent presidential campaigns have had significant similarities. The general themes and strategies I have examined in this chapter were as important in the 1950's as they were in the 1980s, and with minor modification could be applied to the elections dating back to 1832. The single most important factor remains the candidate's ability to sell him or herself to the voters. And the single most effective way to do that is through campaign rhetoric—the rhetoric of change, when the center wants it (as in 1932), and the rhetoric of stability, when the center wants it (as in 1972 and 1984).

But above all, we need to realize that political parties function in America to moderate the process of reform. Only rarely, and only when parties have ceased to represent their constituencies, have they been cast aside for new parties. The Democratic party stands as an effective model of institutional adaptation. Through most of our history it has enveloped those dissidents who would form separate movements. Each party has performed as the loyal opposition; both parties also breed leaders for the future. Through primaries and conventions, they provide a framework for selecting candidates. They are the institutional guardians of the political arena. It is within that arena that the weapons of political persuasion have to be arrayed and used.

I have surveyed what is going on in national political persuasion in the latter part of the twentieth century. Three things stand out specially:

(1) Modern political persuasion in the United States entails very complex, highly organized, and sociologically and psychologically sophisticated processes that even well informed citizens understand only vaguely.

(2) The erosion of blind party loyalty and the stability of the two-party system have rendered modern political persuasion more, not less, centrist.

(3) Most attempts to elevate such values as "equality" or "opportunity," "financial equality," "truth," and "ethics" to positions above the traditional value of freedom of expression have in fact *restricted* political freedoms; on the other hand, where freedom of expression has been preserved it has usually brought with it its own self-corrective mechanisms.

Viewed over time, modern, national, political persuasion in the United States has not been seriously divisive; it has contributed to, rather than endangered, both freedom and stability. If there is danger to democratic values, it comes from usually well-intentioned attempts to "purify" the idiosyncracies that the First Amendment promises to protect for *all*.

NOTES

1. Theodore H. White, *The Making of the President 1964,* (New York: The New American Library, 1966), 409.

2. George McGovern, Campaign Speech, Nov. 2, 1972.

3. Nationally television speech, Nov. 5, 1972.

4. Campaign speech, Nov. 5, 1972. McGovern's charge that Nixon had contrived the illusion of peace was neatly answered by Agnew who pointed out that Hanoi had first revealed the peace package.

5. Campaign speech on "Economic Issues," Oct. 19, 1972.

6. "Economic Issues."

7. George McGovern, text of acceptance of Democratic Nomination, delivered July 14, 1972.

8. "Economic Issues."

9. Acceptance Speech.

10. "Integrity in Government," aired Oct. 25, 1972.

11. "Vietnam Negotiations," aired Nov. 3, 1972.

12. "Integrity in Government."

13. Richard Nixon, Aired Oct. 28, 1972.

14. "Philosophy of Government," aired Oct. 21, 1972.

15. For example, Nixon received 47 percent of the vote in cities 10,000 to 50,000 in population in 1968. His percentage in 1972 was 61.

16. For some specific observations on these considerations inside and outside of the campaign environment, see Judith S. Trent and Robert V. Friedenburg, *Political Campaign Communication: Principles and Practices* (New York: Praeger, 1983), 84–118.

17. Wallace admitted to me that this was his version of Huey Long's attack on the Republicans and Democrats in 1934 and 35. Long said that one party stood for "highpopulorum" and the other stood for "lopopuhighum. I told Wallace that at least he had changed the phrasing. Long had stolen the "everyman a king" phrase from William Jennings Bryan, who had visited Winn Parrish, Louisiana, Long's home area, in 1908.

18. Almost one-half of those voting for Hubert Humphrey in the primary, voted for Nixon in the general election. "Humphrey Backers in State Switch to Nixon, Poll Shows," *Los Angeles Times* (Dec. 22, 1972), 3. In the nation the trend was similar: George Gallup found that "one-third of Democratic voters went for President Nixon. . . ." "Poll Finds 33% of Democrats Chose Nixon," *Los Angeles Times* (Dec. 18, 1972), 5.

19. The Eagleton affair reinforces my thesis that McGovern was caught between doing what he thought was correct and doing v t he thought would get votes. Originally, he was committed to standing by Eagleton but then he shifted when party regulars advised it. See also Milton Viorst, "Did Tom Eagleton Do Anything Wrong?" *Esquire* (Feb., 1973), 144.

20. Kevin Phillips, "How Nixon Will Win," *The New York Times Magazine* (Aug. 6, 1972), 36.

21. By August 1972, Harris reported that Nixon's popularity had risen to 59%, up from 47% in November, 1970. But more important, Nixon was also up in the ratings related to specific problems. Louis Harris, "Nixon Rating from Public is Near Peak," *Miami Herald* (Aug. 21, 1972), 32.

22. Many of the public relations people who arranged Nixon's 1972 convention were in Dallas in 1984 to script Reagan's. Both Nixon and Reagan had speechwriter Ken Khachigian, though Khachigian was far more influential in 1984 than he had been in 1972 when he served under Patrick Buchanan.

23. Clark MacGregor, "Press Release," Oct. 9, 1972.

24. Richard Kleindienst, "Press Release," Oct. 28, 1972.

25. Spiro Agnew, Campaign speech, Aug. 25, 1972.

26. Campaign speech, Oct. 24, 1972.

27. Campaign speech, Oct. 18, 1972.

28. It is estimated that Proposition 13 cut property tax revenues by $228 billion over the last decade. See Jay Mathews, "California Transformed by 'Prop 13,'" *Washington Post* (May 23, 1988), p. A1.

29. The sample ballot for November 4, 1986 contained pages of candidates for different offices including governor, lieutenant governor, secretary of state, controller, treasurer, attorney general, state board of equalization, U.S. Senator, U.S. Representative, state senator, state assembly, college district trustees, school district members, and country tax collector. It then called for votes on retention

of eight judges and thirteen ballot propositions on the *state* level. (Counties could add their own.)

30. Andrew Kohut, president of the Gallup organization, explained it this way: "Consider the American public a large bowl of soup. You only need one spoon full to get an accurate taste." Kohut was badly embarrassed by the results of the New Hampshire primary of 1988. Gallup predicted a Dole victory of nine percentage points. When the final votes were in, Bush had won by eight percentage points.

31. Carter's tracking polls were remarkably close to Gallup's until the last week of the campaign.

32. Kenneth Burke says, "[T]he commercial rhetorician looks not merely for persuasive devices in general, but for the topics that will appeal to the particular 'income group' most likely to be interested in his product. . . ." in *A Grammar of Motives and a Rhetoric of Motives* (Cleveland: Meridian, 1962), 588.

33. PACs contributed $640,000; 17,000 individuals gave $1,000 a piece; 3,000 individuals gave between $500 and $1000 a piece.

34. "Penny-Savers" and suburban newspapers are multiplying, however, and have begun to take political advertising from major newspapers.

35. In Tampa, in 1986, a 30-second advertisement on "The Cosby Show," the nation's most viewed program, cost $6,500 and was viewed by 383,000 women and 262,000 men, according to ratings. A 30-second ad on "St. Elsewhere," a prime time show viewed by a smaller, better educated audience, cost only $1,750. A commercial on "Wheel of Fortune," a game show drawing blue collar families, cost $2,000.

36. These figures only reflect what was spent on placing the commercials in the media; they do not include the cost of production for the commercials. See "Chasing the Political Ad Dollar on TV," *Channels* (Feb., 1988), 92.

37. This step would restore some measure of order to a system that verges on the chaotic. As I stated in the introduction, balancing freedom and order is no easy task.

38. One reason is that Senators who plan to seek reelection do not want members of the House "to get a free ride" in the even years when they would not be up for election. Should a Senator's term end at such a point, the new rules would make it easier for a sitting member of Congress to challenge him or her. Senator Kassebaum of Kansas has sought to overcome this situation by proposing that when House terms are extended to four years, Senate terms be extended to eight and both be up for reelection only in presidential election years. Under the Kassebaum plan the entire House and half the Senate would be up for election in every presidential election year. Thus, to challenge a Senator, a member of the House would have to resign his or her seat.

39. "The evidence from the past several elections . . . indicates that paid media generally count for comparatively little in determining the turning points or the outcome of any given presidential campaign. . . . [In 1980] Bush did best where he advertised the least." The same is true for Robert Kennedy in 1968. *The American Elections of 1980,* Austin Ranney, editor (Washington, D.C.: American Enterprise Institute, 1981), 179–82.

40. Based on interviews with John Holum, aide to Senator McGovern, Robert Schrum, speech writer for Muskie and then McGovern, and Rose Economu,

163

advance-person for Muskie in New Hampshire. The interviews were conducted at the Democratic National Convention in 1972.

41. "Dole Shoring Up Support," *Washington Post* (Jan. 31, 1988) p. A14.

42. In fact, the media phrase, "The Reagan Revolution" was taken up by his staff during the first terms as the new slogan.

6

INADVERTENT AND
DISGUISED PERSUASION

To a considerable degree, modern politics is what the media of mass communication portray as the political actions of political figures and institutions. This means that the "news of the day" is the major means of persuading politically. According to numerous opinion polls, the primary source of news for a majority of Americans is televised news;[1] therefore, we will not understand modern political persuasion without understanding the explicit and implicit persuasive features of political news when telecast. Political figures and organizations understand this, and they spend most thought and money on generating and managing filmic and televised information.

Prior to the 1930s, understanding mass political persuasion required study of information spread primarily by speaking personally to audiences and by means of the printed media. That is not an adequate way to understand contemporary political persuasion. Audiovisual media persuade in numerous ways that we are prone to overlook. Because contemporary persuaders concentrate on influencing public opinion chiefly through news making and news production, I shall focus this chapter on audiovisual news.

A first fact about political and other information gained from television is that a great many persuasive influences are embedded in and are sometimes implanted in televised and filmic communication. These I am calling sources of "disguised" or "inadvertent" persuasion, and in the present chapter I propose to enumerate, explain, and illustrate the most prominent.

We must first notice the obvious fact that television and film are *visual* as well as auditory media. They *narrate;* they do not "argue" directly as we do with words; they show people doing and things, events being done *through time.* Because the television and motion pictures are *stories,* there exists in these media some persuasiveness that is simply inevitable in this form of presenting. For example, these media communicate with pictures, and without thinking about it, we usually take what we see pictured as more "real" and "true" than what we are told with words alone. Imagine the difference between having *seen* the Kennedy assassination coverage or the space shuttle explosion and having simply read about those events. In short, audiovisual communication persuades by seeming to present "reality."

There are many points at which persuasive elements can be implanted in audiovisual media. In this chapter, I concentrate on televised news, but everything from movies for television to documentaries on PBS can be used to persuade. For example, the television movie *An Early Frost* softened attitudes toward AIDS victims by sympathetically portraying their plight. The PBS documentary series *The World of Nature* inadvertently reinforces the concerns of environmentalists.

The central fact is that filmic and televised information comes to us as *narration*. "What's the Watergate story?" "What's the Iran scandal story?" "Who are the major characters?" "Who knew what, when?" These are common journalistic questions, and journalists write or produce *stories* as answers to them. We may or may not perceive the subtle persuasive qualities of those accounts, but our environment of public information *is* an environment of stories narrated in print, on screen, and on radios.

The boon that such an environment yields is that freely developed and used technologies help us get more information to more people in a short time. Naturally enough, in totalitarian societies the technologies for disseminating information are carefully controlled, but with exceptions such as I have discussed, the technologies of communication have evolved freely and their use has been minimally regulated in American society.

The subtle "powers" of the various media of communication have frightened some Americans, including the Congress. Persuasion is said to be "hidden" and therefore subversive. This is a reason I choose here to explore directly the kinds of "disguised" persuasion in modern media. Once "disguised" and inadvertent persuasion is understood, there will be less reason to fear the "powers" of media because citizens will be better equipped to understand and respond to the environment of stories in which we live. There is, I shall suggest, less reason to fear the persuasive forces of media than the popular term "hidden persuaders" has implied to a generation of Americans.

HOW THE DISGUISE WORKS

Technologies—whether of printing, broadcasting, filming, or other—always result in some disguising, masking, and/or distorting of realities

166

because every technology provides users with obvious and also with largely hidden resources and constraints on what can be communicated. The full suggestiveness of sound and color cannot be conveyed in print, and one cannot easily present *pictures* of abstractions. Such facts make possible both intentional and unintentional "manipulation" of information. "Manipulation" does not always imply deception. Each medium of communication *inevitably* and uniquely "manipulates" content and meaning. If "a picture is worth a 1,000 words," it is because (1) we respond with special sensitivity to visual re-presentations of phenomena of the world, and (2) we are not as ready to believe a camera can be mistaken as we are to believe that words (less vivid than pictures) can misrepresent the "facts" of the world. On the other hand, some concepts such as *justice* or *freedom* simply cannot be pictured as readily as they can be talked about, and some concepts such as *child* or *office building* will be more clearly and specifically communicated through pictures and drawings than through words.

One reason we are often unaware of persuasive influences is that we conceive of "persuasion" too narrowly. We think of "persuasion" as transparent, obvious action, as when a politician appeals for votes or someone advertises products or services. In these cases, we usually know the goal of the creators is to "persuade." To assure that consumers recognize the creators' purposes, our society has even adopted regulations that equate non-obvious advertising with being "deceptive, misleading, or false." But here, again, is the too-simple notion that everything that "persuades" can and ought to be recognized as deliberately intended to persuade. Such recognition-of-purpose is not always easily achieved. To be told something we already know tends to persuade us to believe it more firmly. Also, all communication is persuasive in the sense that its content, organization, and manner of presentation were *selected*. Every communicator chooses among options for the effect he or she believes the choices will have. In this section I focus on the influences of communication that *show* ongoing events visually.

Movies and the news media have long played an important role in providing entertainment with informative content. Using entertainment as a vehicle, filmmakers have played on values in efforts to change the ways we think and behave or to reinforce attitudes already in place. The special power of disguised persuasion lies in the capacity of the medium and of structural patterns to lend authority to arguments and claims without doing so argumentatively. Many films, novels, and even poems have hidden messages. For example, a narrative can present both sides of an issue but portray the representatives of one side with greater sympathy and appeal. This is not a new phenomenon, of course, Fables, Greek dramas, epic poems such as *Paradise Lost,* and the political novels that became popular, especially in England, in the nineteenth century all had the dual qualities of entertaining and persuading. In the twentieth century, films and televised narratives, "docu-dramas," documentaries, and even audiovisual reportage have exploited their technologies' opportunities to persuade without arguing directly.

The silent film *City Lights* is by today's standards a less than subtle attempt by Charles Chaplin to advance his views on social policy. At the beginning of the film, Chaplin disrupts a ceremony at which a statue is to be unveiled. In the course of dismounting the statue, Chaplin insults the establishment by sitting on the face of the sculpture and engaging in off-color activity with its sword. Later in the movie, homosexual themes are developed: Chaplin sleeps with his male host, who when drunk kisses Chaplin on the face, but when sober throws Chaplin out of bed. Later, because Chaplin is behaving effeminately in a men's locker room, a boxer refuses to disrobe as long as Chaplin is watching. Still later, one character changes from a man into a woman. All the while, Chaplin puts down the pomposity and hypocrisy of the wealthy while he defends a poor waif who sells flowers. Contemporary films try to be more subtle.

In the movie *Missing,* for example, an American citizen turns to the American ambassador in Chile for help in locating his son amid the chaos of the 1973 revolution that overthrew the Marxist regime of Salvador Allende. By the end of the film it has been clearly implied that American authorities were partially responsible for the young man's murder, and the grieving father has come a long way toward accepting his son's habit of questioning American governmental policy.

Sometimes the news media, under the guise of informing, present both sides of a story with a selective bias toward one. "Sixty Minutes," the most highly rated weekly news series in history, often faces lawsuits for alleged bias due to editorial slants that surface in the show's segments.

In these and many other cases, we are prone to think that if we see an entire series of events laid out before us, we can suspend critical judgments about selectivity because we have what we take to be "objective" rhetorical account with artistic merit. Furthermore, we grant art the privilege of subjective interpretation, but in the presence of a narrative we often forget that *interpretation* is always *persuasive* if we attend to it. *Paradise Lost,* the epic poem by John Milton, is a famous case in point. It is a great artistic work, but many who read it forget that its art was intended to enhance a certain theological point of view. The same thing happens with contemporary audiences at the movies or in their living rooms as they watch television programs and video cassettes. Persuasion, we naïvely believe, does not occur in sublime presentation.

168

Because I want to focus on relatively new media of communication, I will begin by examining how one case of filmic narrative influenced American values. In dealing with filmic narration, however, I will focus on television because the audiovisual media of mass communication now draw most of the controversialists' attention and money when they plan public persuasion.

FILMIC NARRATION

Through films, television, and cassettes the persuasive powers of dramatic narration are enhanced because they are pictorial narratives that have become parts of almost everyone's experience, and so can persuade enormously large and varied audiences. We have an instance of sophisticated persuasion in the landmark 1967 film *Bonnie and Clyde*. It is a fictionalized account of the activities of Bonnie Parker and Clyde Barrow, who robbed and murdered people throughout the Midwest in the 1930s and who were finally killed by a hail of bullets in a police ambush. In raw fact, the pair were undoubted murderers and robbers. They were not in reality either physically or personally attractive. Their exploits were erratic and their purposes were to all appearances motivated by antisocial feelings and by greed. Understood in this way, the saga of Bonnie and Clyde does not make an appealing "story." The creators of the film knew this; they *created* a script *based on selected facts* about Bonnie and Clyde but with extensive material and interpretations not supplied by the pair's history.

The film begins by defining the leading characters in such a way that we can identify with them. This technique is used in most successful films and dramas because if an audience cannot identify with a least one character, they are unlikely to be entertained, let alone persuaded. Men who watch *Gone with the Wind,* for example, tend to identify with Rhett Butler, and are then drawn into the film. Women tend to identify with Scarlet O'Hara, and then come to think of themselves as part of the plot. Secondary characters can be portrayed to reinforce central identifications, or to attract members of the audience who failed to identify with the leading characters. Thus, Ashley Wilkes and Cousin Melanie serve to bring into the story subsets of the audiences for *Gone with the Wind.*

Bonnie and Clyde develops five characters with whom an audience might identify. Clyde Barrow, the shy, daring, and handsome hero, has doubts about his masculinity, but none about how he wants to run his life. Warren Beatty plays this character so convincingly that he was nominated for an Academy Award. Buck Barrow, Clyde's older brother, who enthusiastically joins the robbery spree, is played by Gene Hackman, who was nominated for an Oscar for his role. The role of C. W. Moss, a young gas station attendant who revolts against the authority of his dominating father and joins the Barrow gang, is played by Michael Pollard, who also garnered an Oscar nomination. He portrays the gang's sidekick and jester. These three characters represent three major male psyches: hardly a male in the audience could not find a character with whom to identify at least partially.

Bonnie Parker is portrayed as a bright and sensually beautiful, small-town girl aching for an exciting life. In this role Faye Dunaway became a star and nearly won the Academy Award for Best Actress. Buck's wife is the one character who voices fear of and dissatisfaction with the gang's marauding. Her constant worry makes her character a foil to Bonnie's impetuosity and a measure of the real nature of the gang's activities. Estelle Parsons won the Academy Award for this supporting role. Thus, women have two major but different characters with whom to identify.

Through these identifications, the film advances three arguments. Bonnie and Clyde represent "life force." The risk-taking, the hand-to-mouth existence, and the killing are depicted as vigorous and vital, and therefore "alive." It is not new to use the tension of daring death through the way one lives to further identification. John Donne used it in poems and sermons. In chapter 2, I pointed to it in a sermon by Jonathan Edwards. In those cases, the speaker or writer worked with *words* to elicit a response that would cause the listeners or readers to imagine pictures and feelings. Film is more powerful because the picture is literally placed in front of the auditor. The eye must be closed to block the image rather than closed to imagine it.

Bonnie and Clyde argues that to live truly is to become "someone." Bonnie and Clyde are portrayed as individuals who, through their acts, escape humdrum lives and really live. Finally, those killed by Bonnie and Clyde do not "live properly," as defined within the film. To that extent, they deserve death. For the hero and heroine, others simply do not exist as people and eventually they cease to exist as "real" people for the audience. They become objects. By these processes, Bonnie and Clyde are portrayed as scarcely more guilty of murder than a man who swats a fly.

Through this set of very indirect arguments, the film makes its double appeal to values. The first major theme is that it is better to be a vital person than to be nonexistent, no matter how vitality is achieved. The filmmaker intentionally supports this theme by portraying the "non-living" beings as unsympathetic characters: bank tellers are bland and law enforcement officials are ridiculous. These individuals do not have

170

any sense of the vital life force, so they can plausibly be sacrificed to those who pursue it.

Furthermore, persons who come into intimate contact with the Barrow gang are transformed into "living" beings. C. W. Moss, bored with his nonexistence, experiences a giddy sense of freedom as the gang's getaway driver. "Living" is better than "existing." When Moss betrays the gang near the end, he is returned to his meaninglessness.

The second major theme of *Bonnie and Clyde* is that love comes only to the "living." Clyde overcomes his initial impotence and Bonnie, formerly a whore, argues for family life and writes poetry. Buck's wife, forced to choose between her religious past and the man she has married, finds a vibrant love for him for the first time. Thus, the characters in *Bonnie and Clyde* create meaning in an absurd world. They advance major thematic material.

USING CINEMATOGRAPHY TO REINFORCE ARGUMENT

The life-force appeal of *Bonnie and Clyde* is strengthened by film-makers' techniques. That the gang members are vitally alive is undeniable after we see the tenacity with which they cling to life until the final scene. Buck dies a long, cruel death. His wife, never killed, is blinded literally as well as figuratively when taken from the gang. Bonnie and Clyde escape several times and are killed only after they are betrayed by Moss, who represents a once vital force now slipped back into nonexistence under the thumb of his father. These events move themes forward within the plot structure, perhaps unintentionally. But other techniques are clearly intentional.

The slow-motion filming of the final scene is not a sadistic flourish but a reinforcement of the life-force argument. The longer it takes to kill Bonnie and Clyde, the more likely we are to see the power of the life force in them. "Cops" fall like duckpins in the movie, but the characters with whom we are taught to identify are very difficult to kill.

The movie also suggests subtle parallels between how Bonnie and Clyde lived and how audiences live their lives. Viewers are moved to rethink their own values, at least partially, if they identify with Bonnie's attempts at poetry, her dreams of settling down, and her sense of commitment to Clyde. They can warm to Clyde's boyish charm and empathize with his romantic shortcomings. Bonnie and Clyde, despite their crimes, emerge as warm and loving personalities tragically doomed in a harsh world that refuses to condone their way out of the mundane. Audiences doubtless saw at least parts of themselves on the screen, where

171

Bonnie and Clyde lead lives more exciting and vibrant than their own realities.

At first blush, portraying life-death tensions, with death ultimately the outcome, can seem an improvident strategy in persuasion, but it is neither new nor demonstrably unsuccessful. The life that appeals even though it leads to violent death has been portrayed repeatedly as preferable to pursuing *safety*. George Bernard Shaw's *Joan of Arc* is one parallel case. Joan is nobler martyred than she ever could be had she escaped execution. In life and in death she represents the "spiritual force" that Shaw, though an atheist, believed in and invited his audiences to admire. The crucial persuasive question in such dramatic representations is whether or not the message is constructed so that audiences can believe in, identify with, and at least temporarily approve the *principle* that governs the life that leads to death. In *Bonnie and Clyde,* audiences are invited to believe that aspiring to be "someone" rather than "nobody" is admirable. Whoever accepts that proposition can put the characters' bloody acts at the periphery of perception and their determined pursuit of "life" or "spirit" at the center. Living is set against existing, and the extent to which we accept the persuasion is determined by our—at least temporary—adherence to the notion that "living" is in all ways preferable. The belief becomes still more inviting if, as in this film, an oppressive, insensitive world is portrayed as to blame for the characters' inability to find a better way to "be someone."

Bonnie and Clyde was a huge box office success in 1967. It was particularly popular with college audiences. To what extent the film reinforced the "new freedom" that swept campuses in the late 1960s and early 1970s is impossible to determine. Whether its creators had such a purpose in mind is unclear. Yet, given the cleverness of its appeals, one may speculate that the movie contributed to a social climate in which risk taking, freedom seeking, and individualism were heartily endorsed.

Motion pictures of all sorts provide role models, value structures, and guidance for audiences. As techniques have matured, persuasion through film seems to have become more powerful. *Becket* calls us to a spiritual life beyond the world of politics. *Who's Afraid of Virginia Woolf* questions whether one should make life endurable by filling it with constructed fictions and cruel games. The *Star Wars* trilogy argues that deep contemplation can lead one's soul to the moral force of the universe. And once possessed of this force, even magical powers are possible. *Star Wars* also makes advanced weaponry spectacularly attractive to some and while doing so, may reinforce political calls for space exploration or Reagan's Strategic Defense Initiative, dubbed "Star Wars" by the media. *Gandhi* blatantly rewrites the life of the prophet to attack imperialism and endorse passive resistance.

Filmic narration is a potent force in the marketplace of ideas because narrative presentation always *implies* that it tells *all that is important* about the story, although it is always and necessarily selective. This is a major reason we overlook narratives' persuasive force. We think, until we correct ourselves, that a "story" is a full "account." *Bonnie and Clyde* illustrates a filmic redoing of history by converting reality into narrative form. For the film to be appealing and allow identification it needs to have villains and heroes, valleys and climaxes—whether the actual lives had them or not. Documentaries similarly imply that what they present is really the full and accurate "report" without redoing history. Nonetheless, if documentation through narration is to succeed, there must be some drama in it. Walt Disney's documentaries about coyotes, bobcats, and other animals attracted large audiences because the "story" of the animal was highly personified and dramatized. Yet history and lives are often less than dramatic in fact, hence artists rewrite the facts in order to succeed.

In short, quite aside from what one can do persuasively with camera shots, slow motion, etc., narrational dramatization persuades because it appears to give a *coherent* accounting.[2] This account is supported by filmic imagery—whether of dramas or the lives of beasts—because we believe what we see. Thus, some of the persuasiveness is inevitable because a narrative implies that it is complete, and a pictorialized account implies that it shows everything important. These facts about the narrative media of communication also open opportunities (that we overlook) for the makers of films to insert deliberately persuasive devices and selections. In *Bonnie and Clyde,* these persuasive elements included a full blown argument on how one should lead one's life, supported by a whole series of substrategies. The same can be done in whole or in part in any report presented in narrative form.

THE EVENING NEWS

Filmic narration provides remarkable examples of disguised persuasion, but the influence of films is limited to those who choose to see a particular film. The average American watched about 30 hours of television a week in 1986, according to the Nielsen rating service. Each network news program reaches about ten million households a night, spend $300 million a year on news operations, and employs over 1,000 persons in its news division. Televised news, then, is an enormous enterprise with probably the greatest influence of all mass media on political perceptions in our society. In the paragraphs to follow, I concentrate on the evening news broadcasts by CBS, NBC, and ABC because I have direct knowledge of these three. I emphasize, however, that almost everything I say about networks' nightly newscasting is also true of televised news at any time of day or night, whether by networks, independent broadcasters, or local stations.

Whether intentionally or not, every televised communication distorts reality and is laden with persuasive strategies. This is true whether we think of the selections of ideas and words, the tones of voice used, the broadcaster's control of colors, or any other component of audiovisual communication. It is, for example, a most elemental feature of televised news that there can be no *televised* representation of anything that occurs where sun or artificial light cannot be introduced. For television per se, then, there can be no "news" in total darkness. Speech, writing, and simulations must communicate whatever information is disseminated about such events. Since producers of televised information are naturally partial to what can be presented imagistically, the result is that a great deal of "living" gets excluded from televised "news." Still more importantly, most citizens think of news reporting as "informative" rather than "persuasive," and this perception means that any persuasion entering newscasting, whether inevitably or intentionally, is disguised by the viewers' preconceptions that they are receiving something other than persuasion.

The illusion persists for several reasons. Newscasts are perceived as merely adding to our knowledge. They invoke authority by employing the rhetoric of objectivity. They use a fact-oriented, descriptive format.[3] The illusion that reporting is not persuasion is reflected in the oft-cited standards of journalism. In 1896, when he became publisher of the *New York Times,* Adolph Ochs said that journalists must "give the news impartially, without fear or favor, regardless of any party, sect or interest involved." The same terms are repeated today. Joseph Pulitzer, for whom the Pulitzer Prize is named, dictated in 1907 that journalists must "never belong to any party" and "always be drastically independent." Contemporary newscasters similarly and consciously cultivate the impression that they "mirror reality."[4]

To "mirror reality" is taken to mean one "informs" without "persuading." "Informing" evokes a greater sense of credibility than does the term "persuading." That is one reason we tend to permit newscasts to work their persuasive spells unnoticed and unchecked. With information we associate factuality, objectivity, and honesty. We also tend to associate

174

these same qualities with scientific and technological presentations but, as I shall show, televised news reporting is presented in a unique technological setting replete with gadgetry that fosters the illusion of "factuality" while it actually provides special means of persuasion— intentional as well as inescapable.[5] In all of these ways and in others, televised news programs indirectly teach us to expect objectivity and comprehensiveness—without any persuasion, manipulation, coercion, or salesmanship. There is no gainsaying that responsible reporters and anchorpersons *try* to approach the ideal of "objectivity," but I want to emphasize the fact that the nature of human communication, the medium of television, and factors external to "the news" all prevent the ideal from ever being fully attained.

A special external pressure on televised news presentation is the battle for ratings. Ratings reflect the audience's allegiances and the status of networks and their affiliated stations. If high, ratings attract advertisers, which means greater income for the network as a corporation. Even though network news departments are separate units within the network structures, they still are parts of those overall structures and they cannot be oblivious to the race for popularity and income.[6]

The news gatherers' fundamental concern for audience approval generates many persuasive aspects of televised news reporting. Selective bias, time limitations, and entertainment factors explain some strategies, but these are subcategories of the major thrust of televised news manipulation, the object of which is to attract and hold a large audience. Let me emphasize that this objective overrides any inclination toward political bias, or toward attacking a given party, policy, or public figure. I have found very little evidence of intentional political bias in network news broadcasting. In the pages that follow, I will, therefore, concentrate on the most important *strategies* that lead to distortion.

TECHNOLOGY'S IMPACT ON CREDIBILITY

Networks work hard with both technology and rhetoric to convince us that they are the best source of news and information. They do this out of pride, professionalism, and the desire to attract large audiences. The larger the audience, the bigger the revenue from advertising sales, and the larger the budget for news production. The size of a network news team's budget is no inconsequential matter. The budget determines the number of reporters, bureaus, and programs the network will field and produce. The network with bureaus in Miami, Atlanta, Dallas, and New Orleans is normally going to do a better job of covering the news in the South than the network with only a bureau in Atlanta. Thus audience size as determined by ratings is important to the *quality* of news programming, and hence increasing viewership is a legitimate goal of the networks.

Whether they are correct or not, networks are under the impression that technical devices in general, and computer graphics specifically, help them keep and expand their audiences. To begin with, consider how the teleprompter changed news broadcasts. This simple device makes a text available to a reporter as he or she looks into the camera lens. It has eliminated the "scriptedness" of presentations and enhanced the credibility of reporters and the smoothness of virtually all broadcasters.

Most networks and other news shows place a "magic window" behind their anchorpersons for the evening news, for convention coverage, and for election-night reporting. At various times, this screen is used to show personalities being interviewed, statistics, shots of action, slides, etc. The "window" is in fact a huge screen. The surface is one solid color, usually blue. The images seen on the screen are "mixed" into the television picture by a process called "chromakeying." A separate camera, keyed on screen color, substitutes what it is pointing at for the screen behind the anchorperson. (If the anchorperson were to wear a blue tie of the proper hue, the interviewee would appear on the tie.)

Having a newsmaker actually *appear* on the evening news inadvertently reinforces the feeling that one is witnessing history. And on occasion history has been made under such circumstances. Walter Cronkite coaxed Menachem Begin into accepting Anwar Sadat's rather tentative suggestion that he visit Jerusalem; Cronkite did so while both were being interviewed on the chromakey screen during the evening news hosted by Cronkite. In most cases, however, the screen is used to show slides or graphics that accentuate stories.

Perhaps the most spectacular use of computer graphics to date occurred on election night 1986 when CBS, unlike NBC and ABC, decided to give the elections a full night's coverage. CBS spent large amounts of money and several days of rehearsal time to find ways to make the election results not only clear but scintillating. Banks of computerized tote boards relying on precinct analyses flashed up "winner"; states popped up out of maps and turned different colors to indicate which party had won the race; percentages were translated into bar graphs that elongated before our eyes. The recomposition of the Senate and turnover in governorships were represented in several ways, the most spectacular of which was a block filled with color cubes; one block was used for governorships, another for Senate seats. Each small cube within the blocks had the abbreviation of a state on it and was

176

colored to match the party in control of the particular office represented by the block—red for Republicans, blue for Democrats. First, the block of cubes would appear as the Senate or governorships stood before the election; red cubes on the right, blue cubes on the left inside the block. Then the cubes would reorder themselves to reveal the current standing. Blank cubes indicated undecided states. By the end of the evening, each cube was filled with a color and a numerical graphic at the bottom revealed the net gain or loss of each party. With the addition of computer graphics and other technological possibilities, new productions can take our breath away with dazzling displays. At such moments, an audience is highly impressionable and very receptive to persuasion.

Chyron machines print text over the picture; Adda consoles hold graphics at the ready for quick use; Quantel computers make inset pictures spin, expand, or shrink. Inserted slides can be made to whirl, flip, and combine with other pictures and slides. There is an enormous arsenal of devices at the disposal of the executive producer of the evening news or a special events program such as a convention or election night.

One can hardly blame audiences for being fascinated with displays of technological versatility. Furthermore, since these graphics make it easier for the viewer to understand what is happening in a given election or at a given convention, they make presentation of the news more efficient even if at times it may be oversimplified.

But these technical advances have given rise to problems. At an earlier time in our history, Theodore White and others would spend months doing intensive interviews in key precincts and report to us on the substance and the qualities of outlooks and desires of voters. Some argue that we have little of that today and that quantification and visual display are suppressing attention to the *reasons* for voters' judgments. The machines have a bias toward numbers, objects, and quantification.

Such complaints ignore several realities. There is nothing stopping researchers from writing a Theodore White type of account of our elections today. Jack Germond and Jules Witcover did it with *Marathon* in 1976 and *Wake Me When It's Over* in 1984; others plan in-depth looks at the 1988 effort. Second, exit polls have allowed network news to get at voters' motivations in more detail and with more accuracy than even the intuitive insights of a Theodore White. Despite the problems of sheer speed and volume of information, CBS has managed on each election night to have a "trend-desk" that does nothing but look behind the data to seek out underlying causes of voting patterns. While not all trend-desk stories get on the air, some very significant ones do. For example, in 1986, CBS was able to determine that concern over the

Social Security system was crucial to the outcome of Senate elections in Alabama, Georgia, Louisiana, and North Carolina. Exit polls showed that it was either the most or the second most cited problem in those states, unlike other states. Among voters who cited Social Security worries, almost two-thirds voted for the Democratic candidate. In those states, the Democratic candidates had run advertising attacking their Republican opponents' record on Social Security. In states where no such advertisements were run, the issue did not rank nearly as high on the list of voters' concerns nor cut as drastically against the Republicans.

Technology has not only helped networks display results better, it has helped them project the results earlier and with more accuracy. In 1986, CBS conducted a national exit poll on issues, demographics, and party preferences, and state-wide exit polls where critical races for Senator and Governor were occurring. CBS has been surveying voters as they leave the polls for over a decade because it has found the technique more accurate than randomly sampling actual votes. In a close race, both methods are combined and tempered with past election results in the state to provide a more accurate prediction. In 1986, for example, while other networks inaccurately predicted races in Missouri, Georgia, Alabama, and North Dakota, CBS waited to see if its random sampling in "indicator precincts" would verify its exit polls. Thus, in no case did CBS make an inaccurate prediction during its 1986 coverage. The credibility of CBS's predictions, of course, was enhanced by computer graphics. And since no predictions were made about a particular state until its polls were closed, harmfully influencing voters was not possible.

Some have argued that in past presidential elections network predictions have influenced the vote. In 1980, for example, NBC, very early in the evening, declared that Ronald Reagan had won enough states to produce a victory in the electoral college. A congressional committee later questioned Richard Scammon, NBC's chief predictor, about how the prediction was made, since several states placed in the Reagan column had closed their polls only moments before NBC declared the result. Scammon said that he had relied on exit polls, earlier poll data, and raw returns. Unfortunately, no congressman asked Scammon if all three methods or even two of them were used in *each* state. There is some evidence that NBC called some elections using only one of the methods Scammon cited.

The congressmen were upset because they believed NBC's early call, which was later joined by the other networks, had discouraged eligible voters in the West from going to the polls. Witnesses said once word got out that the election outcome was determined, they walked away from

178

polling places without voting. But hard data do not support these allegations. And the allegations are somewhat compromised by the fact that President Carter himself conceded the election just after NBC made its prediction. Furthermore, a close study of voting patterns in presidential elections reveals that there usually is a vote fall off in the West *regardless* of whether the election has been called or not. Finally, where voters have said they did not go to the polls because the election was already determined, they split evenly between winning and losing candidates. This fact would seem to argue against any damage having been caused to a single party by the persuasiveness of networks' predictions.

Some argue, however, that driving voters from the polls with early predictions damages the electoral process further by discouraging voting in other races and on propositions on the ballot. To this one might reply that if a voter's commitment to those other candidates and propositions is so weak that he or she is no longer motivated to vote once a network has declared a presidential candidate the winner, then perhaps those voters should be discouraged from voting in the first place. Such a voter is likely to be the least informed on the other issues and candidates.

Supporting the exit pollsters' and predictors' activities is the claim of the public's right to know. Among questions raised are: What are you telling the public when you rely on an exit poll, and when do you have enough verifiable data to tell them something? The matter is further complicated by the fact that viewers may change channels if they believe they are not receiving up-to-the-minute reports. We can go back to the 1980 presidential race for a case in point. As word got around that NBC had predicted that Reagan would win the presidency, NBC's ratings went up at the expense of CBS, CNN, and ABC. While critics may object to predictions, the American public seems to prefer the network that makes them the fastest. Thus, the fault, if there is one, may not be with the networks, but with the audience itself.

This situation raises a constitutional question. The courts have ruled that the people have a "right to know" the news and how the government operates. But the problem here is not whether they have a right to know, it is *when* they have a right to know. Specifically, do they have a right to know results *before* the polls close? And are those results real?

The press's right to report such information is inviolable. We regularly see polls predicting an outcome, often citing their margin of error. Since polls are not infrequently wrong, we tend to view them with skepticism. But whether it is desirable to broadcast an election prediction before the polls are closed based on what voters *said* they did in the voting booth is another question. I have already pointed out that broadcasters *are* subject to content regulations if such regulations can be shown to be "in the public interest." That is because in the *Red Lion Case* (see chapter 4), the Supreme Court ruled that due to a scarcity of broadcast outlets, the Federal Communications Commission was within its rights to declare broadcasters "public fiduciaries" and therefore subject to content controls. Congress is now considering strengthening the "public interest standard" (on the books since 1927) by mandating that broadcasters not predict elections in a given state before the polls close. The constitutionality of such a law would be particularly interesting, given the erosion of the scarcity rationale.

Technology has made the reporting of election results fascinating, persuasive, and efficient. But, as I have shown, its use has again raised the question of whether the electronic media should be treated differently from the press, which usually must wait until the next day to print election results. If ratings are any indication of their preference, the American audience does not want the electronic media restricted in this regard. Certainly, the voters of New York will not willingly tolerate waiting until the polls close in Hawaii to be told who won the election.

This problem may be solved by imposing a twenty-four or forty-eight hour voting period that ends at the same Greenwich mean time in all states. Even if such a law is not passed, censoring broadcasters hardly seems necessary, based on the studies completed so far concerning the problem. Furthermore, the constitutional questions associated with imposing a ban on electoral reporting should deter lawmakers. Some jurisdictions have tried to forbid exit polling, but the courts have generally overturned these laws as clear violations of the First Amendment. Certainly a reporter, or anyone else for that matter, has a right to ask someone who they voted for. The voter is free not to answer, to lie, or to reveal a preference for a candidate. Once more we see that the disguised persuasiveness of reporting data is what gives rise to tensions between the value of freedom and expediency in policy making.

Since the exit poll is here to stay, the question becomes how to prevent a broadcaster from mentioning it in an irresponsible way. Self-enforcement would seem more desirable than government fiat. Broadcasters who gamble and use the information recklessly will damage not only their reputations, but the credibility of anyone relying on exit poll data in the future. Consistently, those networks that have made inaccurate predictions have suffered the critical slings and arrows of their competitors and of the press. At CBS, where I have served as a consultant, reporters are warned to choose language describing election

180

results with great care. Lengthy memos on the subject are required reading just before election night. Once on the air, CBS has made very clear what information provides the basis for their election predictions. If the call is based on exit polls, the audience is told that; if the call is based on swing precincts, they are told that. Once again, knowledge of what goes on and the pressures of the marketplace and competition seem to be a better way to ensure accurate news reporting than to censor information that in all likelihood will get by the censors on constitutional grounds or because of the clever wording of a newscaster.

CASTING AND CREDIBILITY

Casting is another strategy to broaden the audience and enhance the credibility of news presentations. Networks once strove to find newscasters with authority to anchor their news shows. Age seemed an important criterion from 1962 to 1980. The team on the American Broadcasting Company's news was silver-haired. A stolid and aging Walter Cronkite of CBS became one of the most trusted men in America and was even considered as a vice presidential candidate by George McGovern in 1972. Eric Sevareid, appearing with Cronkite as a commentator, became renowned for his commentaries and for the fact that he looked like Andrew Jackson's portrait on the $20 bill. Even when the wry David Brinkley was elevated to anchorman by NBC, he was balanced by the more somber Chet Huntley, whose writers made him sound more conservative.[7] In the 1980s, the decade of the Yuppies and the Baby Boomers, the emphasis seems to be on youth. Who would have thought Dan Rather would be the oldest of the three major anchormen in 1988? Tom Brokaw really does look and sound almost adolescent. Peter Jennings, the most urbane of the three, is also the most dashing.

Even dress is treated as a means of persuasion. Roone Arledge, who took over ABC News after great success with sports production, went so far as to suggest to Frank Reynolds, an ABC anchor for a few years, what color suits should be worn during the evening news broadcast. Dan Rather wore sweaters during the evening news to "warm" his image and caused a good deal of commentary.

Here again we have a perceptual difference between the press and the electronic media. When one reads a news item in the *New York Times* or a local paper, one normally has no idea what the reporter looks like. On television the news is presented by a personality; even on radio there is a human voice. Personality colors the story through vocal tone, facial expression, and many other non-verbal cues.

Since the Nixon Administration, politicians, and particularly presidents, have not been shy about criticizing the news media. They tend to focus their criticism on individual members of the electronic media. This phenomenon, combined with the fact that broadcasters have become akin to movie stars, their lives covered by magazine and gossip columns, has reduced their credibility as newscasters to the point where printed stories in the daily press can have more impact, more credibility, and more persuasive effect than the same story uttered by a Lesley Stahl or a Sam Donaldson. It is significant that recent studies indicate that while most Americans receive their news from television, if something interests them or they want something reinforced or verified, they tend to seek further information in the printed press. It may be that the broadcasters' push to bring star quality to their correspondents has reduced their credibility. Diane Sawyer is a serious, hard working reporter, but she is also glamorous and often pictured in such magazines as *Vanity Fair* and such tabloids as *The Star*. She is seen going to parties and there is rampant speculation about her private life. To a degree, the reporter's credibility as a serious investigator of news becomes equated with that of Robert Redford or Kathleen Turner. It may be that where broadcasters have moved to hold audiences by fascinating them, they have also risked undercutting the believability of their news programming.[8]

In any case, there can be no question that broadcasters try to make news more appealing by enhancing their public images, which is a form of persuasion that can work either positively or negatively on credibility of broadcast journalism.

SUSTAINING THE ILLUSION OF COMPLETENESS

Many rhetorical choices made by newscasters imply that the news is *fully* covered in each broadcast. The more candid reporters readily grant, off-camera, that this is not true. But devices that imply otherwise are numerous. Reporters usually conclude their reports by telling us where they are and who they are: "This is Phil Jones, CBS News, Capitol Hill." An implication for the unwary is that Jones is *there,* therefore he's covered all the news of importance up to this minute. Anyone familiar with the many committees of the Congress knows that comprehensive coverage is impossible to provide. But anchorpersons often have a standard sign off that implies full and ample coverage: "And that's the way it is, January 30, 1975," or "Central Pennsylvania's largest news service." Showing clips of stories yet to come implies that we will later get the *full* coverage. Segues are carefully rehearsed so that presentations are without bald shifts of attention that might suggest incompleteness.

Strategies with special potential for controlling or even misleading viewers occur when interviews are edited, and they usually are. Interviews are often rehearsed or rearranged; interviewers sometimes reword and then insert questions into films and tapes of already completed interviews; scenes are refilmed, at different times, using different people in different places but the scenes are treated as connected with a single, linear, initial story. As long as the event did occur somewhere, the Federal Communications Commission makes no objections to these simulations. This is especially strange since visual representations of simulated events such as a space vehicles' voyages are always labeled "Simulation." Reenactments of events are not uncommon, although they, too, are usually so labeled. Stories that are difficult to handle are likely to be handled in standard ways. For example, complicated causes for stock-market changes are reduced to "uneasiness about interest rates," as though the entire nation of buyers and sellers had been polled. In fact, reporters quickly interviewed some market analysts, and the answers easiest to understand and most economically expressed were fit into the brief time allotted to the market report.

Most of these subtly persuasive orchestrations of newscasts are done with regard for accuracy, but they are not carried out with much regard for *full* coverage of what has happened and why. The behind-the-scenes designing is intended to make a smooth, convincing, and entertaining show.[9] Each choice I have mentioned *implicitly* invites belief that the reporters are fully knowledgeable, expert at reportage, and are committed to giving us all that is worth knowing about today's news.

Television newscasts are usually "packaged" in a thirty-minute format. This "packaging" gives the impression that the newscasters have time to cover all or most of the important news. We can scarcely imagine a network anchorman ending his thirty-minute show with: "And that's all the news we have time for tonight."[10] That, however, is usually the fact, but telecasting does not contain that kind of language except in segments devoted to the news of sports. For the most part, the illusion of total coverage is carefully sustained. Neither do many of us stop to reflect that, of the events reported, few are given adequate exposure to place the facts in their actual context. Speeches and press conferences are excerpted unmercifully; events are viewed and described from one reporter's perspective most of the time. (To his credit, Walter Cronkite consistently urged viewers to read newspapers, magazines, and journals to get the whole story.)

The televised news Americans see and hear helps them make political decisions. Televised news is delivered by a person who has been cast for the role, may enhance his or her reputation through dress, publicity, and other appeals to the audience, and tries to give the impression that what is reported is complete. Thus, televised news is set in rhetorical situations latent with inadvertent persuasion that may affect the public's perception of events. But the "disguised persuasion" does not stop there.

SELECTING AND EDITING

Beyond personal strategies is another set of constraints imposed by the host of decision makers who *select* news to be broadcast. First, we need to understand that after it is "discovered," a news story is shaped and reshaped as it passes through a chain of command. All other things being equal, a story stands a better chance of being included on the evening news if it is visual, that is, captured on videotape. That means that normally a story will be "covered" by a reporter and a "cameraman." The first *selecting* takes place when the producer decides to cover a story. On rare occasions, an event may occur in such a way that a reporter makes this decision on his or her own. For example, a plane may crash or a volcano may erupt; a trained reporter will assume that such events are newsworthy. The second selecting takes place when the reporter decides how he or she wants to tell the story. The cameraman then tries to support that story. For example, if a presidential candidate delivers a speech in which he or she announces a new position, the reporter will probably build the story around the new announcement and ask the cameraman to tape the "sound bite" containing the articulation of the new position. However, the videotaping process itself can help to reshape the story if something unusual, such as an assassination attempt or a demonstration, interrupts the "set" story. In that case, the reporter would rebuild the story around the new or unscheduled events. Thus, at the very basic level of firsthand coverage, a dynamic interrelationship exists among reporter, cameraman, and event. Their interplay allows reconstruction guided by the criteria established for getting a story on the air: The need for a *dramatic* narrative that is important and interesting.

Once the story is sent to the network, more selecting and choosing among alternatives takes place.[11] At the editorial level, another set of priorities comes into play. They, too, help explain how the news is inadvertently distorted. Each story sent in from the field must be compared to other such stories ready for that evening's news. If it is a "slow" news day, that is, one on which not much is happening, a story coming in not only has a better chance of being included in the broadcast, but will receive more actual air time. If it is a "fast" or "hot" news day, a

184

given story may be shortened, "bumped down the schedule," grouped with other stories, reduced to a quick line or two by the anchorperson, or dropped altogether. In the latter two cases, the story is often sent to affiliated stations where it can be used as a feature on the local news.

The pressure to construct a lively, informative, fascinating, and therefore persuasive evening news program leads to arranging, cutting and newswriting that severely reshapes each news item.[12] The need for efficiency because of the limited time and the need for effective dramatic appeal to build ratings make the news editor's job a crucial one. These editors become, as one admitted, masters of making sense out of the chaos of film, videotape, and information that flood them. "Given at random, say, half a dozen shots of a different nature and subject, there are any number of possible combinations of the six that, with the right twist of commentary, could make film sense."[13] And "film sense" means a coherent, dramatic narrative that becomes an effort to persuade the audience that the network's (i.e., editors') view of the world is correct. The anchorperson adds yet another layer of editorial discretion to the process. Walter Cronkite confessed: "Every word that's said goes through my hands and is usually touched by my hands in some way. I edit almost every piece, rewrite many of them and originally write some of them." David Brinkley went even further: "The anchorman does have the power to steer public attention in one direction or another."[14]

Again, dynamic interactions are at work to shape "information" persuasively. There are tensions between the data of the raw, uncut story and the "creator's" desire to be believable and fascinating to an audience. The broadcasters try to create a "good" story by "making sense" through rendering each account faithful to what the audience knows about human affairs and by making the whole account cohere, as narrative. This is "argument" by means of "narrative logic."[15] Where the narration is audiovisual, the creators of news accounts have the special persuasive advantage of working with symbols that place the narrative before the listeners' own eyes, thereby further vouching for its "reality." These are inevitable persuasive forces that operate as strongly in accounts of political affairs as in any other, for political events are re-presented as audiovisual *narratives*.

Cost constraints have recently been tightened by industry-wide consolidation and by management changes. General Electric has taken over NBC; Capital Cities has taken over ABC; and CBS, in order to avoid a takeover by Ted Turner, allowed a member of its board of directors, Laurence Tisch, to buy almost 25 percent of its stock and become its chief executive officer. In each case, news budgets were severely cut.

185

Network news has also lost a worrisome share of the audience to alternative news systems, such as CNN, and to other programming, mainly provided by cable. In 1980, the three network news broadcasts had a combined audience share of 72 percent of television sets in use. By 1987, that share had dropped to 63 percent. Where the CBS Evening News reached fifteen million households a night in the mid-1970s, it now reaches about eleven million a night. Financial pressure has thus been added to the time constraints that make efficiency the byword of network coverage of news.

Even before the recent round of austerity measures, efficiency in operations had led to some bad habits. For example, each network uses a relatively small band of correspondents to report the news. In one year, "ten correspondents reported 68 percent of the film stories at NBC, 56 percent at ABC, and 51 percent at CBS."[16] Television relies heavily on wire service stories to save time and money, and keep up with fast-breaking news. In turn, when the networks prepare stories for the evening news and send "daily feeds" to their affiliates, the affiliates are in most cases getting stories that were drawn off the wires. The total result of the drive for efficiency is a pyramid of news initiation with United Press International, Associated Press, and, perhaps, Reuters, at its foundation. Though on occasion a network reporter or analyst may expand or supplement such stories, it is clear that the sources of most news stories have been narrower than the public believes. Presumably the new austerity will intensify this tendency.

When the networks do initiate their own stories, the devices and procedures I have identified can result in illusion building. Network coverage of the 1968 Republican Convention illustrates the point.[17] That Governors Rockefeller and Reagan had made an agreement to stop Nixon's campaign for nomination was known and reported. Researchers working for one network discovered that the attack on Nixon's base of support would concentrate on the Florida delegation.[18] Because of its position in the roll call and because of its self-imposed unit rule, if Florida's delegates held for Nixon, delegates in the Georgia, Mississippi, South Carolina, and Texas delegations would probably hold too. If Florida broke for Reagan, so would other delegations from the South. A total of over one hundred delegates were involved, enough to stop Nixon on the first ballot. (He won by only twenty-five delegates.) Thus, during the nomination process, Ronald Reagan called each Florida delegate to his trailer off the convention floor and begged for support. He then made a special plea in a caucus room to the Mississippi delegates; tears formed in Reagan's eyes as he spoke and several delegates openly wept.[19] Little of this was reported to the public, and illusions were fostered.

186

Since the Florida delegation was half female, Reagan had his name put in nomination by Ivy Baker Priest. One reporter, unaware of the composition of the Florida delegation, claimed Reagan was being nominated by Priest because he couldn't get anyone more important to do it. The major political professionals spoke before the Florida caucus. Despite memos and news stories sent to the news desk from the research team, CBS correspondents continued to report that Nixon had the nomination locked up.

The Florida delegation was polled several times before the actual balloting. Each time the Nixon majority held by a smaller and smaller margin. Finally, just before the balloting on the convention floor, the Nixon margin was down to a single vote (18–16—a change of one vote would have meant a 17–17 tie). It was that one vote that gave Nixon the delegates necessary to win the nomination on the first ballot. If that one vote had changed, would other delegations have abandoned Nixon? One does not know. All three networks reported "reality" as they saw it. At CBS those who selected what information to put on the air created the illusion that there was never a doubt that Nixon would win the Convention's nomination. What went unreported to the viewing audience was that the 1968 Republican Convention was indeed open, and there were moments of dramatic and suspenseful political maneuvering during which some on the scene realized the nomination might well be decided by a single vote in the Florida delegation.

The reporting of the 1968 Republican Convention is typical of the, perhaps unconscious, tendency of the news media to maintain their initial views of what stories are likely or unlikely to develop. Evidence that supports prior predictions gets favored over evidence that does not. For example, in 1984 the networks decided that the Republican Convention that would nominate Reagan in Dallas was going to be boring—and it was. But in the process of reporting, the networks filled so much time with their own analysts and stories that they missed some truly interesting events of the convention. CBS, for example, never showed the six Olympic medalists who came into the convention, or football star Rosie Greer, in whose arms Robert Kennedy died, accompany a blind "special" Olympian to the podium. CBS put not one minute of the blind Olympian's speech on the air, even though that speech clearly stirred the "bored" delegates. Neither did they cover gold medalist Nancy Hogshead plunging into the crowd and giving a speech from the floor of the convention. Although CBS stayed on the air after 11 P.M. to cover Jennifer Holliday's closing song to the Democratic Convention, they went off the air during Ray Charles' version of "America the Beautiful" at the Republican Convention. They thereby missed one of the convention's most spontaneous moments—Nancy Reagan helping the blind Charles to the podium as the cheers of the delegates washed over him. They did not miss this event out of animus for the First Lady; instead, they were trying to make affiliates happy by giving the evening back to them at 11 P.M. for local news.[20] The affiliates had been angry when at the end of sessions of the Democratic Convention, CBS went past 11 P.M. in its coverage.

In the inescapably multiple processes of selecting and editing information to be broadcast to the pubic, *expectations* and journalistic *habits* give order, clarity, and bias to news presentations. The research and planning done prior to covering a major political event help to make the coverage informed and interesting. I have just illustrated, however, that preparations can lead to "tunnel vision" reportage. Broadcasters, especially, need to develop stronger corrective systems than they now have so that spontaneous and unexpected events are covered as well as the planned and expected. Broadcasters need to resist the temptation to fill air time with preplanned commentary and exposition when they could be searching out *immediately important* live events. Our system of generally free communication is developing some correctives, however. Major newspapers and magazines, and even some television programs such as "Entertainment Tonight," now offer critiques of televised coverage of everything from individual speeches to sporting events. Such critiques are a healthy influence on broadcasters' planning and execution of "the news of the day," including political news. Networks are also developing "program post-mortems" through which reporters and producers can learn to achieve credibility through *both* pre-program planning and spontaneous coverage.

Editing and selecting are persuasive actions. They *must* occur in creating information of any sort. We are reasonably aware of this fact when we encounter printed media. But as new and ubiquitous audiovisual technologies develop, listener/viewers need to alert themselves to the fact that the "reality" of every picture is no less freighted with selection-that-persuades than the front page of a newspaper.

SYMBOLIC PICTURES, PREDICTION, AND THEMATIC PROGRAMMING

There are three common ways by which a presentation can *create* "realities." An item may be charged with *symbolic* meaning. A prediction can create a futuristic "reality." Thematic reportage can give *created* meaning to phenomena that are not necessarily so related. This section looks at the uses made of these communicative strategies in broadcast news.

188

Any item that comes to represent more than its literal meaning is a symbol. The flag is a symbol of the nation. In much the same way, a picture or verbal description can be offered as "standing for" something more complex and emotionally touching. If we hear a story about hunger in Africa, our culture has taught us to expect to see starving children in a telecast report. It is neither as easy nor as expected, however, to see illiteracy symbolized, but it can be done. A widely televised vignette in 1986 invited support for literacy programs by showing a man in early middle age trying to read to his child and stumbling over the simplest words. The vignette symbolized the embarrassment of being unable to read. As these examples show, in covering the news, as well as in advertising, attempts are often made to create symbols out of persons or events. An interview with one black man is offered as representing the feelings of blacks throughout the nation; mass transit problems in Detroit are presented as symbolic of mass transit problems in all urban areas; the plight of a refugee family in Los Angeles is offered as representative of the problems of all refugees—at least all refugees of that family's national origin.

Symbolic representations in film or writing give color and emotion to presentations of real conditions, but as consumers we seldom remember that *symbolic representations always minimize differences among individuals in the symbolized class.* Nonetheless, as Reuven Frank, once President of NBC News, said of the starving-child image, "The picture is not a fact but a symbol."[21] But if portions of the news are symbolic rather than real, the audience is being persuaded to conclusions that are much larger than the facts used to support them. Here, I believe, is one of the most dangerous kinds of news distortion. Suppose a reporter discovers that the Defense Department is paying twice as much for number 6 nails than the average consumer. Suppose, without checking on other purchases, the reporter or the network generalizes that the Defense Department regularly pays twice as much as everybody else for supplies. Most of us would say this was an irresponsibly drawn conclusion. Such examples are rare, but not so rare is the use of one telling human example to build a conclusion about the welfare system, about a foreign war, or about the staff surrounding the president. Again, the need for a dramatic story and the constraints of efficient operation make such leaps of logic more common than they should be.

Luckily, fallacious reasoning occurs in an open marketplace of ideas where correctives abound. A competing reporter will often file a story contradicting the incorrect one. The Defense Department, or any other offended agency, can remedy the situation by refuting errors through their own press offices. There is also the growing phenomenon of

189

"revisionist journalism" wherein a story that is generally accepted as true is scrutinized to see if it is accurate. "Sixty Minutes," for example, scheduled a story on labor conditions in Joseph Coors' nonunion brewery in Golden, Colorado. Persons involved with the production readily admitted that they thought they would find conditions worse than in union shops, and so would be able to symbolize the dangers of right-to-work laws. Once the story was fully researched, it became clear that Coors' workers were better off than union workers and were generally happy with their working conditions. To its credit, "Sixty Minutes" ran the story based on the evidence it actually obtained.

Pictorial symbols tend to oversimplify. Predictions, however, can either oversimplify events or make them seem more complex or more or less certain than they really are. Predictions *persuade* in one direction or another by building the illusion that a level of certainty exists about what is as yet unknown. Where political affairs are concerned, predictions can acquire credibility in several ways.

First, audiences rarely check after an event to see which predictors were correct and which were not. Predictions therefore tend to stand as probably true whether or not they are borne out. Second, predictions can become self-fulfilling wishes. A prediction, once made, may "promise" an outcome that will generate a bandwagon effect, drawing people to its support and to actions likely to make the prediction a "fact." Many cults have been born in this way; and in politics, a prediction of success or failure can enhance or diminish supporters' enthusiasm. Third, predictions fascinate audiences. Predictions suggest "inside information" and create an aura of suspense. Partly for this reason, in covering presidential campaigns, networks make *events* out of releasing predictions—of "delegate counts," election winners, and the like. Reporters predict *when* announcements will be made, *when* a treaty will be signed, *what* it will contain, and likely outcomes of trials. "Instant analysis" of speeches is another format for predictions about intentions, qualities, and effects.[22] Also, predicting allows commentators to be more colorful. The typical pattern is to throw out a few truisms to get listeners/viewers in a mood of agreement, than a metaphor is spun, and finally a prediction or judgment is issued.[23]

In political reporting, in-house prediction can have the effect of pre-programming reportage in thematic ways. Enormous preparatory work yields estimates that this or that is likely to happen or that certain persons, groups, or issues will be crucial to the outcome of a convention or campaign. The result of these estimates can be that reporters carry those probabilities in their minds as predictions and then interpret unfolding events in light of the initial estimates.

Consider a major example. CBS distributes a handbook on the conventions and elections. It goes to CBS's reporters, correspondents, and their aids. The purpose of the handbook is to provide background information, biographical data, and profiles of delegates (or state demographics on election nights). The information is drawn primarily from interviews, from in-house analysts, and from clippings from the *Wall Street Journal,* the *Washington Post,* and the *New York Times.* The project is impressive and includes a "delegate count." Every delegate has been interviewed once, and 90 percent of them are interviewed twice. The cost of preparing this report is staggering. It was created to give correspondents something to talk about when convention proceedings get boring, which is often. More significantly, it also tends to preprogram the reporters' explanations of news events and to make their explanations better than the competition's, or so CBS hopes.

What can be misleading for convention coverage is the way the "delegate count" is used. Reporters on the floor of a political convention sometimes begin interviewing leaders of delegations by saying, "We have projected this delegation to break forty-six to fifteen for Humphrey; that doesn't square with your figures. Where are you going to get the needed delegates?" Or, "Our network has computed that McGovern is already over the top. Don't you think that will start a bandwagon?" In actual fact, *these approaches led delegates to believe the reporters,* and in several crucial cases, delegates changed their votes in view of what they heard. It was the leaders' responsibility to know their delegations better than anyone. When they did not, viewers and leaders alike took a pre-convention estimate as an actual measure.

I have been focusing on how "realities" that are not actual get created in political analysis and reporting. Phenomena and persons are rendered symbolic and hence represent "deeper" realities. Predictions generate a false sense of truth and certainty. Early analyses of probabilities suggest story lines that may or may not prove real in the event. These are not necessarily deliberate distortions of reality; they are simply examples of ways in which the outlooks of news makers and news interpreters can *create* persuasive interpretations of what is.[24]

SECRET SOURCES

News programs often cite undisclosed "secret," "major," or "reliable" sources. This tactic can have important persuasive impact. The unrevealed sources are usually referred to as "high government officials," "an aide close to the president," etc. Sometimes they take on geographic personae: "Washington has it that . . . ," "Saigon rumored today

. . . ," "Moscow released word that. . . ." Such phrasings can give authority to what is being reported. Officials frequently prefer the use of such language by refusing to be quoted with their identity revealed. The effects of the verbal tactic are not changed by that fact. Among the press corps, for example, sources at the State Department are well known, even though their names are not used when they are quoted. The practice is part of a diplomatic game played by most nations, and it often serves to provide channels for "unidentified communication" between states. On the other hand, the usage can have the rhetorical effect of giving a political story "the right spin" or implication. And the practice has the further effect of forcing a symbiotic relationship between reporters and their sources. That fact creates mutual opportunities (sometimes obligations) to further diplomatic relations as domestic information is disseminated.

The question of when sources ought to be revealed in political reporting is a legal as well as a rhetorical and ethical question. Our Constitution guarantees freedom of press and speech, but as our laws have evolved they have come to assert that use of undisclosed sources cannot be allowed to impinge on other constitutional rights unless a major *public* interest is at stake. When the freedom of journalists to protect their sources comes into conflict with, say, constitutional assurances for a fair trial, as much tension is created in the political system as when freedom of speech and press come into conflict with protection of national security. These difficulties were dramatized when William Farr, a *Los Angeles Times* reporter, was jailed for refusing to divulge his source for a story about the Pentagon Papers trial. The trial judge ruled that Farr's withholding information endangered a fair trial. Supreme Court Justice Potter Stewart reviewed the judge's ruling and said, "The Court has also been called upon to decide whether a newspaper reporter has a First Amendment privilege to disclose his confidential sources to a grand jury. By a divided vote, the Court found no such privilege to exist in the circumstances of the cases before it."[25]

Journalists thus face a dilemma. They are taught that sources are crucial to their stories and to provide the public with information. Often, unless a reporter can cite a source for his or her story, it will not be used. Indeed, a journalistic rule of thumb is that *two* sources are needed to confirm a "fact." On the other hand, if reporters have to reveal their sources, some of their most valuable sources may dry up. Reporting based on undisclosed sources uncovered the Watergate scandal. But it also led to further criticism of Senator Thomas Eagleton as a vice presidential candidate in the 1972 campaign when it was falsely alleged

192

he had a drinking and driving record as well as having received psychiatric treatment for depression. What readers and viewers are likely to overlook is that, especially where interpretations of "the facts" are controversial, both public figures and news agencies make use of the ambiguities concerning revealing sources.

On the other side of the coin, sources can use reporters to create versions of reality. This can sometimes be beneficial; at other times it is not. *Time* magazine revealed how Henry Kissinger had manipulated the press in his quest for a settlement in the Middle East:

> Whenever he was asked how far along the negotiations had come, Kissinger would answer, "Oh, 60 percent completed." The next time it was 75 percent and the next, 90 percent. As the two sides kept reading these daily stories, they could not help being nudged into believing that a settlement was nearly at hand. "He played the press like a cello," recalls one reporter. "We created all the background music he needed."[26]

Ultimately, of course, relations in the Middle East were "normalized" because Kissinger succeeded in his private bargaining.

The same strategies can be harmful. When, before the election of 1972, CBS was pressured by Charles Colson to balance their Watergate coverage, I was assigned the task of researching and writing about any scandals related to the McGovern campaign. The White House sources I consulted were only too cooperative in supplying information. After double-checking, I wrote a five-page story listing McGovern "scandals," including McGovern's use of phony slates in the Illinois primary and his use of spies in the Muskie campaign in New Hampshire. The report was never put on the air. Instead, the second Watergate news segment, originally scheduled for fifteen minutes on the next night's news, was substantially cut.[27]

Clearly, the communications system as it now exists is subject to manipulation. Sources can use reporters to get their versions of a story to the public or to foreign diplomats. In fact, Nancy Reagan, during her battle with her husband's chief of staff, Donald Regan, used the press to leak stories about Regan's incompetence. Regan retaliated by leaking a story about how he had hung up on the First Lady twice.[28] The adversaries were using the press for their own purposes, not to make news; they were, in effect, sending signals to rally various members of the administration to their sides. Donald Regan eventually was forced to resign.

193

Reporters can use sources to bolster their own credibility and convince the public of certain "facts." The best check in such a system is the competition between network news teams. Gaffs, misstatements, errors in judgment, and media manipulation are frequently the subjects of editorials, commentaries, and news stories. For example, *Time* magazine ran a story in October of 1986 criticizing all three networks and much of the print media for "hyping" the problem with the drug "crack." Wrote *Time*:

> But the [Drug Enforcement Administration], after a city-by-city survey of crack's availability, asserted in a report that the result of media attention "has been a distortion of the public perception of the extent of crack use." The DEA said the drug "generally is not available" in some major cities, including Chicago, Philadelphia, and New Orleans, and is not widely available in many other metropolitan areas.[29]

TV Guide, the most widely read magazine in America, regularly takes television news programs to task. For example, in its March 28, 1987 edition, the weekly program guide criticized Dan Rather for stealing a line from comedian Mark Russell and using it without a credit on the evening news. In a more lengthy article, *TV Guide* evaluated "Sixty Minutes"; here are some of the more critical comments:

> Time and again, it seems, TV's leading newsmagazine show doesn't ask the critical questions that will provide important insights or a sense of fair play. . . . Reasoner did fewer stories than any of the other correspondents, and the stories he did do often seemed thin, lacking crucial elements. . . . Bradley also did a puzzlingly incomplete story on a Maine businessman who had been accused of organized-crime ties. . . . Wallace didn't ask anyone from the White House to comment about this bizarre situation. . . . I had the same feeling of "But what does the other side say?" when Sawyer did a story on ballerina Gelsey Kirkland. . . . There were other notable omissions in *60 Minutes* stories, omissions that had less to do with fair play than with insight, perspective or even sharp edge. . . . Safer was similarly uncritical in a story on a public-housing project in St. Louis that's run by its tenants.[30]

Criticism of television news is also common in reviews in daily newspapers. Competition provides the American public with readily available means by which to correct improper impressions and the effect of

194

persuasive strategies in television news. On the other hand, competition can also cause distortions in the presentation of news and special events.

HOW COMPETITION CAUSES DISTORTION

I begin by examining competition *within* news divisions. Each reporter wants to advance his or her career, and the way to move up is to find newsworthy stories. This means a reporter will try to structure a story so as to make superiors think it newsworthy. The Kerner Report on civil disorders pointed to some of the unavoidable results of reportorial competition:

> Most errors involved mistakes of fact, exaggerations of events, overplaying of particular stories, or prominently displayed speculation about unfounded rumors of potential trouble. . . . An experienced riot reporter told the commission that initial wire service reports tend to be inflated.[31]

At other times, competition produces heroic results, as it has in reporting from various battlefields. As still other times, the results are comic, as when Mike Wallace of CBS stole his way past secret service agents on the podium at the 1968 Republican Convention and revealed to the nation on camera that security was not all it was cracked up to be. Sometimes the competition impels reporters to create their own news. The Kerner Report tells how reporters interfered with police activities during the Newark riots in 1967, and even encouraged rioters to commit acts of violence "for the cameras."[32] The Walker Report on violent disturbances associated with the 1968 Democratic Convention also revealed staged events.[33]

Inter-network competition is even more fierce. Having worked on news sets on election nights and during conventions, I can say from personal experience that everyone from the lowest researcher to the president of the news division follows the ratings. Despite disclaimers, correspondents as well as executive producers understand that higher ratings mean not only better salaries but larger budgets with which to work. Each rating point is worth over $15 million a year in advertising revenue. Fifteen years ago, each network news operation lost about $20 million a year; those divisions now sometimes make over $50 million a year for their respective networks, even though their annual budgets run about $300 million.[34]

Competition for ratings also encourages coverage of non-events and sensational reporting. We have all witnessed attempts to make the news more "attractive" and "lighter." Televised news magazines such as "Sixty Minutes" and "20/20" compete against each other and also with print weeklies like *Time* and *Newsweek*.[35] Eagerness to "do better than the competition" inevitably influences selection and presentation of the "news." It may also influence the way anchorpersons perform and what assignments they undertake. For example, in late 1987, Tom Brokaw "scooped" his competition by gaining an exclusive interview with Soviet Premier Gorbachev and by moderating a two hour, two-party debate live on national television. Such success may have influenced Dan Rather's decision to interview Vice President Bush live on the CBS Evening News on January 25, 1988. The ensuing nine minute running battle between Bush and Rather made national headlines and improved Rather's ratings. Just how competitive influences work depends on specific situations and persons, but competitive influences are persuasively present in *all* the media of mass communication.

In sum, on a network's news program there are only twenty-two minutes of news, if you subtract the time given to commercials, just as there are only so many square inches of news and feature space on the front page of a newspaper. Reporters and newsmakers compete to get into those spaces, and publishers and network presidents compete to insure that the public comes to them for news. But "the news" is always *selectively* presented. News that doesn't break quickly and spectacularly by the East coast's deadline usually gets left out of the nightly news across the nation.

THE MYTHOS OF THE PRESIDENTIAL DEBATES

In addition to competition, geography, and technological advances that shape what we learn about politics through the media of mass communication, myths shape the "realities" portrayed for us. This is no new development. In the days when this republic was consolidating, it was common to portray the relation of the colonies to their "mother country" as the relation of child to parent. In his history of pre-revolutionary rhetoric, Stephen E. Lucas has pointed out how this mythical image of relationships had to be altered through public rhetoric before independence could be fully justified:

Across the years 1765–75 [Whig leaders] persuasively redefined the status and obligations of both members of the British political family in a fashion that broadened the acceptable sphere of resistance to an unjust parent, provided a more exalted depiction of the growing American child, and gradually highlighted the inherently revolutionary implications of the analogy.[36]

Analogies, images, and myths have always colored perceptions of political issues and actions. They influence presentations of "facts," and they *persuade* in our own day just as significantly as they did just before the American Revolution.

This principle is interestingly and specifically illustrated today in public treatments of presidential debates. Images of what "debates" are or ought to be together with frequently naïve interpretations of the "lessons" to be drawn from their relatively short modern history shape what we learn about presidential candidates from the media of mass communication. What has happened concerning presidential debates and what are the results?

The first modern, televised presidential debates took place between John F. Kennedy and Richard M. Nixon in 1960. In the ensuing election, Nixon lost by only 112,000 popular votes out of 40 million votes cast. Immediately, a series of myths about presidential debates began to develop as reporters and commentators ruminated on why Kennedy won and why Nixon lost. Almost everyone has by now heard that Nixon lost the election because he looked terrible in the first debate with Kennedy. This "common wisdom" originated with those composing and reporting the "news" about the debates. In fact, scholars in various fields have shown that this assessment must be significantly qualified. They have pointed out that people who heard the first debate on radio thought Nixon won it,[39] that the circumstances of the first debate were thoroughly penalizing for Nixon in respect to his health, his makeup, and the setting that was used in the debate. Nixon was perceived as winning or drawing with Kennedy in the next three debates; however, each of those debates was watched by only half as many people as watched the first debate. The conclusion one ought to draw from these careful analyses is that Nixon's appearance in the first debate probably had something to do with his ultimate loss by a narrow margin, but that the causes for the voters' decisions were much more numerous and complex than his appearance in the first of four televised debates. Nonetheless, almost all mass media reports accept and project into our own time the simplistic explanation for Nixon's defeat.

That oversimplification of causes occurs under the pressures of reporting the news is not surprising, but even with years to review their analyses, reporters have spun out a series of generalizations about televised presidential debates—all based on the simplistic analysis of the first Nixon-Kennedy debate. They apply these generalizations to each set of later presidential debates. Here are some of those myths that virtually every reader of this book has heard expounded as a "must" for presidential debaters.

Wear Makeup. After each modern presidential debate, reporters spend almost as much time reporting what people wore and how they looked as reporting what was said. Why? In the first place, of course, it is easier to describe the obvious than analyze issues and exchanges in debate. But it is also repeatedly recalled that in the first Nixon-Kennedy debate, Nixon refused to wear makeup and made a poor impression.[38] But technology has changed in twenty-five years. The cathode tube used in black and white television cameras in 1960 penetrated Nixon's first layer of skin and revealed his black stubble beard. He not only looked dirty and somewhat sinister, his televised visage seemed to confirm mean caricatures of him done by Herb Block and other cartoonists. But despite advances in television's technology, many contemporary reporters still infer that Nixon's difficulties in the first televised debate *prove* the vital importance of makeup. In 1984, in the second Reagan-Mondale debate, Mondale was badly lighted and thus seemed to be wearing too much makeup. Most of the networks' post-debate commentaries dwelled on Mondale's looks. This emphasis was partially set up by a joke Reagan had made a few days earlier. When asked if he was bothered that Mondale looked younger than Reagan in the first debate, Reagan responded that he would look younger to if he had worn "all that makeup." The significant thing is that the time spent on Mondale's facial appearance crowded out full reportage of what the two men said.

Reporting on the Bush-Ferraro debate of 1984 suffered from a disproportionate amount of speculation on the Congresswoman's choice of clothes. In 1987, the bad habits of the electronic media were emulated by the printed press. Two columns in the *Washington Post* on the debate among Democratic presidential candidates in Houston focused on appearance and demeanor at the expense of issues. In each, the paragraphs about Senator Paul Simon mentioned that he had large earlobes but probably was not hurt by the fact that he wore a bow tie.[39]

No one would deny that how a political speaker *appears* when telecasting his or her appeals is one of the forces that dispose viewers favorably or unfavorably, but constant stress on the special importance of facial makeup in televised debates tends to persuade the audience to pay less attention to what gets said than to how "natural" speakers look.

198

Don't Answer the Question They Ask You, Answer the Question You Want to Answer. The notion that this is the way "good" question-answer debates should be carried on by candidates is apparently traceable to the fact that, in 1960, John Kennedy answered the questions he chose to answer and Nixon, the ex-college debater and lawyer, was copious in answering the questions asked. In press conferences, too, Kennedy often ignored specific questions and talked about something he wanted to address. Apparently for these reasons, questioners in presidential debates seldom press for direct answers. I cannot remember ever hearing a reporter say, "But, sir, that is not responsive to the question I asked." Thus, a mythic "rule" has come down that candidates do well to say what they want in debate instead of answering specific questions. Hence, in 1984, neither Mondale nor Reagan was criticized for avoiding questions. In fact, both were praised for being strategically clever enough to get their own best points across. In 1988, Senator Dan Quayle believed the myth, evaded several critical questions, and badly lost his debate with Senator Lloyd Bentsen. In this case, the tepid criticism of Quayle by the media immediately following the debate was altered later when public sentiment ran heavily against Quayle's performance.

Where televised question-answer debates are concerned, it appears we have reached a point where candidates are praised for speaking in ways we would ordinarily call evasive at best and immoral at worst. A myth apparently traceable to 1960 has become "institutionalized" to the extent that what might reveal the specific opinions and states of knowledge of candidates is, as it were, tacitly excluded from the political forum. If candidates are free to do so, they will most certainly exercise persuasion through selecting what to answer.

Ignore Your Opponent and the Questioner Once He or She Is Finished Asking a Question; Then Address the National Audience. This "rule" arises from the fact that Kennedy consistently looked into the camera in 1960, while Nixon, ever the debater, looked at Kennedy when making or refuting a point. The worst moment for Senator Biden in the July 1, 1987 Houston debate came when he said, "I was going to address the audience, but since the camera is over here. . . ." He then turned away from the audience and delivered his concluding remarks to the fixed television camera. Apparently, he was unaware that roving cameras would have picked up his face no matter which way he faced.

It seems to me this "rule" will have to be modified in light of President Reagan's approach to debate situations. Reagan has been gracious to questioners; he has often looked at them while answering their questions. He has watched his opponents answer. He has often talked *to* his opponent, particularly when delivering one of his little correctives, such as "There you go again." What pundits will make of these facts in making "rules" for future presidential debates we shall have to wait to see, but the generalization derived from 1960 is not sound.

A Debate Will Be Remembered More for Points Scored than for One Line or One Mistake. The Ford-Dole team lost a close election to the Carter-Mondale team in 1976. Errors made in debates were interpreted as *causes* for the loss. Ford, who had been ridiculed by comedians as being clumsy and dumb, had overcome that problem with a strong acceptance speech and a credible showing in his first debate with Jimmy Carter. But, at least as publicly reported, all of this was lost when in the second debate Ford misspoke himself and said Poland was not under Soviet domination. The rest of that debate was ignored by most reporters; for the most part they dwelt on one answer to a single question. I do not imply that the mistaken answer was unimportant. I simply point out that to be accurate in reporting, the mistake needed to be placed in context. It was an answer to a follow-up question in which Ford talked about the independence of Yugoslavia, and the movement of Romania and Poland away from the Soviet Union on some policy matters.

In the Dole-Mondale debate of 1976, the clever Dole was easily holding his own with Mondale until Mondale pointed out that Dole had run the Republican Party when Watergate took place. Angrily, Dole shot back that blaming the Republicans for Watergate would be like blaming the Democrats for World War II. With indignation and probably purposely misunderstanding Dole's remark, Mondale replied at length that for Dole to blame Democrats for World War II was unfair and unjust.

Since that occasion in 1976, reporters have spent more time waiting for the "big gaffe" or other big moment than they have attending to the substance of the debates. In the 1980 New Hampshire primary, for example, George Bush was scheduled to debate Ronald Reagan one-on-one. But just before the debate, Reagan tried to change the rules to admit the other Republican contenders. When the moderator tried to shut down Reagan's microphone, Reagan yelled, "I paid for this microphone, Mr. Green." The face of the angry Reagan, who had borrowed a line delivered by Spencer Tracy in the movie "State of the Union," made every news broadcast; the debate that followed was anticlimactic and was hardly reported at all. Bush was the victim of the same kind of

200

selectivity in 1984 when the networks repeated again and again Geraldine Ferraro's, "Don't patronize me," a line everyone, including George Bush and the media, knew was coming at some point in the debate. In the July 1, 1987 Houston debate, Senator Albert Gore referred to dark-horse Tennessee candidate James Knox, meaning James K. Polk. Several commentators said this revealed that Tennesseean Gore was a converted Northerner, raised in Washington, D.C. and educated at Harvard.

Tom Shales, normally the reviewer of television entertainment programming for the *Washington Post,* has been used to review political debates. The results make the television commentators look substantive by comparison. For example, in his review of the two-party debate on NBC on December 1, 1987, Shales spent more time discussing "Tom 'Superboy' Brokaw" than on any single candidate. When he did talk about the candidates, he focused on their delivery, style, and appearance:

> They talked and talked, and soon a viewer couldn't be blamed for playing the game of who does he remind me of? Albert Gore still strongly resembles Clark Kent, only he never hops into a phone booth to become somebody more interesting. Paul Simon is looking less like Orville Redenbacher and more like Oscar Levant. Al Haig comes across as if he were a larky creation of the late Al Capp. Pete DuPont is Blake Carrington, but as weird Bruce Dern would portray him. Bruce Babbitt is Jimmy Stewart playing Jimmy Carter. Richard Gephardt blends right into the woodwork, as if he had been colorized but it didn't take. Pat Robertson is as shifty-eyed as ever, oddly avoiding direct contact with the camera. In George Bush there is just a trace—just a trace, mind you—of Jack Nicholson. The surliness is inescapable. And Dole is a tantalizing cross between former NBC newsman Lloyd Dobyns and Hurd Hatfield, who starred in the "Picture of Dorian Gray."[40]

Glib columns like this one may entertain readers but they do not contribute much to their understanding of the issues debated. Worse, they encourage the candidates to pay more attention to style than to substance.

If the media communicators continue to watch for and emphasize single moments in debates, and other campaign appearances, candidates will continue to rehearse "one liners" to capture attention of the media. Presidential debates, along with press conferences, no doubt, will be reduced to a series of simple-minded responses such as "Don't patronize me. . . . Whine on harvest moon! . . . Where's the beef? . . . There you go again. . . . That answer was as clear as Boston harbor!" Such responses do not serve the public well, nor does the reporting of them to the exclusion of other more thoughtful material. As is the case with other debate "myths," the notion that candidates must have "one liners" is a case where "rules" set down by reporters and the constraints of televised news have intruded on the debates themselves by changing the behaviors of the participants.

The Underdog Will Lose. Reporters have a bias in favor of underdogs for several reasons. The unexpected is presumed to be more newsworthy than the expected. Election contests are seen as "races," and debates among candidates are reduced to elemental win-lose occasions. And, of course, it is somewhat an American characteristic to favor underdogs. Such considerations have had a distorting effect on coverage of presidential debates on television. Reportage about campaigns is about the win-lose contest more than about exchanges and their meanings. In almost every case where the press and pundits have declared one candidate the probable winner of a debate, the other has been proclaimed the actual winner of that debate. Kennedy's victory over Nixon in the 1960's first debate was treated as remarkable because Kennedy was initially presumed to be the inferior debater of the two candidates. In the first debate between Gerald Ford and Jimmy Carter, Carter was predicted the probable winner because he had been portrayed as bright, quick, and knowledgeable, and Ford had been portrayed as plodding. Ford's advantage in that first debate was therefore treated as an "upset." The pursuit of "upsets" in reporting presidential debates has persisted. Reagan "upset" Carter. Mondale "upset" Reagan in their first debate and so was treated as the probable winner of the next debate; therefore, when Reagan appeared to have the advantage in that debate, he "upset" Mondale.

My point is not that the bias for underdogs in political reportage is *political;* my contention is that because reporters need to have news and news is tacitly defined as the *unusual,* accounts of presidential debates and campaigns are composed in order to persuade readers and viewers that the contests are like jousting matches or foot races. The significance of what is said in the debates thus becomes hidden from us. If we fail to recognize that this disguised persuasion is normally present in media accounts, we shall misperceive what actually happens in politics.

Whoever Wins the Debate Wins the Election. The attribution of Nixon's 1960 loss to his performance in the first debate with Kennedy strikes fear in the heart of every candidate who agrees to debate his or her opponent. But what politicians and reporters often fail to realize is that a candidate can win a debate but lose the sympathy of the voters. For example, in 1980 Ronald Reagan debated Republican-turned-Independent John B. Anderson on national television. Debate coaches, reporters, and the public in general thought Anderson convincingly won the debate. But what reporters failed to note was that, in the process of winning the debate, Anderson had taken positions inimical to his Republican roots and to the beliefs of many conservative Independent voters. So while polls showed that Anderson was perceived as the winner of the *debate,* his popularity in presidential *preference* polls rapidly declined. Moderate Republicans and conservative Independent voters preferred Reagan.

A similar phenomenon occurred after the first debate between George Bush and Michael Dukakis. In the Gallup poll following the debate, 38 percent of those interviewed thought Dukakis "did a better job" in the debate as opposed to 29 percent who said Bush did a better job in the debate. But the Gallup poll measuring presidential preference that was taken two days later, gave Bush a lead of 47 percent to 42 percent, virtually the same lead he enjoyed in the Gallup poll of September 11th two weeks before the debate. Reporters need to be much more sensitive to the reality that a debate is not the election, and the winners of debates may not be preferred in the vote that follows.

The mythos that has developed around presidential debates is unhealthy. The myths that the media have spun out are being taken as rules that candidates should follow. But coverage works to make the myths real. The glib will defeat the thorough. A single line is remembered more than the rest of the debate. Strategies that actually interfere with effective communication on issues are praised, while attention to detail is criticized. The realities of debates and campaigns are not the "realities" the media of mass communication are apt to report.

The most important myth may be that these joint press conferences are real debates. They are not. The format prevents the candidates and hence the voters from focusing on a single issue. Furthermore, politicians, seeking the least common denominator among the public, are reluctant to take specific stands. The short answer times give them the chance to avoid detail. This tactic, combined with the media bias toward the dramatic, humorous, and brief, saps the "debate" of its educational possibilities.

Surely, the complexities and the shifts of thought can be better reported than they usually are. And it is important to do so because, except for acceptance speeches where candidates are in control of the substance and the form of what they say, the modern televised "debate" provides the mass of voters with their best opportunity to assess candidates' characters, their abilities to think on their feet, and, most important, their stands on particular issues. The goal of political reporting ought to be to describe and interpret the *interactions* of a public debate rather than to declare a "winner" and a "loser." Failing that, a citizen's best defense against the oversimplifying persuasion of political reportage is to attend personally to such rhetorical events and to make independent judgments of the candidates facing one another. In the days of the often cited Lincoln-Douglas debates, political bias in reporting was rampant, as it is not today. Then and now, the fundamental democratic principle that justifies debates is that each individual voter is expected to *seek out* reliable information concerning candidates and issues. Debates themselves, not reports *about* them, render this principle practical and realistic if only voters will watch them and force candidates to take positions.

COMMON PERSUASIVE STRATEGIES
IN TECHNOLOGICAL MEDIA

I hope to have shown in this book that persuasion has always been pervasive in American public life. Most people readily recognize this. With the development of national, even international, coverage of events by audiovisual media of mass communication, all of the familiar means of persuasion continue to exist and to them are added an almost bewildering array of new opportunities, resources, and strategies for persuading about theology, individual freedom, political policies, campaigning for office, advertising products and services, disseminating news, and so on. That is why in this chapter I have pointed out the non-obvious ways in which communication that is *mediated* by audiovisual technologies persuades—either inevitably, inadvertently, or by design. Accordingly, I want to conclude the chapter by recapitulating the strategies I have been examining, this time identifying questions that are useful in analyzing what is "really there" in audiovisual communication. The questions I shall provide can open up the substance of disguised persuasion, making possible *informed* judgment of the merits of what is being presented.

I will begin with filmic presentations, whether fictional or "documentary." When watching a film, one ought to ask the following questions to uncover latent strategies of persuasion:

204

1. Are the characters specifically designed for you to identify with? Are there characters for other people to identify with? If you identified with a character, to what extent did you feel the character's attitudes and values were applicable to your situation? In the 1950s, many young people identified with James Dean in his classic films *Rebel Without A Cause* and *Giant*. Yet, the characters Dean played often broke the law. Is the character you identify with acting in ways that are inimical to your values, or in ways that reinforce your values? In retrospect, did this experience change your attitudes or values? If so, *what* made you change?

2. Did the film have a "message" beyond the story? That is, did you feel the need to do or think about something beyond simply enjoying the film? For example, many people who saw the *Star Wars* trilogy enjoyed it, but saw no need to change their lives or go out to support a cause. On the other hand, some who saw the film thought of the character Yoda as a Zen Master who neatly summarized the spiritual message of the films. Still others were reinforced in their quest for metaphysical meaning in life. Many who saw the movie *Norma Rae* became much more sympathetic to unions; many who saw *Wall Street* became more distrustful of big businessmen.

3. Were cinemagraphic techniques used to influence your perception of the "message"? First, think about such techniques as: slow-motion filming, backlighting, filming through gauze to soften features, using color or black and white photography. Can you link any such techniques to persuasion being worked? Were the characters you identified with filmed in flattering ways in contrast to the less sympathetic characters? Is black and white used, as in *Who's Afraid of Virginia Woolf,* or *The Last Picture Show,* to make the film more stark and the message clearer?

4. What tensions, if any, were raised by the film between your values and those espoused or portrayed in the film? What actions, ideas, or values that you typically reject seemed more acceptable after seeing the film? Why? What values that you hold were reinforced? How?

When watching television news, consider these questions to see whether you were being persuaded and, if so, how:

1. Were the reporters trying to dress a persuasive message in objective or informative clothing? Often we are told by a reporter that he or she is trying to get at the truth. If so, were all

sides given a voice? Were all the facts presented with equal emphasis or were you being asked to make a judgment based on isolated examples, biased or unknown sources, or selective witnesses? Were you checking what you saw and heard on television against what you read in the newspaper and magazines?

2. Were the news teams or the people they covered "playing" to the audience? Was the story being dramatized or shortened to hold your attention? Was a politician *staging* and timing his or her event to get on the news?

3. Were you deluged by technical effects that enhanced credibility but distorted the substance presented? For example, election results should be just that—results, but we are often led to believe that "exit polls," "random samples," and other projections give the results as accurately and more quickly than the actual vote. Most of the time they come close; but misses happen every election night on some network. Have flashing screens, colorful graphics, and statistics helped you understand the facts and ideas better, or did they obscure important information?

4. Did constraints such as time-of-day or where-the-largest-audience-is produce imbalances in news coverage? For example, the sun rises over New York three hours before its rays warm Los Angeles, so each day the news "starts" in the East first, and the East has a much larger total population. Did the news show you watched emphasize Eastern news? Were the stories in the newscast covered for their *importance to viewers* or because they could be conveniently covered by television or because they fit the limited time slots in the program? Ask yourself whether you missed anything of importance because of these kinds of time and demographic pressures on newscasting.

5. Was there evidence that the news was "packaged" to suit a theme or point of view? Did items or events seem "arranged" to sustain a particular kind of story line? If so, do you know of any facts that run counter to the theme that was developed? Did the selection of stories seem to show any pattern or outlook that would not be supported if stories had been selected simply for their importance?

6. Is the story you were listening to a prediction or based on hard fact? How did the reporter know the prediction would come true? and when? Write the prediction down and check to see if the reporter was right.

7. What impact was competition having on this story? Was the story being put on the air to raise the ratings of the news show?

Was the story the result of competition between two reporters at the same network trying to get more "air time"? What motivated the reporters to get involved in this story? What motivated the network to cover the story?

To track these possibilities requires diligent and critical listening and viewing, but if we want to minimize the degree to which we are manipulated, we have little choice but to attend to such questions in order to unmask disguised persuasion. From the days of Puritan New England until the era of Joseph McCarthy, most political persuasion in America was achieved through face-to-face communication or through print. In this chapter I have focused on the multitude of new communicative possibilities that operate persuasively because we now have giant information systems that are electronically mediated and therefore are freighted with new persuasive possibilities. These new systems supplement and in some circumstances displace face-to-face talk and print as instruments of political persuasion. That is why it is important to be sensitive to the overt and the disguised means of expounding and weaving the fabric of political life in the United States.

Myths, mores, and ideals introduce persuasion into electronic reporting, as they do in print journalism. The ideals of journalism include impartiality, accuracy, comprehensiveness, and truthfulness. These very ideals and the traditions associated with them are sources of subtle persuasion because they are claimed as virtues of what we are told, yet they are never totally realized, nor can they be. Nonetheless, to the extent that a reader or viewer or listener believes reportage is impartial, accurate, comprehensive, and true, he or she is persuaded to believe realities are *as they are presented*. That has always been the case with political journalism, but now vast amounts of political reportage and persuasion are brought before us *electronically*. As a result, there are special ways in which *broadcast* news will fall short of total impartiality, complete accuracy, comprehensiveness, and truthfulness.

To summarize, audiovisual narration leads to special, subtle kinds of persuasion. The desire to make news into "stories" leads to distorting reality in order to make accounts more fascinating and to make them cohere. Often the story is then punctuated with cinemagraphic techniques borrowed from movie makers. Slow-motion filming, fading to black at the end of a tragic story, and using "freeze frames" to "lock in on" an image are techniques that blur the line between fact and fiction. Editing, selecting, competition, and the constraints of time and money inevitably shape the "realities" that can be portrayed, and they also yield possibilities for deliberate persuasion.

Persons present broadcast news; they will be cast in their parts with the hope that they will give attractiveness and credibility to content. What we think of the people who function in various roles as broadcasters will affect our receptivity to the information they give. In addition, claims made about news sources can persuade us positively or negatively. The reputation of a network or station and its news department persuades us toward belief or disbelief.

Finally, a number of practices common in newscasting persuade. These include the use of sweeping language, selectivity because of deadlines, predisposing predictions that are made by news gatherers and interpreters, and adherence to myths, either of the society or of what is "good" presentation.

Thomas Jefferson's dream of a properly functioning democratic republic was premised on the establishment of an educated citizenry. The public becomes informed by partaking of the free marketplace of ideas. In the final analysis, it is up to the public to demand the best news and information services, and to sift all that is offered for latent persuasive strategies in each. Under those circumstances, we can fulfill Jefferson's dream "[T]o follow truth wherever it may lead, nor to tolerate any error so long as reason is left free to combat it."

NOTES

1. I focus on television news because of its wide impact, but newspapers, radio, and magazines could be used to make the same point. See Robert L. Bishop, "The Rush to Chain Ownership," *Columbia Journalism Review* (Nov./ Dec. 1972), 10–19. The ability of news magazines to force selection of Wilkie as a presidential candidate in 1940 and the collapse of newspaper competition today are reviewed by Bishop. He explains also how reliance on news services (UPI, AP, and Reuters), chain ownership (Scripps-Howard, Knight-Ridder, Cowles), and chain editorialists (Will, Kilpatrick, Broder) have led to a certain uniformity. This trend has been accelerated by corporate leaders such as Al Neuharth, who created *USA Today,* and Rupert Murdoch, who has assembled a vast media empire that spans the globe. In 1987 there were only 1,600 daily newspapers and only 434 of those were independently owned. An Elmo Roper poll in 1971 revealed that 60 percent of those polled depended primarily on television for their news; see Marvin Barrett, ed. *Survey of Broadcast Journalism* (New York, 1971), 7. Gallup took a poll in April of 1984 that showed that 62 percent of the public said that television was their most important source of news and information. This is true even though Professor John Robinson of the Department of Sociology at the University of Maryland found that on a typical day 67 percent of respondents read a newspaper while 52 percent saw a "local or national TV newscast." See "Myths About the Media," *TV Guide (May 30, 1987),* 3.

2. *In his Human Communication as Narration* (Columbia: University of South Carolina Press, 1987), Walter R. Fisher argues that from childhood we learn to apply two tests of "narrative rationality": "Human communication is tested against the principles of probability (coherence) and fidelity (truthfulness and reliability)." The quotation given here appears on page 47; see especially his pages 47–49. By "fidelity" Fisher means truthfulness to experience as we know it. In the "logical" analysis I have presented in this section, I have argued that viewers of *Bonnie and Clyde* would apply to the filmic narrative substantially what Fisher calls the tests of "narrative rationality."

3. See John C. Merrill and Ralph Lowenstein, *Media, Messages and Men: New Perspectives in Communication* (New York, 1971), 228–41. Joseph T. Klapper, *The Effects of Mass Communication* (Glencoe, Illinois, 1960), 250–61. John Robinson and Mark Levy, *The Main Source: Learning from Television News* (Beverly Hills: Sage, 1986), Chapter 6.

4. Edward J. Epstein, *News from Nowhere* (New York, 1973), 13. Epstein goes on to point out that at NBC, "only 41% of the news films depicted events on the day they occurred" 15. The figure is similar for CBS and ABC. The illusion of mirroring reality is maintained in network in-house publications: see, for example, ABC's *Manual of Standards and Policies, 1966*.

5. At times special-events anchorpersons become more concerned with *how* the news is being presented than with the news itself. In telecasting conventions, the introduction of mini-cameras and radio-wave headgear is explained to the audience. For space shots, everything from camera angles to long range flight tracking is discussed in terms of greater coverage and accuracy.

6. News presidents, anchorpersons, reporters, producers, directors, etc.—all have been removed or hired at the whim of corporate executives on the basis of the ratings received by the individual or their broadcasts.

7. These observations are based on interviews of NBC newswriters conducted by the author in 1968.

8. Daniel Schorr told me that "television does not have a liberal bias, only a bias toward the dramatic, the simplistic, the confrontations—toward whatever raises ratings. In short, a bias toward success in a competitive free market of images and information." (Interviewed by the author July 18, 1986).

9. The *New York Times* makes some kind of admission when it claims it reports "All the news that's *fit* to print." See Richard Lee, ed., *Politics and the Press* (New York, 1970). Fred Friendly, *Due to Circumstances Beyond Our Control* (New York, 1968); Ben Bagdikian, *The Effete Conspiracy* (New York, 1972); Newton Minow, et al., *Presidential Television* (New York, 1973); John Hohenberg, *Free Press; Free People* (New York, 1971); Kurt and Gladys Lang, *Politics and Television* (New York, 1968); Sig Michelson, *The Electric Mirror* (New York, 1972); James Reston, *The Artillery of the Press* (New York, 1967); William Small, *Political Power and the Press* (New York, 1972); Robert T. Bower, *Television and the Public* (New York, 1973).

10. In an interview with *Playboy,* Walter Cronkite claimed that the "number of words spoken in a half-hour evening news broadcast—words spoken by interviewees, interviewers, me, everybody—came out to be the same number of words as occupy two thirds of the front page of the standard newspaper." *Playboy* (June, 1972), 77. See also Hohenberg, *Free Press*, 487 and Epstein, *News from Nowhere*, 113–14.

11. See Edith Efron, *The News Twisters* (Los Angeles, 1971), 18, 23–25. Maury Green, *Television News: Anatomy and Process* (Belmont, Calif., 1969).

12. *Future Shock* (New York, 1971), 164. Toffler continues the discussion of packaging the news for several more pages. See also Efron, *News Twisters*, 8–9; Ben Bagdikian, *The Information Machines* (New York, 1971), 90; Douglas Cater, *Power in Washington* (New York, 1964), 223–24; and Maxwell McCombs and Donald Shaw, "The Agenda Setting Function of the Mass Media," *Public Opinion Quarterly* (Summer 1972), vol. 36, 167–87; and Epstein, *News from Nowhere*, 17.

13. Epstein, *News from Nowhere*, 174–75.

14. For Cronkite's comment see *Playboy*, (June, 1972), 84. For Brinkley's comment see the *Washington Post* (Apr. 1, 1974), p. A-22.

15. Fisher, *Human Communication as Narration*, 47–49.

16. Epstein, *News from Nowhere*, 138. See also 149. In 1986, NBC's Chris Wallace made 122 appearances on that network's evening news. ABC's Sam Donaldson made 113; CBS's Bill Plante made 110. ABC's John McWethy and CBS' David Martin made 101. NBC's Robert Hager made 91; CBS's Bruce Morton and ABC's Brit Hume made 81; CBS's Eric Engberg had 78. The first correspondent in the top 20 from outside the Washington area was CBS's Allen Pizzey who covers the Mediterranean and the Middle East; he had 75 appearances. He is followed by Phil Jones of CBS, with 72 appearances, all related to his congressional beat. The rest of the top 20 in terms of appearances include: Dan Cordtz, ABC, 68; John Cochran, NBC, 65; Rita Braver, CBS, 60; Tom Fenton, CBS, 59; John Martin, ABC, 58; Lesley Stahl, CBS, 78; Ray Brady, CBS, 56; Susan Spencer, CBS, 56; and Dean Reynolds, ABC, 56. Note that Wallace made more than twice as many appearances as even the fifteenth ranked correspondent. When these figures are divided up by network, it becomes very clear that a few correspondents dominate the evening news broadcasts. These figures were compiled by Joe S. Foote, Chair, Department of Radio and Television, Southern Illinois University.

17. Epstein cites many other examples.

18. The author was employed as a consultant by CBS News for the 1968, 1972, and 1984 political conventions, coverage of the election nights in 1972, 1974, 1982, 1984, 1986, and 1988, and coverage of the 1985 Inaugural.

19. A Mississippi delegate allowed me to enter the caucus room; it was closed to the press.

20. These events were staged at both conventions in order to appeal to voters. They are persuasive in their own right and CBS has the right to pick and choose which it will televise. However, that selection process was not equitable in this case due to economic considerations.

21. Epstein, *News from Nowhere*, 5. See also 10–13. The strategy is not only to symbolize but to nationalize a given story. The media claim that one local story "typifies" the entire national problem. See Epstein, 58, 242.

22. See Dennis T. Lowery, "Agnew and the Network TV News: A Before/After Content Analysis," *Journalism Quarterly*, 41 (1971), 209–10.

23. See also Patrick Buchanan's critique of Tom Pettit's report on Ramsey Clark on the "Today Show" in "News Watch," *TV Guide* (Nov. 16–22, 1974), pp. A3-4.

24. See also Epstein, *News from Nowhere*, 129.

25. In "The Role and Rights of the Press," *Washington Post* (Nov. 11, 1974), p. A-20. Fred Graham of CBS News defends the press in "Gagging the Press in the Courtroom," *Washington Post* (Nov. 17, 1974), p. C-3. Graham reviews the increasing number of constraints placed on the press by judges over the last ten years. For previous and more standard accounts, see Don R. Pember, *Privacy and the Press: The Law, the Mass Media, and the First Amendment* (Seattle, 1972). Frederick Seaton Siebert, *The Rights and Privileges of the Press* (Westport, Conn., 1970).

26. *Time,* Apr. 1, 1974, 31.

27. See Philip J. Hilts, "Eye on the White House," *Potomac Magazine* (*Washington Post:* Apr. 21, 1974), 28.

28. Many in Washington, D.C. believed this leak by Regan or his staff was injudicious and did not serve him well. Regan's object in having the story come out was to portray his strength in the face of the First Lady's irrationality.

29. *Time* (Oct. 6, 1986), 73.

30. On September 19, 1987 *TV Guide* ran an article entitled, "Is TV News Too Tough—or Too Easy—on Israel?" See also Edwin Diamond, A. Biddle Duke, and Isabella Anacker, "Can We Expect TV News to Correct Its Mistakes," *TV Guide* (Dec. 5, 1987) 4–10.

31. The Commission goes on to catalogue such reports. See *Report of the National Advisory Commission on Civil Disorders* (Kerner Report) (New York, 1968), 372.

32. Kerner Report, 377.

33. Daniel Walker, *Rights in Conflict* (Task Force Report to the National Commission on the Causes and Prevention of Violence) (New York, 1968), 303. The Kerner Report gives another example: "The television newscasters during the period of actual disorders in 1967 intended to emphasize law enforcement activities, thereby over-shadowing underlying grievances and tensions." 369.

34. CBS now has more regularly scheduled news than any network in the history of television. Its list includes the "Morning News," "The CBS Evening News," "Nightwatch," "60 Minutes," "West 57th," "Sunday Morning," "Face the Nation," and "48 Hours."

35. See Bagdikian's comment on competition, 105. See U.S. House of Representatives, *Broadcasting Ratings* (Hearings before the Subcommittee of the Committee on Interstate and Foreign Commerce) 88th Congress, 1st session, 1963).

36. Stephen E. Lucas, *Portents of Rebellion* (Philadelphia: Temple University Press, 1976), 145.

37. For an opposing view see David L. Vancil and Sue D. Pendell, "The Myth of Viewer-Listener Disagreement in the First Kennedy-Nixon Debate," *Central States Speech Journal,* (Spring, 1987), vol. 38, no. 1, 16–27.

38. Kennedy had refused makeup because he was tan from a vacation in Palm Beach. Nixon, not wanting to appear less manly and fearing the Kennedy campaign would point out that Nixon wore cosmetics, also refused makeup for the broadcast.

39. See Tom Shales, "The Diverting Democrats," *Washington Post* (July 3, 1987) B1, B6; and David Broder, "Gephardt, Simon, Dukakis Score Well Among Viewers," *Washington Post* (July 3, 1987), A1, A16. At least Shales' column was confined to the "Style" section. The July 1 "debate" was broadcast on PBS as part

211

of the *Firing Line* program hosted by William F. Buckley. This precluded the commercial networks from carrying the "debate" and being able to comment immediately.

40. "Candidates' Debate," *Washington Post* (Dec. 2, 1987), p. B4.

7

RESOLVING THE TENSIONS

Since adventurers and pilgrims first set foot on this continent, Americans have been persuading one another to make decisions. From John Smith's, "If you don't work, you don't eat," to Ronald Reagan's appeal for an "Economic Bill of Rights," persuasion has played an enormous role in national decision making. When that persuasion is closely examined, the tensions that permeate persuasion in America are revealed.

Tensions are inevitable in free societies. Liberty, if it guarantees anything at all, guarantees the right to disagree, and disagreement leads to tension. Where everyone is free to persuade, some are certain to argue against the freedom of *all* to persuade freely on *all* subjects in *all* ways. Some believe that the speech of those espousing subversive ideas should be restricted. Some believe certain subjects should be forbidden in the marketplace of ideas. Some believe persuasion over one medium should be restricted while persuasion over another should not. The debate over who can persuade about what, when, and over which medium is the root of all the specific "tensions" portrayed in this book.

The tensions in American political persuasion are of three main sorts. First, tension exists between freedom of expression and restrictions on political subject matters. Throughout American history political leaders have tried to exclude from the marketplace what they considered subversive ideas. As I have shown, this has sometimes been done in the name of religion and sometimes in the name of political stability. As I write, the battle over what is "indecent," or "pornographic" rages, as does the battle over which of these kinds of communication should be censored, in what media, and by whom. The issues are political as well as social and moral. Some studies have suggested that pornography has unhealthy consequences for individuals and/or society; others argue just the reverse. The subject is too involved to consider here except by pointing out that court decisions concerning these matters have been and still are in the process of change, as they have been for decades.[1]

As I have stressed, a second set of tensions exists between freedom and the regulation of certain media of communication. Political persuasion has for the most part escaped censorship since the 1960s, but actions of the 1950s signal that attempts to create political constraints are as possible in modern time as they were in the days of the Alien and Sedition Acts. And, as I have also shown, opportunities for political persuasion are indirectly restricted by the policies of a government that regulates the content of news and editorial programming of the electronic media.

A third set of tensions arises from the conflict between freedom of political expression and restrictions on communicative objectives. Policies concerning "libel" illustrate both the presence and the complexity of these kinds of tensions. If it can be shown that an author intended to defame another person, that author's work may be restricted, and he or she may be forced to make restitution to the injured party. However, if the injured party is a "public person" of some standing, a more lenient standard is applied to the offending author's work. This leniency provides a protection for genuinely investigative reporting that may reveal corruption or other illegalities. On the other hand, there are restrictions on "fighting words," racial, ethnic, and sexist slurs. These are justified on grounds that divisive, ignorant, and pejorative objectives ought to be curtailed in the marketplace of ideas. It is thus clear that issues concerning what is politically "legitimate" in American society are far from settled.

Freedom does not exist in pure form even in a "free" society. At times it exists in conflict with other social goals that encroach on freedom's domain. American political persuasion is influenced by constraints arising from all three classes of tensions. As the means of public communication become more complex and subtle, the points of tension become more complex and numerous, and new "reasons" for regulation of public discourse arise. New technologies and strategies motivate political leaders to try to place new restrictions on public discourse, on freedom to use that discourse, and on where and when the discourse may legitimately take place. I have stressed the inconsistencies of regulative policies that do not extend the "print model" of the First Amendment to electronic media of mass communication and that restrict television stations as they do not restrict teletext or television cable operations. Both political and nonpolitical communication is thereby confusingly restrained and the marketplace of ideas is illogically constructed.

I have argued throughout this book that an open marketplace for political ideas is necessary to the proper functioning of a free, democratic-republican society. This position is not a new one. In his *Rhetoric,*

214

Aristotle contended that the ultimate end of rhetorical activity ought to be to construct and to maintain social systems and that, other things being equal, truth will prevail in society because truth is observed, based on reality, and not fabricated. There, "truth" can prevail if fully, artfully, and adaptively promoted and defended. Falsehoods or imagined matters, he said, are invented and so require greater skills—including rhetorical skills—to sustain them. This proposition is the foundation of the occidental system of jurisprudence. When both sides are represented by *qualified* spokespersons or lawyers, the judge and/or jury is presumed able to determine the truth or justice of the matter at hand. Aristotle contended that truth or its best approximation will prevail *if argued for with full rhetorical skill,* and our system of justice even incorporates that qualification through its prescription that if it can be shown that an incompetent lawyer represented one side or the other in a case, that is cause for ordering a new trial.

Of course, this system is not perfect; due to mitigating circumstances, hidden interests, or errors in judgment, the truth may suffer on occasion. But over time, the system corrects itself, especially when it is open to public scrutiny. In fact, television cameras are allowed to cover some trials these days for just that reason.

Thomas Jefferson, among others, added a new dimension to this argument by postulating that an open marketplace of ideas fosters public awareness and contributes to education of the electorate. That, in turn, strengthens democracy against those who would suppress it. Through vigorous and spirited public debate citizens become informed about the actions of their government, and they can react responsibly. An unencumbered press, Jefferson thought, is essential to this process. He wrote:

> No experiment can be more interesting than that we are now trying, and which we trust will end in establishing the fact that man may be governed by reason and truth. Our first object should therefore be to leave open to him all the avenues to truth. The most effectual hitherto found, is freedom of the press.[2]

Jefferson believed that open debate can better expose corruption and prevent falsehood than can any set of laws.

A free marketplace of ideas is not only an aspect of democratic theory, it is a presupposition of American constitutionalism. The question is not whether we shall have a free marketplace of ideas, the question is how best to maintain it. One way is to resolve the tensions that plague it in favor of openness wherever possible. Another way is to ground the

215

tensions of pragmatic, workable applications of public policy instead of ideological conceptualizations.[3]

Historically, tensions have been "resolved" over the long run by the emergence of compromiser-synthesizers who moderate dogmatic positions. Theodore Roosevelt modified the radical demands of the Populist platform in such ways as to make them palatable to a wider audience. The modification included stripping away the most radical proposals and then couching the new program in a rhetoric that did not threaten mainstream voters. That rhetorical adaptation tied the new programs to traditional institutions and themes.

In the United States, institutional forces have provided remarkable stability, and these stabilizing forces have worked for the most part to confine conflicts to verbal confrontations. The cases I have examined show how the American guarantee of free speech and free press has contributed to the viability of the political marketplace. I began with the arduous argumentation of Puritan preachers and the Populists to illustrate how philosophical confrontations alter the values of Americans. Philosophical confrontations between defenders of freedom and those seeking to impose a theology on society ultimately reinforced individualism, while, at the same time, allowing a national acceptance of diversity to develop. The Populists' experience illustrated that while politics can be elevated to a philosophical level by those seeking reform, such a strategy tends to result in reform of a more pragmatic kind that was envisioned by the ideological instigators of the movement.

Next, I examined three cases of suppression, each of which may seem less important to Americans today than to those who suffered through the crises. However, such suppression could happen again, and the strategies used to defeat the censors in these three instances are important to the preservation of free political persuasion in America. If some Founders could be seduced into subverting the First Amendment in its seventh year of existence, if the men who won the Civil War could pervert its ends by subjugating liberty in the South, and if such legendary figures as Dwight Eisenhower could appear at a political rally with a demagogue like Joe McCarthy, we have reason to believe that repression could rise again. We are well advised, then, to remember the strategies of radical elements whether of right or left and to emulate those who succeeded in defeating the radicals.

A free marketplace of ideas provides a forum for correcting extremism in our society, and it also encourages the pragmatic side of political persuasion. The American political system reduces philosophical and ideological positions to pragmatic political proposals. We are a *prag-*

matically conservative people. Political persuasion has had to "come down" out of the philosophical and be situationally pragmatic and personal in order to be effective.[4] While philosophical persuasion can set the bearing or lay down fundamental premises, political persuasion has to be about what to do and how to do it if it is to move the American audience. For the most part, the public wants to know *how* the government is going to be run to assure economic prosperity and national security.

Perennial contests among democratic values have had a major impact on pragmatic operations of the political system. As I have shown, some argue that "equal voices with equal access" to the media of communication is a more important value than free and unrestricted participation in the political system. Others argue that "fairness," by which they mean government-ordered presentation of "contrasting views," is more important than complete freedom of expression. The problem is that social agendas that elevate values above freedom lead to control of political and cultural content. The Alien and Sedition Acts were primarily aimed at controlling internal subversion fomented by foreign agents, but soon American editors and politicians who criticized President Adams and his party found themselves in jail. The same occurred during and after the Civil War, during the "Red Scare" under Woodrow Wilson and Warren Harding, and during the McCarthy era in the early 1950s.

Current attempts to curtail political expression should cause concern because they often affect the content of messages and thereby threaten the free marketplace of ideas. In reaction to the Watergate crisis, campaign reforms opened the political marketplace in ways that accomplished some good. An example is the requirement that all contributions to a political campaign be promptly reported to the Federal Election Commission and made available by the Commission to the press, the public, and opposing candidates. That step guarantees that the public knows who is supporting whom with what amounts of funds. The information is available to all. Such a requirement does not hinder the free flow of ideas, nor does it restrict anyone's ability to raise money in any way other than "under the table." It is a regulation that opens the process to scrutiny and contributes to political dialogue.

As I indicated in chapter 4, the same reform bill also imposed restrictions that limit the free flow of ideas. It limited how much could be spent on a political campaign. This part of the measure was struck down by the Supreme Court as an unconstitutional restriction. Other "reforms" that restrict political persuasion remain, and still others are proposed, all presumably in the interest of purifying political life. There now exists a restriction on how much one person or one group can contribute to a political campaign, and proposals that would limit citizens' participation through political action committees (PACs) were placed before the 100th Congress in 1987.[5] These and other restrictions on political freedom arise from the opinion that if persons and groups are free to support political activity as they wish, some will acquire too much power and influence. That kind of fear is as old as the Constitution itself. At times such fears have served the democracy well. On one hand, it was fear of the power of "the wealthy" that led to abandonment of property qualifications for voters that originally existed in the constitutions of many of the early states. But the same impulse, in the form of suspicions of powerful PACs and of the influences of wealth, have led to restrictions on *everyone's* rights to participate fully and freely in the political marketplace. These are but recent examples of the constant tensions between such honorable values as the equal-voice-for-all-citizens and the *first* American freedom—freedom of speech and press.

Government's assuming the power of licensing electronic media illustrates how power of "authorization" can be converted to control over content. Laws affecting the electronic media can be used by those in power to suppress the rights of others. Key operatives of John Kennedy, Lyndon Johnson, Richard Nixon, the CIA, and members of the Federal Communications Commission have all proposed to use government-sanctioned controls over content to stamp out opposition in the electronic media and to intimidate publishers who own television and radio stations.

Further, the "red tape" of even the best intended regulation slows development of new media of communication. Controls are slowing the advance of new technologies, such as videotex and teletext,[6] because those technologies fall under regulation by the Federal Communications Commission. The danger increases that controls over content will be applied even to newsprint now "broadcast" by satellite to printing locations. News information obtained by satellite sensors can be restricted by other government agencies. As new technologies emerge out of old ones, or as they are assimilated into the publication process, the laws that restrict technology become potential limitations on publication.

This danger is compounded by agenda-setters and elitists who would use restrictions to promote their own programs. To argue for a given agenda or cultural value is a guaranteed right in a free society. Proponents have the right of expression even if their programs would restrict the rights of others. But agenda-setters and elitists become impatient with the evolutionary nature of our system. Their goals are more speedily

218

attainable through *controlling* channels of communication than through the slower but systematic workings of *competition* among ideas and channels.

Those who seek to set a national social agenda have been especially zealous in defending governmental controls over the content of the electronic media. Controlling the airwaves is a powerful way to promote ideas and policies. The tactic is not new, but it is dangerous. Hitler used a press law not unlike the Fairness Doctrine to organize the printed and electronic media in monolithic support for the Third Reich. One of the first things rebel groups do to solidify a coup is seize radio and television stations. The United States was the first country in the history of the world to include in its Constitution guarantees of freedom of expression. Paradoxically, in regard to the electronic media, the United States is more like the England of Henry VIII than it is like the United States of 1791, the year we adopted the Bill of Rights.

Elitists who would restrict communicative systems do not trust the public to make its own evaluations. Or worse, they would impose their own views on the "masses." In the former case, the principles of restriction become translated into familiar practical forms: The public should see so much news each night, the composition of that news should meet governmentally determined standards, and editorial opinion should cover certain issues and carry "contrasting views."[7] From elitists there is less talk about doing good "in the public interest," and more suggestions that people of the elitist sort know more and could rule better if unfettered by the demands of average citizens. Like Plato's philosopher kings, elitists would propagandize citizens to ennoble them.[8] In managing the airwaves, elitists would select the programming or at least "quantify" how much of each type of programming should be allowed on the air. In fact, elitists have used government controls over content in the media to discourage documentaries, news, and programming that is alien to their ideals.

Those who would manage *political* content and/or *cultural* content are anti-democratic because they do not trust citizens to decide issues or select communicative materials for themselves. Both groups have used their freedom to persuade as a means of fostering their beliefs at the expense of others' beliefs and preferences. Frequently some moral, cultural, or political value is pronounced more important than untrammeled freedom to express and to consume what is expressed. But once this is done, the very values the regulators put forward can also be subverted because freedom to argue about the relative merits of public values is then chilled. In the early years of Pennsylvania's statehood, it

219

took a decade to establish the principle that all Pennsylvanians were free to discuss and to alter their state government as they wished. This came about because radical democrats legislated that their original Constitution, called "The Frame of 1776," was sacrosanct and that legislators were not free to discuss the basic law of the state. The paradox ended only with ratification of the federal Constitution. In our own days, other values have been placed above freedom to express. The Congress has placed fairness, access, equity, and other values above freedom of expression for licensed media. The result is that they have put in place or have advocated tools that can be used to suppress speech generally.

In opposition to regulative lines of thinking, this book has been an attempt to show by historical illustration that free and open competition among values and policies has been, in the long run, the better alternative. This is true in part because freedom compels competition among the media and among those who have invested in them. The different potentialities and constraints of the several media of communication work against monopolies of views, unfairness in communication, long-term distortions in reportage, and suppression of political persuasion. Where communication and use of media are entirely free, overt and disguised modes of persuasion succeed or fail to persuade *according to the judgments of the persuadees.* This is the communicative condition that the fundamental principles of republican democracy presuppose. If we are to operate under democratic assumptions, we must trust citizens to make proper decisions based on the information they have. And the best way to assure that the information they receive is unadulterated is to make sure it comes from an open, uncensored, unpatronizing marketplace of ideas.

For the system to work well, citizens and their leaders should be able to persuade publicly about any matter of governmental policy. To have this freedom, we must tolerate attacks on it. Sometimes we must endure bad taste. Always we must try to make what we consider the "best" ideas fully and artfully presented in the competition of ideas. And we must also be vigilant lest freedom be taken from us or periodically suppressed by those who would play on our distaste for some of the communication that is bound to arise in a free and open marketplace.

I believe I have shown how freedom of political expression has led to compromise and synthesis, hence relative stability in our society. Freedom of political expression is the value our historic institutions were created to foster. The system of checks and balances, so fundamental in our political structure, creates a bias in favor of resolving tensions by compromise and synthesis. Separation of powers presupposes *negotiated*

220

decisions reached through competition among ideas, entities, and leaders. And that method, though frequently frustrating, has worked for two hundred years to institutionalize *pragmatic moderation.*

Our traditional dialectic between order and freedom has encouraged a two-party system. That system is powerfully encouraged by the structure of our national government. There is *one* executive, not several as some proposed when the Constitution was being framed. That means *one* political point of view will preside over the executive branch at any given time. The Supreme Court always reflects several executives' political persuasions because of the judges' appointments for life. The two legislative houses have to be presided over by *majority* leaders. With all of this checking and balancing, there is scarcely any opportunity for ideologues' action because it is almost inconceivable that an ideology other than the balance-of-power doctrine could command more than one branch of government at any given time. Ideologies, for the most part, are supported by minorities. To have impact, such minorities are forced to operate within the larger structures of our political parties. There they must compromise or become isolated.

So how must the system work? Only by persuasion about who is going to do what. The Enlightenment's homage to reason was transformed into a pragmatic government in the Declaration of Independence, the Constitution, the Bill of Rights, and the Emancipation Proclamation. Each of these documents not only buttresses our government, but lends credibility to the citizen orator by *certifying his or her right to persuade.* This right is underscored by the Founders' commitment to personal accountability. A reading of the reports of the Constitutional Convention and the Ratification Debates makes clear that the Founders' view of human nature was rooted in personal accountability. Over and over a major theme of debate was how federal officers were to be held responsible for their actions. The main answers settled on were: by frequent elections and by separation of powers. The plan finally adopted greatly reduced the relevance of ideology in political debate. Ideologies might lie behind proposals, but the proposals themselves had to be sold on grounds of specific benefits and minimal costs in economics and fairness. Placing personal accountability above party or group accountability made it imperative for political persuasion to be pragmatic in order to succeed. The basic American political issue was and remains: Who is going to do what, how and with what probable result? When the French cried "Liberty, Equality, and Fraternity" from the barricades, Americans then and since have consistently asked *who* was most likely to forward such ideals *under the constraints and freedoms of the written Constitution.*

221

The result has been that political persuasion in America is very different from persuasion in parliamentary governments, even in England and Canada. The doctrine of balanced and separated powers, the tradition of personal responsibility, and the conditions under which leadership is attained in the national government all mitigate against ideological and numerous political parties.

How could, say, five ideologically different parties function under our system? To achieve power, several parties would have to agree on one presidential candidate, on a majority leader in the Senate, on a Speaker of the House, and on a vice president. That would be virtually impossible. What happened to the Populists is almost certain to happen to any ideological party of strength. They may even find a charismatic leader who can gain a fair percentage of presidential votes, but providing consensus leadership in the House and Senate will be difficult if not impossible. What happened to the Populists was not exceptional. The same has happened to the Socialists, the Communists, and to other ideologically oriented groups. The very structure of our political system strongly encourages a two-party system, and that, in turn, means that the most successful political persuasion must be centrist, bearing somewhat to the left or right. Only so can "independents" be swung in one direction or the other while persuaders maintain their basic cores of left-leaning or right-leaning partisans.[9] Finally, the institutions of primary elections and national party conventions are not constitutionally mandated but have existed for more than a century. They, too, encourage *two* but discourage many political parties.

Our system and our traditions also emphasize adjustment over disruption. Decision by debate is the institutional ideal. Conflict is therefore usually worked out in dialogue and ultimately resolved by the acquiescence of the popular audience. We have a tradition that political persuasion is preferable to force, so a particular debate may go on over many years, as did the debate over the right of women to vote. And no matter how long the debate, political persuaders must address each other's arguments or face the charge of violating "the rules" of politics. Many have "taken to the streets," but political leadership does not come in America *directly* from "street" activity. Witness the intervals that had to elapse between Jesse Jackson's and Tom Hayden's "street" activities and their acceptance as established political actors. *Adjustment* is a major mark of persuasion *within* American political institutions.

Adjustment is encouraged in another way. Most of our democratic goals and assumptions are ambiguous. For example, Judeo-Christian values inform our system, but Judeo-Christian *doctrines* do not. Our

Constitution dictates a democratic *republic,* not a pure democracy. The separation of church and state is dictated by the Constitution but the applications of that principle are perennially argued. We are devoted to pluralism but have evolved a "civil religion." In a paradoxical way, these and other ambiguities absorb calls for change. The Populist platform is compromised into the Democratic; the Progressive into the Republican and Democratic; the Socialist into the New Deal. Revolution is prevented by the fact that ideals are not fixed and all conceptions are open to scrutiny and interpretation by a diverse public. Thus, progress is made slowly within a framework of general assumptions interpreted, enforced, and reinforced rhetorically so that change is usually evolutionary rather than revolutionary.

Checks and balances, inter- and intra-party rivalries, robust public debate, traditional procedures in government, and pluralism compel compromise and synthesis. Multiplication of media of communication introduces more competition and more checking and balancing information. The news media and the competition among them introduce checks on abuses, unfairness, and error. Each source keeps an eye on the others, challenging where "error" or "misrepresentation" is found.

The multiplicity of persuasive sources also introduces a multiplicity of methods. Hence "new" or "technical" persuasive forces and procedures come into being and need to be learned and understood. To a considerable degree, the media of communication "teach" those methods. The movies *The Candidate* and *Power* exposed numerous campaign practices of which the general public had not before been fully aware. News media regularly discuss sophisticated uses of polls, cinematography, and political fund raising. Expert practitioners are interviewed about their work in the press and on television and radio. Given the conservatism of the American *polis* and the multitude of informational checking systems, only regulation can introduce long-ranged bias into public information and decision making.

The "civil religion" dictated by our "sacred" documents and institutions defies all ideologies except the ideology of freedom of expression. Other ideologies must fail as long as political institutions confine politics to pragmatic choice among entities, ideas, and persons. With open competition among ideas and sources of information, politics becomes the art of *adaptation,* and adaptation is anti-ideological.

I have tried to identify and explain the major features of modern political persuasion in America. I have done so because, as our Founders wrote, "To secure these rights, governments are instituted among men, deriving their just powers from the consent of the governed." "Consent of the governed" is attained by political persuasion. I have examined the means, methods, and general effects of historic and modern political persuasive practices in the United States. I have done so in the hope of adding to the general understanding of the political environment in which we live and act.

NOTES

1. See, for example, the changing standards in *U.S. v. Roth, Miller v. California, Jenkins v. Georgia,* and *Pope et. al. v. Illinois.* At least these standards are fairer and less arbitrary than the heavy-handed and over-broad recommendations of government commissions such as the one recently chaired by Attorney General Meese.

2. Letter to Judge John Tyler from Thomas Jefferson, June 28, 1804, reprinted in *Thomas Jefferson Writings,* ed. M. Peterson (Literary Classics of the United States: New York, 1984).

3. The Fairness Doctrine is an excellent case in point. As advocates argue over the philosophical goals of the Doctrine, it sounds like an idea that guarantees diversity in the marketplace. But once the practical operation of the Doctrine is examined, it becomes readily apparent that the Doctrine has a chilling effect on the marketplace of ideas.

4. This phenomenon explains why rhetorical skills are so important in our society. Rhetoric is an art that deals in specific situations, audiences, speakers, and topics; it is concerned with universals only in so far as they are useful as persuasive tools in specific situations.

5. See particularly S.2, introduced by Senator Boren in 1987.

6. See M. Joel Bolstein, *The First Amendment in the Information Age: Regulation and the Videotex-Teletext Industries* (Freedom of Expression Foundation and The Media Institute, Washington, D.C. 1987).

7. See *Hearings on Comparative Renewal Process for Broadcast Licensees* before the Senate Committee on Commerce, Science, and Transportation, 100th Congress, 1st Session, July 17, 20, 1987.

8. I was interviewed on Wisconsin Public Radio by Margaret Andreason on August 10, 1987. Ms. Andreason expressed the belief that more people would watch PBS if more people "were exposed to it." I replied that people certainly were "aware" of it and capable of turning to it to see if they wanted to watch it. She replied that children wouldn't "eat spinach unless they were exposed" to it by their parents. I responded that she was equating television viewers with children that needed to be force-fed in order to know "what was good for them." Her assumption was that PBS is better for viewers and listeners than commercial network programming. To assist with the force feeding, Ms. Andreason suggested that the federal government subsidize the cost of advertising programming so that each system, PBS, CBS, ABC, and NBC, had "equal advertising budgets." Her belief was that equal advertising budgets would result in equal shares of the audience. Since PBS television has a 6 percent share now that is increasing while each commercial network has about a 20 percent share that is declining despite heavy advertising, statistics do not support her assumptions.

9. Some say that either Ronald Reagan, as an example on the right, or

Franklin Roosevelt, as an example on the left, are exceptions to the rule of centrisity. I disagree. First, what was defined as conservative and liberal by the public when each man was elected was very different than the standard used by historians. When Ronald Reagan was elected, a high percentage of voters saw him in line with their beliefs, and defined themselves as conservatives in greater numbers than they had in polls in the last twenty years. While polls did not exist at the time of FDR's first election, it is probably true that in reaction to the depression the public had moved to the left, making FDR more of a centrist than some historians assume. Second, both presidents have highly pragmatic records that the public normally perceives to be in the centrist part of the political spectrum. Roosevelt continually experimented in a pragmatic way to overcome the economic difficulties he faced and campaigned on a platform of states' rights in his first campaign. Reagan's tax reforms were born in the Senate and nurtured by such moderates as Senators Bradley and Packwood. Perhaps no other anecdote than Reagan's facility at quoting FDR makes clearer how stable our system is.

INDEX

Index

Index